Katharine Coman

The Growth of the English Nation

Katharine Coman

The Growth of the English Nation

ISBN/EAN: 9783741186868

Manufactured in Europe, USA, Canada, Australia, Japa

Cover: Foto ©ninafisch / pixelio.de

Manufactured and distributed by brebook publishing software (www.brebook.com)

Katharine Coman

The Growth of the English Nation

OF THE

ENGLISH NATION

BY

KATHARINE COMAN
Professor of History and Economics in Wellesley College

AND

ELIZABETH KENDALL
Associate Professor of History in Wellesley College

MEADVILLE PENNA
FLOOD AND VINCENT
The Chautauqua-Century Press
1894

Copyright, 1894,
By FLOOD & VINCENT.

The Chautauqua-Century Press, Meadville, Pa., U. S. A.
Electrotyped, Printed, and Bound by Flood & Vincent.

PREFACE.

THIS little treatise traces the growth of the English nation from its beginnings in a weak and struggling island community to its present attainment of maritime supremacy and world-wide empire. Such a study must concern itself, primarily, with social, economic, and political conditions, since national achievement is the outcome of national character—the resultant of all the forces operating upon a people. Industrial prosperity, intellectual development, the evolution of methods of self-government, the victory of the moral and spiritual over the brute elements in race temperament—these, and not war nor dynastic intrigue, are the determining factors in national progress. We shall, then, since our space is limited, pay slight heed to the deeds of kings and potentates, that we may give more attention to the deeper influences at work. We shall endeavor to understand the people and those popular movements that shape the statesman's policy.

The treatment must, necessarily, be of the briefest. Readers desiring a fuller narrative are referred to Gardiner's "Student's History of England," Bright's "History of England," and Green's "History of the English People." In the attempt to recreate the life of the past, the historical novel and the historical play lend welcome aid. It is hoped that the illustrative readings indicated in connection with the several chapters will add much to the pleasure of the student's work. Yet a word of caution is necessary. It must be remembered that in any imaginative representation, justice and accuracy are often sacrificed for the sake of dramatic interest. One must test the impressions of the artist by the conclusions of scientific history.

KATHARINE COMAN.

Wellesley, Mass., June 6, 1894.

CONTENTS.

CHAPTER.		PAGE.
I.	THE ISLAND HOME OF THE ENGLISH	9
II.	RACE ELEMENTS OF THE ENGLISH NATION	21
III.	NORMAN ENGLAND	47
IV.	FUSION OF RACES	71
V.	STRUGGLE FOR THE CHARTER	88
VI.	RISE OF THE COMMONS	109
VII.	STRUGGLE FOR THE CROWN	146
VIII.	THE TUDORS AND THE REFORMATION	166
IX.	THE STUARTS AND PURITANISM	196
X.	PARTIES AND PARTY GOVERNMENT	224
XI.	GROWTH OF DEMOCRACY	239
XII.	INDUSTRIAL PROGRESS DURING THE EIGHTEENTH AND NINETEENTH CENTURIES	266
XIII.	THE EXPANSION OF ENGLAND	284
	TABLE OF BRITISH COLONIAL POSSESSIONS.	

LIST OF MAPS.

Physiographical Map of the British Isles	*Frontispiece.*
	PAGE.
England	8
Outline Map of England	15
Outline Map of Wales	17
Outline Map of Scotland	18
Outline Map of Ireland	19
Roman Britain	Facing page 25
Britain in 597	" " 31
The English Empire in the Tenth and Eleventh Centuries	Facing page 41
England and the French Possessions of William I., 1087	Facing page 50
Dominions of the House of Anjou	" " 73
England and Wales in 1643	" " 207
The British Isles in 1881	275
Map of World, Showing British Possessions and Protectorates	Facing page 284

THE GROWTH OF THE ENGLISH NATION.

CHAPTER I.

THE ISLAND HOME OF THE ENGLISH.

THE life-story of a nation, like that of an individual, is in good part determined by inheritance and environment. The national traits inherited from ancestral races and the tendencies impressed by the physical features of the country give to a people its peculiar character. A nation's history, the sum of its achievements, is the essential expression of its individuality. Circumstances may modify its development. Propitious events may further, or hostile interference may thwart, the accomplishment of its destiny, but at no time in the history of a nation is the effect of physical environment and race inheritance wholly obscured.

The home of the English people is a group of islands, 5,000 in number, lying off the west coast of Europe. They look on the map like icebergs floating away from a huge old glacier. Most of them are mere ledges of rock lifting a few acres of grass land beyond reach of the waves. Some are so bare that they only serve as homes for the sea-birds. Many are picturesque and romantic—Staffa and Iona, Holy Isle and the Isle of Wight, have furnished refuge to persecuted saints and kings—but Great Britain and Ireland alone are of sufficient size to have considerable influence on the national character. The area of the

Area.

British Isles is 121,481 square miles, about one four hundred and thirtieth part of the land surface of the globe. In extent they are somewhat larger than New England, somewhat less than Japan. This seems too small a country to cut any very striking figure in the world's history, and yet the English government controls to-day one fourth of the land area of the globe. The population of the British Empire is ten times that of the British Isles. Nineteenth century Englishmen boast, and with good reason, that the sun never sets on Her Majesty's dominions.

How can we account for this extraordinary national development? Much is doubtless due to certain inherent qualities in the English people, but much is the result of physical environment. We need to find out first of all, **Physical make-up.** what in the physical make-up of the British Isles has contributed to the success of the English race. The most apparent fact regarding these islands is that they lie within easy reach of Europe. The Straits of Dover are but twenty miles across. The water is nowhere of great depth, 300 feet in the English Channel and 70 feet in the North Sea. The British Isles, in fact, were originally part of the Continent. What is now the bed of the North Sea was once low-lying plain over which animals now extinct and, it may be, prehistoric men made their way. At no time has communication been impossible, but it has always been attended by hazard. The rudest boat can cross the Chan- **Advantage of insular position.** nel in calm weather without harm, but these are tempestuous seas and such storms may rise as put a man-of-war in peril. Several times in English history this natural isolation has been an effective defense against attack. The great Spanish Armada was dashed in pieces on the Irish coast in Elizabeth's reign, and three centuries later the all-conquering Napoleon shrank from the risk involved in an invasion of England. In the early centuries of its history, Great Britain was frequently overrun and subjugated by her continental neighbors, but the Norman conquerors may be said to have announced England's Monroe doctrine. Thenceforward the British Isles were not open to colonization. From the twelfth century, the inhabitants of these islands have repelled all invaders and stoutly maintained their national integrity. Accessible from the Continent yet easily independent of it, the English people have enjoyed the rare privilege of a free and natural race development. Unhampered by foreign interference, they have dealt with the several problems of political, social, and religious life under conditions comparatively simple, and have arrived at results which, though not perhaps perfect in themselves or of universal application, are at least admirably suited to the national character. On the other hand, this isolation has not been such as to prevent England from sharing in every vital impulse that has stirred the Continent. The Crusades, the Renaissance, the Reformation, the Revolution, each in turn has deeply influenced English life and roused the English race to nobler achievement.

A no less important consequence of its insular situation is the maritime greatness of the English nation. An island people are of necessity seafarers. They must venture across the water in search of what their narrow realm does not provide. Great Britain, as we shall see, is peculiarly fitted to foster a race of mariners. Her firths, estuaries, and river mouths form natural harbors, and her situation is most favorable. Lying over against France, Holland, and the Baltic, is a series of seaports in direct communication with these rich and populous regions of the Continent. The western harbors formed by the Clyde, the Mersey, and the Severn, look toward Ireland and America. During the Middle Ages, Venice was the busi-

Commercial advantages.

ness center of the Occident, and London but a remote trading post lying near the edge of the world; but the discovery of America has opened industrial opportunities hitherto undreamed of, and altered commercial relations. London proves to be at the center of the land surface of the globe, and England lies in the direct highway of modern trade. These are great natural advantages, but England's maritime supremacy has not been won without a struggle. Spain, Holland, and France were before her in the field and must be driven out. Only by dint of a long series of commercial wars has England secured her haughty title of Mistress of the Seas. The people's pride in this hard-won victory is voiced in the national song,

"Rule Britannia! Britannia rules the waves."

These commercial advantages are rendered more valuable by the unusual facilities for internal communication. No part of the country is more than one hundred miles from the coast, and water ways, natural and artificial, give access to the remotest regions. England boasts five navigable rivers, the Yorkshire Ouse, the Trent, the Mersey, the Thames, and the Severn. These reach far into the heart of the country and their head waters are connected by a system of canals. Ships may pass across Scotland from the North to the Irish Sea by the Forth and Clyde canal. Ireland's principal river, the Shannon, is navigable nearly to its source, and is connected by canal with Belfast, Dublin, and Waterford. To-day the railroad has almost superseded water traffic, but the rivers of Britain, these "roads that run," have served an important part in promoting her commercial greatness.

Climate.

This wave-washed realm is further blessed by a most fortunate climate. An island climate is usually moist and equable, but the British Isles are peculiarly favored in that they lie directly in the path of the Gulf Stream.

This great ocean current is a veritable godsend to Britain. Bearing upon its bosom the atmosphere of a subtropical sea, it beats against the western coasts, bringing to a country of the latitude of Labrador the climate of Virginia. Dublin has the mean temperature of Savannah, though two thousand miles farther from the equator. The Gulf Stream brings to this lucky land not merely heat but moisture. The warm west winds break on the mountainous coasts of Ireland, Wales, and Scotland, and discharge abundant supplies of rain. Here the average annual rainfall amounts, in certain districts, to seven feet. The rainfall of England is, however, not half so heavy. The influence of this warm, moist climate not only upon the occupations but upon the habit and thought of the people, can hardly be overestimated. The humidity is a great advantage in certain textile industries—notably cotton-spinning. The winters are rarely so severe as to interfere with field-works or transportation, while the wholesome, bracing atmosphere actually stimulates to exertion.

In natural resources the English race is well endowed. The mineral deposits of the British Isles are not only rich and of great variety, but so placed as to be readily accessible. Long before the English came to Britain, tin and copper were extracted in some rude fashion from the rocks of Cornwall. To-day, not only tin and copper, but coal and iron, lead and zinc, are mined with such success that notwithstanding the more extensive mineral regions of America, Africa, and Australia, Britain is still one of the most productive mining countries in the world. Rarely does a country combine such mineral wealth with so fertile a soil as that of the British Isles. Wales and Scotland, to be sure, can boast but scanty agricultural resources, but there are nowhere more fruitful regions than the pasture lands of Ireland and the gardens and wheat fields of eastern

Physical resources.

Agricultural area amounts to 75 per cent of total area in England. 60 per cent of total area in Wales. 25 per cent of total area in Scotland. 75 per cent of total area in Ireland.

and southern England. Throughout the Middle Ages the soil of Britain not merely fed her own people, but furnished considerable quantities of grain, cattle, and wool to foreign lands. To-day, however, her population has outstripped the food-bearing capacity of her fields, and Britain is obliged to look to Australia and America for supplies. Nineteenth century Britain is the richest country in the Old World. Her present wealth is estimated at $49,000,000,000, or $1,235 for every man, woman, and child in the United Kingdom. The wealth of the United States is reckoned at $64,120,000,000, but our population is so much larger that our average per capita wealth is only $1,050. The wealth-producing facilities of Britain enable her to support a dense population. This surpassing prosperity has a double source. It would be difficult to say which of two coöperating causes has been more influential—Britain's exceptional advantages of situation, soil, and mineral wealth or the pronounced industrial genius of her people.

37,888,153 in 1891.

Political divisions.

The four political divisions of the United Kingdom were originally independent and though they have been under one government for centuries, each still preserves a marked individuality. We can account for this dissimilarity in some measure by race inheritance, since the English are Teutons by origin, while the Irish, Welsh, and Scotch are Celts; but even more is due to the modifying influence of physical conditions. Ireland, Wales, and Scotland have been but shabbily dealt with by Dame Nature, while England has fallen heir to her richest bounties. For example, England has the advantage of situation as regards Europe. The mountains of Great Britain are piled up in the north and west. Scotland, Westmoreland, Wales, and Cornwall are mere masses of rock and moor. From these inhospitable heights the rich plains of England slope eastward to the Channel and the North Sea. Her water courses cross the

England.

country from west to east, forming natural highways for commerce. Four of her navigable rivers, the Tyne, the Tees, the Trent, and the Thames, give direct access to the Channel trade. Their harbors stand like so many open doors, inviting the products, the men, the ideas of Europe. England may be said to turn her back on Ireland and to face the Continent. She is indeed the favored sister. The west winds come to her with warmth and moisture, but not till excess of rain has been precipitated on the rugged heights of the Welsh mountains.

Outline Map of England.

The Channel fogs, it is true, invade the low districts of the eastern coast, but they have this virtue, at least, that they insure England's harvest against drought. Industrially, England is divided into two distinct parts. A line drawn from the estuary of the Humber to the mouth of the Severn would approximately represent the division. Southeast of this line lies agricultural England. The rich lime soil and the gentle rivers of this region make it one of the most productive in the world. No more fertile fields gladden the heart of man than those of the Fen country and the Thames valley, while the pasture lands of the Chiltern Hills, the North and South Downs, and the Cotswold Hills nourish famous breeds of sheep. Northwest of our imaginary line is the mineral wealth of England. Here lie the great coal fields of Northumberland, Durham, Yorkshire, Derby, Stafford, Leicester, Warwick, and Lancashire. They are 1,650 square miles in extent and constitute the mainspring of England's manufacturing industries. In the midst of this immense coal area rises the Pennine chain, a range of mountain and moorland which thrusts itself like a great wedge 200 miles into the heart of England. It is an axis of carboniferous rock and along its barren slopes lie rich mineral deposits, iron, zinc, and lead. This remarkable combination of fuel with mineral resources has attracted to the region the capital and labor force of England. Here are the mining districts of Northumberland and Durham. Here lie the great manufacturing towns of Leeds, Nottingham, Sheffield, Birmingham, and Manchester. The centers of wealth and population were originally in the agricultural regions of the south, but the opening of the coal measures has reversed conditions and the most populous districts of England today lie north of the Trent. The Pennine district does not, however, monopolize the mineral wealth of England. The rocky promontory of Cornwall supports a large mining population. These barren hills bear rich veins of copper, lead, and tin. Many lesser resources have contributed their quota to England's prosperity. In Cheshire, along the valley of the Weaver, lie rich deposits of salt. They have been known for 1,800 years, but have only in modern times been extensively worked. In addition to its coal measures, Staffordshire boasts a fine clay soil admirably adapted to the manufacture of earthenware. Here Wedgwood and many lesser craftsmen have practiced the potter's art. The remarkable success of the industry has won for this district the name of "the Potteries."

Cf. density of population in agricultural county, e. g., Bedford, 348 to sq. m.; with that of mining county, e. g., Durham, 1,004 to sq. m.; or that of manufacturing county, e. g., Lancashire, 1,829 to sq. m.

Wales.

If now we turn from merry England to the little principality of Wales, we shall find a marked contrast. This is a rugged, mountainous country, picturesque and romantic enough, beloved of the tourist, but scantily endowed with industrial resources. These massive peaks, enveloped in mist and rain, afford meager opportunity for pasture or tillage. A circumscribed agricultural district lies along the north coast in the valleys of the Conway and the Clwyd, but the best industrial opportunity of Wales is in the slate quarries of the Cambrian range and the coal mines of the south. The coal fields of Wales are nearly equal in extent to those of England. That of the Black Mountains is 900 square miles in area and 10,000 feet in depth. This has become the center of the smelting industry. A dense population is gathered in a series of smoky towns, Swansea, Cardiff, Merthyr-Tydfil, and Ystradyfodwg. From Cornwall, from France, from North and South America, from Australia, large quantities of metal are brought to the foundries of South Wales. But this prosperity is offset by the poverty of vast mountain wastes. Wales as a whole supports but a sparse population. Her area is one seventh that of England while her population is but one eighteenth as large.

Outline Map of Wales.

Scotland in physical make-up is quite comparable to Wales. It looks but a jagged mass of rock from which broken bits, the Shetlands, the Orkneys, the Hebrides, Skye, Mull, Arran, are crumbling off into the sea. The country is naturally divided into three districts distinguished from one another by marked physical features. First of these is the picturesque northern section, the

Scotland.

Highlands, the land of shootings and salmon rivers. It contains two thirds of Scotland's territory, but very little of her material wealth. Fishing and sheep raising are the principal employments. The Lowland Plain is a long narrow valley, which may once have been an isthmus, running across the country from east to west, from the Firth of Forth to the Firth of Clyde. This region contains the mineral wealth of Scotland. Here are rich deposits of coal and iron which sustain flourishing manufactures. Here, too, are Scotland's harbors and hence her commercial opportunity. The population of this favored region is more than half that of all Scotland. The third natural division is that of the Lowland Hills, Scotland's natural barrier against invasion from England, the "border" of the

Outline Map of Scotland.

ballads and historical romance. These hills are monotonous moorlands. They lack the picturesque beauty of the Highlands and the mineral wealth of the Plain. They are good for little but sheep pasture. The Tweed valley is a more prosperous region; verging on

the coal districts of England, it shares their prosperity.
Of the physical sources of national well-being, Ireland has but a niggardly portion. The island is shaped like a saucer. Along the coasts, north, west, and south, runs a series of low mountain ranges. In the east alone are there considerable stretches of sandy shore and even here the coast line is broken by two mountain masses, the Mourne and the Wicklow hills. The interior is an undulating plain with hardly sufficient slope to afford watershed to its sluggish rivers. It has a limestone foundation and the soil is as fertile as that of England, but it is too wet for successful agriculture and is given over, in great part, to cattle pasture. Numerous lakes and tracts of bog land lie across the heart of the country and reduce its tillable area. Ireland gets the first effect of the warm winds from the Atlantic and the rainfall is excessive. The number of rainy days in a year averages 208. The climate is in consequence warm, damp, and debilitating. Moreover the mineral resources of the country are scant. The immense coal measures that originally covered its surface were carried away ages ago by glacial action. Isolated fragments of the once abundant store are found in the hills, but the output of the mines is quite inadequate to the industrial needs of the country. Ireland possesses rich deposits of iron, but they cannot be worked to advantage because fuel is lack-

Outline Map of Ireland.

Ireland.

Make-up of Ireland:
75 per cent arable land.
9 per cent bog and marsh.
11 per cent barren mountain.
4 per cent water.
1 per cent woods.

ing. The mountains contain other minerals, copper, gold, silver, and lead, and these have been mined at different epochs in Irish history; but the ores are nowhere so rich as those of the Pennine and Cornish districts and the mining industries are to-day actually declining. The fates seem to have conspired against Ireland. Her rivers rarely afford water power sufficient for manufactures. Her natural harbors lie to the west and north where they are of little use. One first-rate harbor lies on the south coast and has become important since the steamship lines running from Liverpool to America have made it a calling station. England stands between Ireland and the Continent. She can control and has thus far stifled the commercial ventures of the weaker country. Deprived of commercial and industrial opportunities, the Irish people are restricted to agriculture. The population is distributed over the land in villages and scattered hamlets. There are but six towns of more than 20,000 inhabitants, Dublin, Belfast, Cork, Limerick, Londonderry, and Waterford. These it will be noticed are all on the seacoast and owe their importance to some commercial advantage. In northern Ireland conditions are more favorable. The climate is bracing, the juxtaposition of two such harbors as Belfast and Glasgow is a spur to commerce, while ready access to the Scotch coal district renders textile manufactures profitable. The poverty of Ireland may be partly accounted for by misgovernment and race weakness, but it is mainly due to the lack of material resources. The comparative prosperity of the political divisions of Britain is clearly indicated by the movement of population. Scotland has always been sparsely settled. The population of Ireland is actually decreasing while that of England and Wales has rapidly increased since the opening up of their mineral resources. Saxony alone of European countries supports a denser population than England.

Queenstown.

Cf. density of population: Scotland, 132 to sq. m. Ireland, 144 to sq. m. Wales, 206 to sq. m. England, 540 to sq. m. Belgium, 540 to sq. m. Saxony, 598 to sq. m.

CHAPTER II.

RACE ELEMENTS OF THE ENGLISH NATION.

Illustrative Readings.
House of the Wolfings; Morris.
Ekkehard; Scheffel.
Alfred the Great; Hughes.
Beowulf.

Important Dates.
55 B. C. Invasion of the Romans.
449 A. D. Landing of the Jutes.
597. Augustine's Mission.
829. Union under Egbert.
871-901. Reign of Alfred.
878. Treaty of Wedmore.
955. Union under Edgar.
1016. Conquest by Cnut.
1042. Saxon Restoration.
1066. Death of Edward.

THE BRITONS AND ROME.

The most ancient descriptions of the island now known as Great Britain show that it must once have been very like northern Russia of to-day, a land of dense forest, barren moor, and desolate fen. The southern coast was lined with forests stretching with scarcely a break from Kent into Devon. Another great woodland bordered the Severn on both sides. The center of the island was covered by forest and thicket. From the Peak to the Tyne rolled almost unbroken woodland and moor, and beyond, impassable forests covered the lowlands between the German Ocean and the hills of Strathclyde. Around the Wash the great fens stretched inland as far as modern Cambridge, cutting off the coast from the interior. To the north and west were barren waste and rugged, inaccessible mountain wilds.

We do not know by what race this desolate land was first inhabited. Traces have been found of a primitive people, cave dwellers, but they have passed away, leaving no clue as to their condition except here and there an etching on a rock, or the engraved tooth of a cave lion. At the

Inhabitants.

earliest time concerning which we have information the country was occupied by two distinct races, the Iberian and the Celt. The Iberians were few in number and were dark-haired and of small stature, a type still surviving perhaps in the swarthy Irish of the west. At one time they held the whole island, but they were driven into the remoter districts or absorbed by the successive waves of Celts that a little later swept over the country.

The Celts.

The bulk of the population was composed of Celts of the Aryan group, a group which includes Teutons, Slavs, Greeks, and some of the ancient races of India and Persia. They were the first Aryans to enter Europe, and, driven onward by the Teutons who came later, are now found chiefly in the more remote parts of the Continent and the adjoining islands, as Brittany, Scotland, Wales, and Ireland. Those who crossed over from the mainland were of two branches, the Gaels, represented now by the Irish and the Highlanders of Scotland, and the Britons who gave the island its name and who were the ancestors of the modern Welsh and Cornishmen. They all spoke the Celtic tongue, and it is still the common speech of Wales and the Scotch Highlands.

55 B. C.

Although the island was visited by men from southern Europe by the fourth century B. C., we nevertheless know almost nothing of its early history. Cæsar relates in his Commentaries that, when he was planning his invasion of Britain, he found it impossible to gain any precise knowledge of the country. "Having, therefore, called together the merchants from all parts of Gaul, they could neither inform him of the largeness of the island, nor what or how powerful were the nations that inhabited it, nor of their customs, or arts of war." Apparently at the beginning of our era the Britons had not passed beyond the tribal stage, and the basis of society was the clan or patriarchal family, those of the

Race characteristics of the Britons.

same blood and having the same totem holding together and shutting out all others. The chief occupation of the tribes of the north was hunting, but they were great fishermen, although they apparently never ventured far out at sea. Cattle constituted their wealth, and with them they wandered from place to place, having no settled home. The Britons of the south were more highly civilized than those of the north. Agriculture was carried on with some skill, the tin mines of Cornwall and Devon were worked, and there was a limited commerce with the Continent. The remains of temples and monuments to the dead, such as Stonehenge in Salisbury Plain, prove that the principles of mechanics were understood.

Totem, a rude picture, as of a bird, beast, or the like; used as a symbolic name or designation of a family.

The religion of the Celts on both sides the Channel was the same. They worshiped many gods, and held sacred certain objects in nature, as the oak and mistletoe. Their priests, called Druids, took an influential part in the government. Cæsar, writing of Gaul, says of them: "The Druids have charge of all matters of religion; they conduct the public and private sacrifices and interpret the omens. They are held in great honor, and many young men come to them for instruction. They decide almost all controversies, public and private. . . . If anyone does not submit to their decision he is made an outlaw. . . . The Druids do not go to war, nor pay tribute with the rest. . . . The leading tenet of the Druids is that the soul does not perish, but passes after death into the body of another person. Thus they incite men to valor by removing the fear of death." In appearance the Celts were tall

Religion.

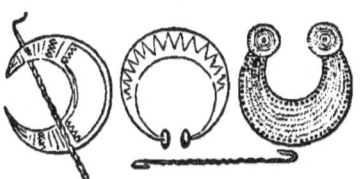

Druidical Ornaments.

and fair. Ptolemy, a Latin writer of the second century, describes them as "impatient of restraint, and fond of liberty; warlike, laborious, fierce and imperious, ingenious and high-spirited."

Roman Conquest.

About the middle of the first century B. C., the Britons came into contact with the power of Rome. Cæsar having completed the conquest of Gaul, "resolved to pass over into Britain, as he had certain intelligence that in all his wars with the Gauls the enemies of the commonwealth had ever received assistance from thence." We have a description in Cæsar's own words of his attempted landing. "He weighed anchor about one in the morning, and about ten o'clock reached the coast of Britain where he saw all the cliffs" (the white cliffs of Dover) "covered with the enemy's forces. The nature of the place was such that, the sea being bounded by steep mountains, the enemy might easily launch their javelins on us from above." Cæsar's first attempt to overcome the Britons was a failure, but in the following year he came again. He met with a stubborn resistance; in a critical moment, however, tribal jealousy broke the strength of the defense, and the Romans won a complete victory. Thereupon they withdrew, having gained their end of putting a check on British interference in Gaul, and for almost a century longer the island was left to itself.

About a hundred years later Rome renewed the attack. Perhaps the Britons opened the way to this by ravaging the neighboring coasts of Gaul. In 43 A. D., a Roman army invaded the island, and by taking advantage of the rivalries of different tribes soon conquered the southern half of the country, including the much coveted tin mines and the most fertile lands. Constant fighting, however, was necessary to secure these conquests. In 58 A. D. Suetonius Paulinus was made governor of

Roman Britain. He at once led an attack on the island of Mona (Anglesey), the stronghold of the Druids and the center of the British resistance. Suetonius was completely successful, but the force of his victory was almost lost through the misgovernment of his subordinates. Oppressed and insulted, the Britons of the south rose against their conquerors and a terrible massacre of the Romans followed. More troops were sent from Gaul, stern vengeance was taken upon the Britons, and at last Roman authority was restored. Agricola, who governed the island during the latter part of the century, pushed the Roman conquests far into the north. To secure what was already held, he felt it necessary to subdue the whole island. He failed in this but he conquered the country as far as the Solway and the Tyne. To protect his conquests he built a line of forts between the Forth and the Clyde, and established a strong garrison at Eboracum (York). Early in the second century the Emperor Hadrian visited the island and strengthened the defenses in the north by building a dyke or earthwall between the Solway and the Tyne, and a few years later a wall of a similar character, known as the Wall of Antoninus, was constructed along the line of Agricola's forts. A final attempt to conquer the wild tribes of the north, the Picts and Scots, was made by Emperor Severus in the beginning of the fourth century. He failed, however, as those before him had done, and he was obliged to content himself with securing the lands south of the Tyne by erecting a wall of stone not far from Hadrian's earth dyke. Parts of these walls remain unto this day.

Throughout the Roman period the Picts and Scots of the north remained unsubdued; south of the firths, however, the island rapidly became a Roman province. The conquered tribes learned to appreciate the benefits of the

Britain under the Romans.

rule of Rome as well as to fear her arms. Peace and good order were maintained. The Romans were great builders and engineers, and they soon covered Britain with a network of fine roads connecting the outlying posts, such as York or Chester, with London and the south coast. Along these roads all the traffic of the country was carried on for centuries, and a comparison of a map of England with a map of Roman Britain shows that even now many of the railways follow the line of the Roman roads. Towns and cities sprang into existence, often about some military station, as is shown by the frequent termination "chester" (Latin *castra*, camp). Along the line of the highways the forests were cleared off and the marshes drained, and in the south much land was brought under cultivation. Agriculture flourished and so much corn was produced that Britain became known as the "Granary of the North." As a result of the closer connection, a brisk trade sprang up with the Continent. The Roman colonists who settled in the country introduced new modes of living. Nowhere within the empire are the remains of villas and town houses more numerous and more splendid. The southern coast was dotted with residences provided with every contrivance for diminishing the unaccustomed rigor of the climate, of which the colonists wrote that it was "rather rainy than snowy, and when it is fine there is a fog." Bath became a popular resort, and the ruins recently uncovered there testify to the luxury of the Roman colonists. Latin was the official language and was spoken at least by those Britons who dwelt in the towns. Roman law, the most perfect legal system the world has seen, was the law of the land both for conqueror and conquered. Druidism was attacked by the Romans because of the determined hostility of the priests to the new rule, and its rites were no longer practiced—at least openly. Under the rule of Constantine in the fourth century Britain became nominally Christian, and the natives to some extent accepted the new religion.

Nevertheless, as a whole, the civilization of Rome did not take a strong hold upon Britain. Even south of the Firth of Forth there must have been large tracts of country untouched by Roman influence, and outside of the towns the bulk of the population probably clung to the old customs, the old language, and the old faith. It is easy to understand why it was so. Remote from Rome, Britain was not readily brought under the influence of Latin civilization. Probably few from southern Europe came to the island. The climate was forbidding and commerce and trade offered but few attractions. To the last Britain must have remained a military colony, a kind of Roman Algeria, the Romans a mere handful among an alien, subject people. But the chief reason for the superficial character of the civilization of the Britons was the short duration of the Roman rule. Britain was the last of Rome's conquests in the west, and was the first to be given up. The efforts to secure Roman Britain against the Picts and Scots had been only in part successful. The walled towns, the large number of troops stationed in the island, show how the tribes of the north were dreaded.

In the fourth century a new danger appeared in the band of pirates that ravaged the eastern coast. The shores of the Continent from the north of the peninsula of Jutland to the mouth of the Ems were occupied by men of the Low German branch of the Teutonic race. Those living in Jutland were called Jutes; in Schleswig and Holstein were the Angles; about the mouth of the Elbe were the Saxons. All these took part in the conquest of Britain, and probably there were Jutes and Angles among the bands that laid waste the eastern coast at this time, though the records speak only of the Saxons. To meet this danger a line of forts was built stretching south from the Wash to Southampton Water, and a special officer, the Count of the Saxon shore, was appointed to take charge of the defenses of the coast. But resistance was vain. The raids of the Saxon pirates were but part of a great westward movement of the Teutons in the fourth century. For centuries Rome had waged an unequal contest with the barbarians; now her foes closed in on her from all sides. The protection of Britain was impossible, and in 410 the Emperor Honorius withdrew the Roman troops and bade the Britons sore-beset look to their own defense.

THE TEUTONIC INVASIONS.

The English Conquest.

For the next forty years the Britons carried on single-handed a desperate struggle with the Picts and Scots on the north and the Saxon pirates on the east. In an appeal to Rome for aid they wrote: "The barbarians drive us to the sea; the sea drives us back to the barbarians; between them we are exposed to two sorts of death; we are either slain or drowned." Contact with the Romans had not increased the power of the Britons to resist their foes. Tribal differences to be sure had disappeared, but the people had not become a nation. Moreover, they had lost the habit of self-government and of self-defense under the paternal rule of Rome. Yet they resisted long and stubbornly. Finally in 449 Vortigern, the ruler of the British, following the example of Rome, tried to play off one foe against another. He used with success the help of a band of Jutish pirates against the Picts, but he then found that he could not so easily get rid of his new allies. They established themselves in the Isle of Thanet and within a few years had overrun the whole of the adjoining mainland as far as Romney Marsh, in Kent.

The coming of the Jutes.

The Jutes were soon followed by other bands of sea rovers. Saxons from the Elbe landed to the west and starved out the strong fortress of Anderida. Still others north of the Thames forced their way inland until brought to a halt by the marshes of the Lea and the fortress of London. Another band of the same great people landing at Southampton pushed through the forest belt, but they were met and defeated by the Britons at Mt. Badon in 520. While the Saxon was thus conquering the southern coast, men of another race, the Angles, coming like the Saxons in small, independent bands, were seizing the land along the eastern shore from Essex, the northernmost Saxon settlement, as far as the Roman wall, and by the early part of the sixth century the whole coast from the Tyne to Southampton Water was held by the Teuton invaders. As yet, however, their settlements were a mere fringe along the shore, and for almost fifty years longer they were held at bay by the desperate resistance of the Britons, aided by the Roman fortresses and the natural defenses of forest and fen.

About the middle of the century there was an advance all along the line. Although the Anglians south of the Wash were still checked by the Great Fen, others making their way up the rivers settled along the Trent. These are known as Mercians, or men of the mark, for their settlement formed a kind of borderland between Britons and Teutons. The records are silent as to how it was done, but sometime before the close of the century the great northern province was conquered by other Angles who established the two strong kingdoms of Bernicia and Deira, together known as Northumberland. In the south, the Saxons pressed forward into the interior taking London and occupying the valleys of the Thames and the Severn. Finally, in 577 the Saxons of the west met the Britons at

The Saxons and Angles

Welsh legends place the reign of Arthur of the Table Round in this period.

Deorham and won a victory which broke the backbone of British resistance.

Britain becomes England.
Step by step the invader had advanced and by the beginning of the seventh century the work of conquest was practically done. The Celts still held their own in the remoter parts of the island, in the north, in Strathclyde and Cumberland, in Wales and Cornwall, but the richest, the most fertile portion of Britain had become Teuton and pagan. For the conquest of Britain was unlike all other Teutonic conquests. Elsewhere the conquerors gradually adopted the language, the religion, the customs of the conquered. But in Britain the invaders held to their old gods, and everywhere they settled the English language and the English customs prevailed.

The reasons for the difference are not far to seek. On the Continent the Teutons came as a united host under one leader, here they came in small, independent bands. On the Continent the natives, weakened by Roman rule, made only a feeble stand, but in the end conquered their conquerors through superior civilization. The half-civilized Celts of Britain, less completely Romanized and aided by their natural defenses, resisted long and stubbornly. The land was won from them only by dint of hard fighting and it took almost one hundred and fifty years to complete the conquest. As a result of the long fierce struggle, a large part of the native population was exterminated, and all traces of Roman civilization being swept away, the land lay bare for the planting of a new nation with its own speech, its own customs, its own institutions.

Saxon Warrior.

The Heptarchy.
The contest between the Teuton and the Celt for possession of Britain had come to an end ; only on the western

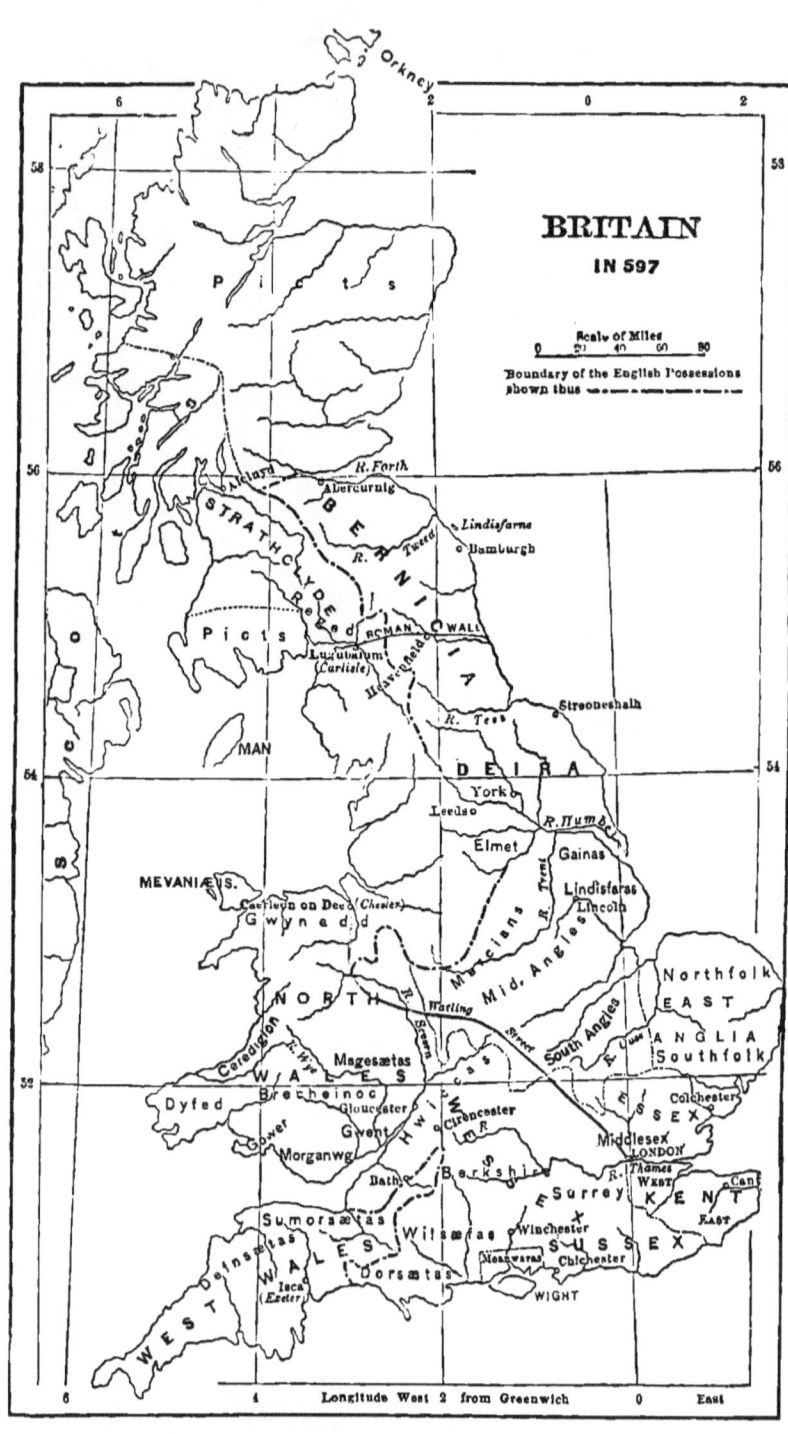

border did the war linger on for a time longer. Peace, however, was not gained. Secure from the Britons, the invaders now turned their arms against one another, and the history of the next two centuries is filled with their strife. Of the many independent Teutonic settlements, seven have a fairly continuous history. Three of these, Northumberland, Mercia, and Wessex, having conquered their weaker neighbors, waged war for supremacy in England. Northumberland under Edwin was the first to rise to power, and early in the seventh century succeeded in conquering all the rest of England except Kent, but it was too weak to maintain its hold. Mercia revolted and under Penda rose rapidly to the foremost place. But the fall of Mercia was as rapid as its rise; it was too exposed, too divided internally to hope to unite England permanently under its rule. That it achieved what it did was due mainly to its great kings, Penda and Offa. In the eighth century Wessex contested the supremacy of the south with Mercia, while Northumberland stood somewhat aloof. For a time Mercia was successful and conquered Essex, Kent, and East Anglia, but early in the ninth century the tide changed, and by 829 the West Saxons under Egbert were masters of the whole country. The kingdoms of the south were directly under the rule of Wessex, while Mercia, East Anglia, and Northumberland retained their own kings; but all alike owned the overlordship of Egbert, and for the moment there was a united England. In looking back over these years of internecine war, it seems a period of much confusion, of apparently meaningless strife, well characterized by Milton as the "battle of kites and crows." The scanty records

Anglo-Saxon Man-at-arms.

show, however, that it was also a time of social and political growth, and that underneath all the turmoil and disorder the English nation was being formed.

THE ANGLO-SAXONS.

The bands of warriors that conquered Britain were but the forerunners of the migration of a people. Wives, children, slaves, cattle even, were brought across the water, and in their island home the Teutonic conquerors reproduced the life they were wont to lead on the banks of the Elbe. They held to the old speech, the old faith, the old laws, the old customs and institutions, and Britain became England, the land of the Angles.

Customs and institutions.

Tyr. Woden Thor. Freyja.

The three tribes that took part in the conquest were much alike. They were heathen, worshiping many gods, some of whose names have come down to us in the days of the week. Their chief delight was in war, and they were equally at home on land and on sea. There were two classes among them, the earls or noblemen, and the simple freemen. Besides these were the people conquered in war and reduced to slavery, who did much of the work of tilling the soil. After the conquest there was a great increase in the number of the unfree, both English and Britons. The leaders were called ealdormen and were marked out from the rest by their wealth or their greater wisdom or prowess. Around each earl gathered his war band. These comrades or *gesiths*, as they were called, were young men whose business in life was war. They lived with their chosen leader and followed him wherever he went, esteeming it their greatest glory to give their lives for him. They probably bore the brunt of the attack on Britain, and after the conquest we find a change in their position. They no longer lived in the house of their leader, but had lands of their own and were called "thegns."

Race Elements of the English Nation. 33

The village.

The life of the Teutons centered in the village. Here families united by the tie of kinship lived together, and each "ham" or "tun" bore the name of the kin that dwelt in it. Thus the town of the Irvings was Irvington. Each village lay isolated by a border of waste or woodland called the mark, a name often applied to the village itself. Every freeman had his own house and strip of plowland, but the woodland and pasture-land surrounding the village were used in common. It is a still unsettled question whether the village lands were owned by the freemen or whether they belonged to some lord to whom the cultivators paid service in return for the use of the land. Each village, whether dependent or free, had its townmoot. Here the freemen met together under a reeve or headman and settled the petty disputes of the neighborhood, just as do the peasants of the Russian village community to-day. Superior to the townmoot was the hundred-moot, the court of a district settled originally perhaps by a hundred families of the same kin. Here the reeve and four best men from each village within the hundred met together to discuss questions arising between township and township, and to give judgment in cases of grave offense and crime.

Gesith.

Justice.

Among the Teutons as among other primitive peoples, justice and order were at first associated with the idea of the family. Each kinsman was his kinsman's keeper, bound to avenge his wrongs, to suffer for his misdeeds. "Life for life" and "eye for eye" ran the hard code of the day. It was a great step in advance when compensation for wrong done might be made at a fixed price, and when the injured man no longer took vengeance into his own hand, but brought his complaint before his neighbors

In the tenth century a king's blood-money was about four times that of an ealdorman, and more than one hundred times that of an ordinary freeman.

in town or hundred-moot. Yet there was nothing like the trial of to-day. If the accused denied the charge he was bound to summon twelve men of the neighborhood, compurgators, who would swear to the worth of his oath. When none would do this, he might appeal to the ordeal or judgment of the gods, and if he could stand the test of walking on hot plowshares or of plunging his arm into boiling water, he was held innocent of the charge against him. Probably but few stood the ordeal, and thus practically judgment depended upon the good or bad repute of a man among his neighbors.

The Tribe. Twice a year the men of the tribe came together in a great folk-moot. Here justice was done between hundred and hundred, and important matters, such as peace and war, were discussed, and the leader of the host was chosen.

Saxon Archer.

One of the ealdormen presided over the moot, the wise men of the tribe spoke, and the freemen standing about shouted "Aye" or "Nay" to what was proposed, or shook their spears and clashed their shields by way of applause. They came prepared to fight as well as to take counsel. Each man had his place in the national force, and just as the folk-moot was the people in council so the host was the people in arms. Kingship among these people was perhaps a result of the conquest. At least we find no earlier traces of it, and within a short time after their coming each settlement had its king. The long, fierce resistance of the Britons forced the invaders to unite under some chief to whom all could look, and to make him something more than a temporary leader. The choice usually fell on the best man of the royal line, but he was still the freely elected leader, bound by the advice of his wise men and the customs of the people.

The seventh century was marked by an event only less important than the conquest itself, the conversion of the English to Christianity. The defeat of the Britons by the Teutons meant the triumph of the faith of Woden over the faith of Christ. The Teutons were not intolerant, however, and when in 597 Roman missionaries landed in Thanet, they met with a patient hearing from Ethelbert, the Kentish king, and he allowed no one to molest them, although he refused to accept the new faith, saying, "Your words are fair, but they are of new and doubtful meaning." Within a few years, however, both king and people accepted the new religion. The royal city of Canterbury became the center of English Christianity, and Augustine, leader of the missionary band, the first English archbishop. The time was favorable to the spread of the new teaching, for under Ethelbert, Kent had established a kind of over-lordship over the surrounding tribes and they accepted the faith of their new rulers.

The conversion of the English to Christianity.

St. Augustin, Archbishop of Canterbury.

The supremacy of Kent ended with the death of Ethelbert, and many of the surrounding states in regaining their independence fell away from the new religion, but Christianity had already begun to make its way in the north through the marriage of a Kentish princess with Edwin the great Northumbrian king. Moved by the entreaties of his wife and the preaching of the chaplain Paulinus, Edwin promised to renounce the faith of Woden if he were successful in war. Returning home victorious, he called upon his people to accept Christianity. His wise men were nothing loath. "So runs the life of man," said one, "as a sparrow's flight through the hall when a man is sitting at meat in winter-tide with the warm fire lighted on the hearth but the chill rain-storm without. The sparrow flies in at one door and tarries for a moment in the light and heat of the hearth-fire, and then flying forth from the other vanishes into the wintry darkness from whence it came. So tarries for a moment the life of man in our sight, but what is before it, what after it, we know not. If this new teaching tell us aught certainly of these, let us follow it." In this spirit the Northumbrian leaders accepted the new faith, and the unthinking crowd followed their example with easy indifference; the old gods had not served them well, the new could at least do no worse.

Baeda's Ecclesiastical History.

But the victory was not yet won. Penda, king of Mercia, came forward as a defender of paganism. He rallied the people of the south around him in a contest which was as much for political freedom as for the ancestral gods. For a quarter of a century the struggle raged. Kingdom after kingdom was torn from the grasp of Northumberland. For a time Penda stood supreme in England and the old gods were restored. But at last, in 655, the great king was defeated and slain by Oswiu, the Northumbrian ruler, at the river Winwaed near the present Leeds. With Penda ended the contest between Christianity and heathenism. The Mercians accepted the religion of the conquerors, Wessex quietly became Christian again, and finally the

Paganism.

South Saxons, the last to yield, renounced the faith of Woden and Thor.

One more danger was to be met. During the fierce struggle with Penda, Northumberland, cut off from Rome, had come under the influence of the Irish Church. At the call of the king, missionaries from the famous monastery of Columba in Iona had come into the country to complete the work of Paulinus. Led by Aidan, who founded the monastery of Lindisfarne, they wandered forth among the hills and dales of Northumberland, winning the rough peasantry to the faith of Christ. For the moment it seemed as though the north would be won by the Irish Church and the separation from Rome would be permanent. Fortunately, in the great synod held at Whitby in 664, to decide the ecclesiastical allegiance of Northumberland, the voice of Oswiu the king was in favor of Rome. The points of difference were slight, but had England held to the Irish Church she would have been spiritually isolated, cut off from all the civilization that centered at Rome. *Synod of Whitby.*

The century that followed was the golden age of the early English Church. Its wealth and influence grew steadily. It was organized into bishoprics and parishes corresponding roughly with the subkingdoms and townships. Throughout the north and on the eastern coast rose stately abbeys and monasteries, the homes of learning as well as religion. Baeda, "the venerable Bede," greatest of early English scholars, and first of English historians, was a monk of Jarrow on the Tyne, and it was at Whitby that Caedmon, the inspired cowherd, first learned the gift of song. While the monasteries became the centers of intellectual life, bishops took their place in the councils of the king, and parish priests moving among the people set the example of purer, gentler living. But it was not simply *Influence of the Church.* *Baeda, 673-735. "Ecclesiastical History of the English Nation."*

through its direct teachings or through the closer connection with the civilization of the Continent brought about by its influence, that the Church became a force in the growth of the English nation. It was the organization of the Church that furnished the model for organization of the State. A united Church under one head, the Archbishop of Canterbury, prepared men for a united State under one king. Ecclesiastical unity was the forerunner of national unity.

ENGLAND AND THE DANES.

Coming of the Northmen. The union of England under Egbert might have passed away as did that established by Penda had it not been for a common danger that bound together the warring states in

Saxon Hawking. Ninth Century.

the ninth century; the completion of Egbert's work was the unwitting achievement of the Northmen.

It is like reading the history of the Anglo-Saxon invasion over again to read of the coming of the Danes. They were Scandinavians and closely akin to the Angles and Saxons. Their faith was the faith of Woden, the sea was their home, and their delight was in war and plunder. Sweeping down from the north they ravaged the eastern coast of England, sacking the towns and plundering the rich monasteries of the fen country. Their object at first was booty, but by the middle of the ninth century the character of the attack changed, they came no longer simply to plunder but to conquer and settle. Within a few years the work of Egbert was undone, only the lands south of the Thames remained subject to the Saxon king, and in 871 the turn of the West Saxons came. The task of saving Wessex, and with it England and the national faith, fell upon Alfred, the young king. For seven years he waged a desperate struggle against the Danes. In 878 all seemed lost. Wessex was overrun, and Alfred with a few followers took refuge in the Isle of Athelney among the marshes of the Parret. But with the spring he came forth, and calling out the men of Somerset and Wilts, he won a complete victory over the Danes at Ethandun, and wrung from them the Treaty of Wedmore. By this they bound themselves to resign to Alfred the lands south of Watling Street. The north and east they kept, and it was henceforth known as the Danelaw, or land of the Danish law.

For the moment it seemed as though all hope of a united England was gone, for Alfred had lost more than half the territory held by his grandfather Egbert. But within what was left, his rule was far more real and substantial. He at once turned his attention to the upbuilding of his realm. He strengthened the defenses by creating a fleet, *Alfred, 871-901.*

Swine Hunting. Ninth Century.

the first English navy, and by reorganizing the fyrd, one half the men of each shire to be always ready for war. With the aid of his wise men the laws were codified and amended, and the courts of justice were revived. His ef- *Fyrd, the national militia, levied by shires.*

forts for the well-being of his realm did not end here. The long wars had resulted in the moral and intellectual degradation of the people, the Church was demoralized, learning had disappeared. "When I began to reign," said Alfred, "I cannot remember one priest south of the Thames who could render his service-book into English." To remedy these evils he rebuilt and founded churches and schools, and brought priests and teachers from the Continent. To meet the need of books in the English language, he himself translated and explained the works of Orosius, Boethius, and Baeda. It is to his desire that his subjects should know their own past that we owe the Anglo-Saxon Chronicle, the earliest history possessed by any Teutonic people in its own tongue. Everywhere he strove with untiring zeal and true wisdom to further the national welfare. "A hero of romance, but to whose character romance has done no more than justice," excelling as warrior, as ruler, as scholar, Alfred stands out as perhaps the most perfect character in history.

A Noble Saxon Youth.

King Edgar.

Conquest of the Danelaw.

Alfred's task was to reorganize and consolidate the lands south of Watling Street. To extend the rule of Wessex into the north, where the Danes had established several independent states, was the work of his son and grandsons. Step by step they reconquered the country, bringing Mercia and Northumbria under their direct rule, reducing the Celts of Wales and Strathclyde to submission, and obliging the Scots to render them some kind of allegiance. When Edgar ascended the throne in

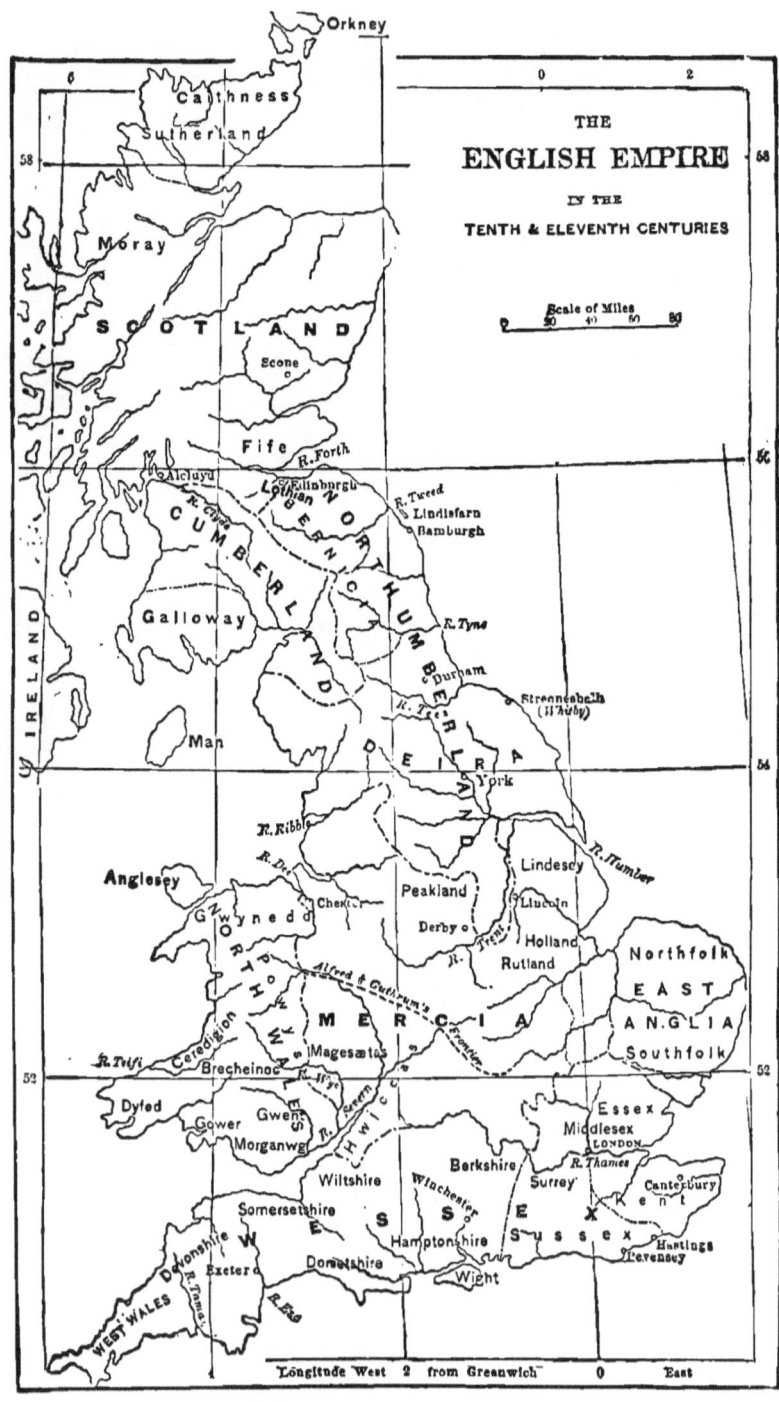

959, he had only to hold what those before him had won by dint of hard fighting, and he spent his peaceful reign in organizing his kingdom and reforming the Church. He had an able coadjutor in Dunstan, Archbishop of Canterbury, the first of England's long line of ecclesiastical statesmen.

The work of reconquest was done; the Dane had accepted rule of the Saxon, and the fusion of races already begun was soon complete. But the effect of the fierce struggle was plain in state and society long after the two peoples had become one. The old provincial jealousies had disappeared before the Dane. Common danger welded the people together, common interest replaced the union of the sword. The new union was symbolized in the king. The strengthening of his authority was a natural result of the war. To him men had looked in their need, their safety was his merit. His thegns leading their dependents to battle had borne the brunt of the fight far more than the unwieldy national force. With enlarged domains his power grew. From afar men looked with increased awe on the Lord's Anointed, the ruler of kings. But the power of the king was still personal, still dependent upon himself. If the king was strong, the crown was strong, but if he was weak, the old provincial jealousies strengthened by new tendencies toward separation at once showed themselves.

The long strife had left its mark on the churl as well as on the king. To protect himself against the Dane he became the dependent of some lord who gave him aid. He followed his lord to battle, tilled his fields, and sought

England in the tenth century.

St. Dunstan.

justice in his courts. He ceased to be free, but yet he was not a slave. He could not leave the land, but on the other hand he could not be sold from the land, nor could it be taken from him. He had also lost whatever political influence he may have had, for the folk-moot had either disappeared altogether, or had become a mere local court, the shire-moot.

Anglo-Saxon Gleeman, Tenth Century.

This same drift toward dependence, toward feudal subordination, showed itself throughout society. Just as the freeman bound himself to his lord, so his lord in turn attached himself to some greater thegn, or to one of the ealdormen who ruled the subject kingdoms. Here lay the great danger to the new union. These ealdormen were like petty kings in their own districts. Athelstan of East Anglia was so powerful that he was called the Half-King. They resented royal interference, and under a weak ruler each went his way, looking rather to his own interest than to the interest of the whole people. They formed also the strongest element in the Witenagemot which had replaced the folkmoots of the subkingdoms, and which now elected the king and made the laws and granted land. Unless the king was a strong man he was a mere tool in their hands. This struggle between the English king and his ealdormen was but a part of the great contest of the century between monarchy and feudalism. In France and on the Continent

Witenagemot—meeting of wise men; an assembly composed of the *bishops and greater thegns*.

A Princess of East Anglia.

generally, feudalism had triumphed; it was only in England that the crown still held its own. But however the issue might turn, the basis of English society was changed, the bulk of the population consisted no longer of freemen owning the land, holding their own courts, forming the backbone of the national forces, but of serfs bound to the soil, tilling the land of another, and doing his will.

The tenth century was for England a brief breathing space between the first and second coming of the Danes. While the descendants of Alfred were gradually bringing under their rule the lands north of Watling Street, the Northmen were spending their energies in making conquests on the Continent. Toward the close of the century they appeared again on the coast of England, coming not in small marauding bands, but as a national host prepared to conquer and to hold.

Anglo-Saxon Harper and Hoppestere. Tenth Century.

Danish Conquest.

Led by Swegen of Denmark.

The throne of England was occupied at this time by Edgar's son Ethelred, the only one of the West-Saxon line lacking in every kingly quality. "Redeless" his generation called him because of his unwillingness to take "rede," or counsel. Not content with his father's position he purposed to make his rule real and direct over all England, but he showed neither force nor judgment in his attempts to carry out his policy. The years of Ethelred's reign were shameful and miserable. On every side was incapacity, treachery. The king feared his subjects more than the Danes, the ealdormen thought only of their own interests, leader of the people there was none. "And forces were often gathered against the Danes, but as soon as they should have joined battle, then was there ever through some cause flight begun." "And when they went to their

Ethelred II., 979-1016.

Anglo-Saxon Chronicle.

ships, then ought the fyrd to have gone out against them until they should land; but then the fyrd went home; and when they went eastward, then was the fyrd kept westward. Then all the Witan were bidden to the king that they might counsel how this land should be guarded. But though they counseled something, it did not stand even one month. And next, there was no man that would gather the fyrd, but each fled as he best might; and next, no shire would even help another."

Cnut, 1016-1035.

That Englishmen could still fight when well led was proved, however, by the success of Edmund Ironsides who succeeded his father Ethelred in 1016. In seven months he fought six battles and in four the Danes were defeated; but death cut short his career, leaving Cnut, the young Danish king, without a rival. The English quietly accepted him as ruler, and once upon the throne he spared no effort to efface the memory of the way in which he had gained it. He strove to rule as an English king, putting Englishmen in high office and reëstablishing the law of Edgar. He sent home his Danish army retaining simply his house-carls, a small standing force, but he disarmed the ealdormen by placing over the four larger kingdoms men whom he could trust.

Anglo-Saxon Men-at-arms.

The greatest of these earls, as they were called, was an Englishman, Godwin of Wessex, henceforth the chosen minister of the king. Cnut gave to England peace and good order, but there was nothing permanent in his work and with his death his empire fell to pieces. For some years his sons reigned in England, but their rule was one of bloodshed and violence, and when in 1042 the Danish line came to an unworthy end men turned with longing to the son of Ethelred living in exile at the Norman court, and "all folk chose Edward to king." But it was as a Norman rather than as an Englishman that Edward came back, and under him far more

Edward the Confessor. 1042-1066.

Cnut and his Queen.

than during Cnut's reign did England learn the meaning of foreign rule. His piety and gentleness won for him the name of "Confessor," and in after years men recalled with longing the "good laws of Edward"; but he was more monk than king, and the real rulers of England during this reign were Godwin of Wessex and his greater son Harold. It was a time of division and discord, local jealousies broke forth again, the great earls strove with each other, the two parties, national and foreign, which divided the court appeared also in the Church. So long as Edward lived outward peace was maintained, but his death gave the signal for a struggle over the succession which laid bare all the elements of weakness in the nation.

Seal of Edward the Confessor.

CHAPTER III.

NORMAN ENGLAND.

Illustrative Readings.
  The Normans in Europe; Johnson.
  The Little Duke; Yonge.
  Hereward, the Last of the English; Kingsley.
  Harold; Tennyson.
  Harold, the Last of the Saxon Kings; Bulwer.
  The White Ship; Rossetti.

Important Dates.
  Reign of William I., 1066-1087.
    1070, Conquest complete.
    1085, Domesday Survey.
    1086, Salisbury Oath.
  Reign of William Rufus, 1087-1100.
    1096-1100, Normandy held in pledge.
  Reign of Henry I., 1100-1135.
    1106, Conquest of Normandy.
  Reign of Stephen, 1135-1154.
    1153, Treaty of Wallingford.

The Norman Line.
  Rollo, the Ganger, 912-927 (?).
  William Longsword, (927(?)-943.
  Richard I., the Fearless, 943-996.
  Richard II., the Good, 996-1026.   Emma m. Ethelred, the Unready.
  Richard III., 1026-1028. Robert, 1028-1035. *Edward the Confessor.
                          *William I., 1035-1067.
                            King of England, 1066-1087.

  Robert, 1087-1106. *William II.   *Henry I.   Adela m. Stephen of Blois.
  Duke of Normandy.   1087-1100.   1100-1135.
                                                  *Stephen, 1135-1154.
                                        Matilda m. Geoffrey Plantagenet,
                                                  Count of Anjou.
                                              *Henry II., 1154-1189.

                                        *Richard, 1189-1199.   *John, 1199-1216.
  *The English kings are starred.

THE CONQUEST.

As in England, so on the Continent, the fierce persistence of the Norse invaders finally prevailed against the more civilized and peace-loving nations with whom they strove, and they secured a firm footing in France, in Sicily, and in Russia. In 912, Charles the Simple, the degenerate

The Normans in Normandy.

descendant of Charlemagne and King of the West Franks, granted to Rollo the Ganger the province lying along the coast on either side the Seine, called from its new masters, Normandy. Rollo thus became a vassal of the Frankish king, but in those turbulent times it was not easy to assert the rights of overlordship, and the Norman dukes gave little heed to their nominal sovereign. The land was apportioned to their followers as booty of war, while the natives, being regarded as a conquered race, were reduced to serfdom. The Norse vikings despised these Romanized and degenerate Franks. Absorbed in hunting and feasting, in making war upon a neighboring lord to extend a boundary, or upon the duke to resist a claim, they contemptuously declined to concern themselves with such slave's business as agriculture and the arts. Yet gradually the superior civilization gained influence among them. They married Frankish women; they began to speak the Franco-Latin language, which, rude as it was, ran smoother than their wild mother tongue; they entered the awe-inspiring Christian

William I. and two Normans. From the Bayeux Tapestry, illustrating the Norman fashion of shaving the back of the head.

churches and forgot the fierce gods of their ancestors; they came under the sway of the clergy and received at their hands not merely a purer religion, a higher morality, but the conceptions of right and order preserved in the Roman law, the traditions of learning and civilization treasured in the monasteries. So it came about that within the 150 years from Rollo the Ganger to William the Norman the rude Norse pirates had become essentially Frenchmen. Losing nothing of their old-time fire and vigor, they had yet adopted the best elements in the civilization of the conquered race. In the tenth century, the Normans were barbarians; in the eleventh, they were the most progressive people in Europe.

During this same 150 years, the English, as we have seen, were retrograding. William of Malmesbury, an eleventh century chronicler of mingled English and Norman blood, compares the character of the Normans with that of the English to the great disadvantage of the latter. He asserts that the "desire after literature and religion had decayed in England," that the English clergy, "contented with a very slight degree of learning, could hardly stammer out the words of the sacraments; and a person who understood grammar was an object of wonder and astonishment." The nobility were given up to luxury and debauch. Gluttony and drunkenness were national vices. The common people, unprotected by the degenerate kings, "became a prey to the most powerful, who amassed fortunes by either seizing on their property or by selling their persons into foreign countries." Yet the wealth so won was spent in wasteful revel. "They consumed their whole substance in mean and despicable houses; unlike the Normans and French who in noble and splendid mansions lived with frugality." "The Normans," says our chronicler, "are proudly appareled, delicate in their food, but not excessive. They are a race inured to war, and can hardly live without it; fierce in rushing against the enemy; and, where strength fails of success, ready to use stratagem or to corrupt by bribery."

A worthy descendant of Rollo was William the Bastard, son of Duke Robert and the pretty daughter of a tanner of Falaise. Flouted by his vassals, William had much difficulty in making good his claim to his father's duchy, since the restless Norman barons seized the opportunity to assert

Contemporary chronicles, The Anglo-Saxon Chronicle. Florence of Worcester. William of Malmesbury. Ingulph. All quotations in this chapter not otherwise specified are taken from the Anglo-Saxon Chronicle.

their independence, but the young duke soon proved himself equal to the situation. He not only reduced his turbulent subjects to submission, but he added to his domains the county of Maine. The vigor and wisdom thus manifested won for him the title of "the Great."

William's claim to the English crown. However, Normandy and Maine together formed but a narrow realm. With the genius for conquest strong within him, William turned his eyes to England. On the death of Edward the Confessor, the Witan had passed by Edgar the Atheling and elected Harold king. The son of Godwin was hardly crowned when William protested the validity of the sacred rite and announced himself as the true successor. The Norman duke brought forward a triple claim to the English crown. Edward had promised to make William his heir; Harold, wrecked on the Norman coast and delivered into the hands of his rival, had sworn on sacred relics to surrender his rights to the throne; finally the pope, offended by English disregard of ecclesiastical law and persuaded that William was a faithful son of the Church, had sanctioned his succession and sent a consecrated banner to further the invasion of England. Yet William's right, as justified by the event, was not Edward's promise, nor Harold's oath, nor yet the papal blessing, but the ability to govern with a strong hand this kingdom torn by civil dissension. Harold was brave and patriotic, but he could never have welded the warring earldoms into national unity. As earl of Wessex, he was but first of the four great ealdormen. His fellow earls were jealous of his ascendancy and his own brother Tostig

Harold II. From the Bayeux Tapestry.

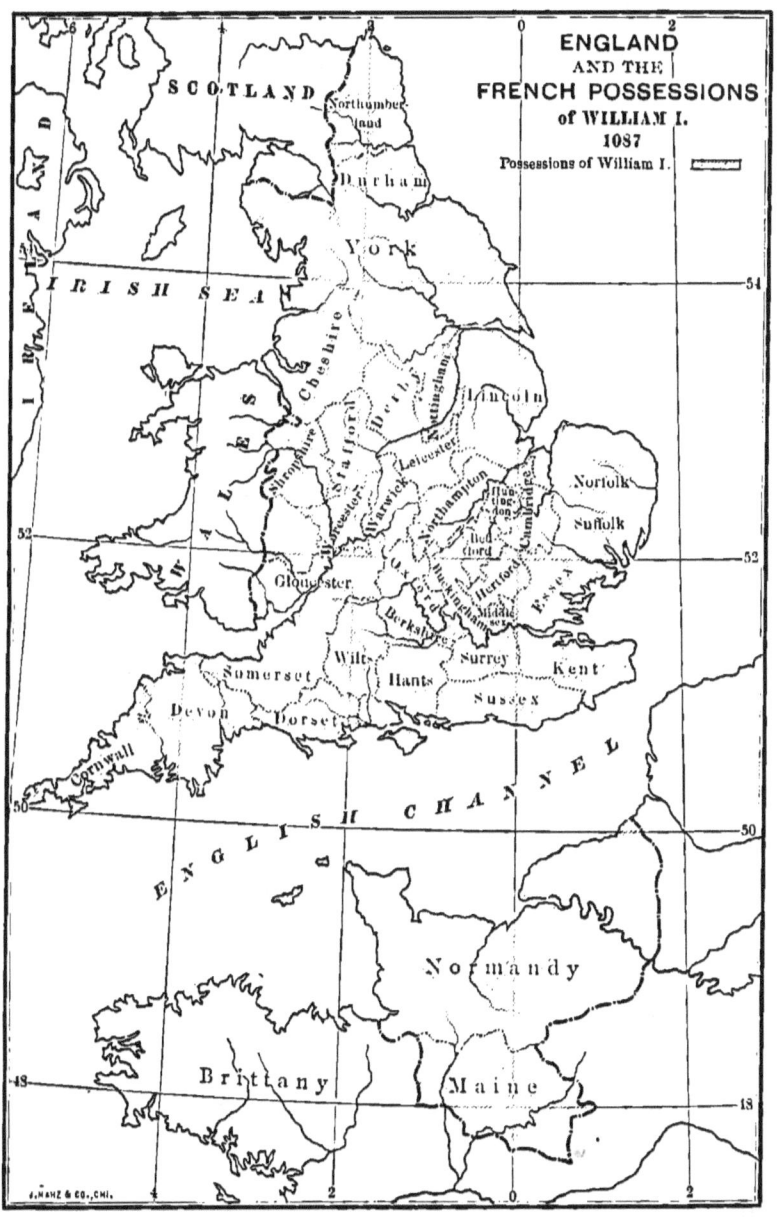

Norman England. 51

was in open rebellion. The Battle of Hastings gave the destinies of England into the hands of William. In the wild rout of Senlac Hill, Harold was slain and his forces scattered.

Battle of Hastings, 1066.

Not yet, however, was the kingdom won. The Witan met at London and elected Edgar Atheling king. Ignoring this action, William marched through Kent and Sussex, ravaging the lands of those who opposed him, up to the very gates of London. He hesitated to lay siege to the city for he wished to present himself not as a conqueror, but as rightful successor to the crown. His forbearance was soon justified. The citizens of London, seeing that the great northern earls made no movement in their behalf, opened their gates to Harold's triumphant rival, and went through the form of electing him king. William was crowned on Christmas day, 1066, in the beautiful abbey built by the Confessor at Westminster. He took oath to "govern the English people as well as any king before him had best done, if they would be faithful to him." The Anglo-Saxon Chronicle, usually so dry and barren of personal details, waxes ardent in the description of William the Conqueror. "This King William was a very wise man

The Conquest.

William I. From the Bayeux Tapestry.

and very powerful, more dignified and strong than any of his predecessors. He was mild to the good men who loved God and over all measure severe to the men who gainsayed his will. . . . . So also was he a very rigid and cruel man so that no one durst do anything against his will. He had earls in his bonds who had acted against his will; bishops he cast from their bishoprics, and

abbots from their abbacies, and thanes into prison. . . .
Among other things is not to be forgotten the good peace
that he made in this land; so that a man who had any
confidence in himself might go through the realm, with his
bosom full of gold, unhurt. . . . Certainly in his time
men had great hardship and very many injuries. Castles
he caused to be made and poor men to be greatly oppressed.
He had fallen into covetousness and altogether loved
greediness. He planted a great preserve for deer, and he
laid down laws therewith, that whosoever should slay hart
or hind should be blinded. He forbade the harts and also
the boars to be killed. As greatly did he love the tall deer
as if he were their father. He also ordained concerning the
hares that they should go free. His great men bewailed it
and the poor men murmured thereat; but he was so ob-
durate that he recked not of the hatred of them all, but
they must wholly follow the king's will if they would
live or have land or property or even
his peace." Such was the man who
had won the crown of England—stern
and masterful, indifferent to the suffering wrought in the execution of his
purpose; but an able administrator,
bent on so governing his realm that
none but the king could oppress the
people.

The New Forest near Winchester. The district was cleared of its inhabitants, whole villages being laid waste to make place for the deer.

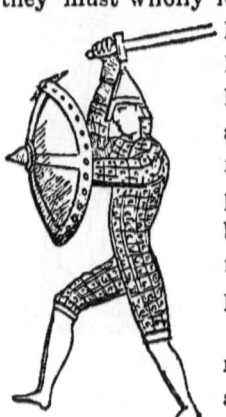

A Saxon Warrior.

When William was crowned at Westminster only the southeastern counties
acknowledged his right to reign. The
west and north held out for Edgar.
The subjugation of the rebellious dis-
tricts occupied the years from 1067 to 1070. Mercia and
Northumbria were reduced to submission, and the unhappy Edgar took refuge in Scotland, where his sister

Margaret was queen. The king handled with merciless severity the miserable lesser folk who had but blindly followed the lead of their Saxon lords. Determined to render another rising impossible, William gave orders that the land should be laid waste. Cities and villages were reduced to ashes and the crops destroyed. The helpless inhabitants were slaughtered or left to die of starvation. "He made a desert and called it peace."

The fame of Norman cruelty and Norman prowess preceded the king even to the frontiers of his terrified kingdom. Chester and the Welsh border submitted without resistance, and Malcolm, king of Scotland, acknowledged William as his overlord. The last stronghold of the English resistance was the Isle of Ely, lying inaccessible in the heart of the Fens. Here the Saxon malcontents rallied under the leadership of Hereward the Wake, who defended his island fortress with desperate but unavailing courage.

THE FOREIGN KINGS.

The people so conquered must now be held in subjection. In the task of governing his newly acquired kingdom, the Norman duke proved himself preëminent in statecraft as he had hitherto been in war. He was most desirous of ruling as an English king, but the chaotic condition of the country necessitated a method of government hardly to be distinguished from a military occupation. The estates of the rebellious Saxon thanes were confiscated and made over to his Norman followers, whose interests were identified with the interest of the king, and who could be relied upon to crush any incipient revolt on the part of the English. William further guaranteed his authority against Saxon and Norman alike by building in all the principal towns castles which he garrisoned with his own men. Many of these are still standing, notably the strong Tower of London.

William I.
1066-1087.

The Conqueror meant that the royal authority should be supreme through the length and breadth of the land. England had known no such kingship, not even in the days of Edgar. The great thanes, assembled in the Witan, had been accustomed to make laws for the nation, having power to elect and even to depose the king, but William and his successors rejected the Anglo-Saxon conception of monarchy. In their interpretation the king was not the elected leader and representative of his people, but lord of the land and master of its inhabitants. Succession to the throne was henceforth by inheritance as to a private estate.

With such conceptions of the royal office, the form of election must soon lapse. William could not allow to any subject such power as had been wielded by Godwin and Harold. He therefore abolished the great earldoms. To a favored few were granted large estates, but these were scattered piecemeal in different parts of the country so that there should be no concentration of power. The king reserved to himself the lion's share of the confiscated territories, and never relinquished his prerogative as original proprietor. In granting lands to his vassals William made the most of his opportunity to impose more stringent conditions than had been customary in England or even in Normandy. Every vassal must pay an annual rent, not however, in money, but in military service. The specific terms of his tenure depended upon his rank and the extent of his fief. If the tenant failed in his duty, the grant might be recalled. In this way every great lord was bound to send his contingent to the king's army. The feudal relation—by which we are to understand the reciprocal obligations of lord and vassal, the lord granting land and protection, the vassal giving a stipulated service—prevailed throughout the Middle Ages both in England and on

Apportionment of land. The king held 1422 manors; Earl of Moretaine, 703; Earl of Bretagne, 442; Bishop of Bayeux, 439; Bishop of Constance, 280. Eleven proprietors held 4,242 of the 9,250 manors in England.

Fief, the estate held on terms of feudal tenure.

Feudalism.

the Continent. It was the characteristic social tie not only between sovereign and tenant-in-chief, but between the king's vassals and their subtenants, between the subtenants and their dependents. King William did not introduce feudalism into England (we have seen that the relation already existed between the landowners and the cultivators of the soil, between the king and his thanes), but he put upon it a new interpretation. Feudalism became, under his vigorous administration, a political system that brought the wealth and fighting force of every landowner in the country under the king's control. He obliged "all the landowners that were of account over all England" to take the oath of personal fealty to him. Every man knelt before him and placing his hands between those of the king swore "to be faithful to the king before all other men." So did the astute Norman check the tendency to disintegration that was the bane of continental feudalism. While the Salisbury oath was observed, no powerful vassal could gather his dependents to make war against his sovereign. All tenants-in-chief were summoned to meet the king in a great council three times a year, at Christmas, at Easter, and at Whitsuntide. This was apparently a continuation of the Witenagemot and indeed the old name was for some time retained. It was, however, no longer a meeting of wise men, the counselors of the king, but of principal landowners who came in feudal array not to advise their sovereign but to render homage. Upon this change of function followed a loss of power. The administration of government was in the hands of the king's officers and the powers of the Witenagemot were absorbed by the Curia Regis.

In order that he might be fully informed as to the value of his new domain, the king had a rent-roll compiled —the so-called Domesday Survey. This concern for accu-

<small>The Salisbury Oath. 1086.</small>

<small>The Great Council.</small>

<small>Curia Regis, standing committee of the great council made up of the king's ministers.</small>

<small>The Domesday Survey.</small>

rate knowledge of his realm is a mark of the highest statesmanship; the Survey was at one and the same time a census, a land register, and a basis of taxation, and remains of the highest value to historians; but the inquiry was deeply resented by the contemporary chronicler. "After this the king had a great council and very deep speech with his Witan about this land, how it was peopled, or by what men; then sent he his men over all England into every shire, and caused to be ascertained how many hundred hides were in the shire, or what land the king himself had, and cattle within the land, or what dues he ought to have, every twelve months from the shire. Also he caused to be written how much land his archbishops had, and his suffragan bishops and his abbots and his earls; and—tho' I may narrate somewhat prolixly—what or how much each man had who was a holder of land in England, in land or in cattle, and how much money it might be worth. So very narrowly he caused it to be traced out, that there was not one single hide, nor one yard of land, nor even—it is a shame to tell, tho' it seemed to him no shame to do—an ox, nor a cow, nor a swine was left that was not set down in his writ."

In the Salisbury oath and the Domesday Survey, the Conqueror's work in England reached its climax. He had succeeded, for the time being, in bringing men of all ranks and races to acknowledge the duty of primary allegiance to the king. The next year he was engaged in war with his own overlord, Philip of France. At the siege of Mantes, he received an injury from which he soon after died. "Alas!" says the pious chronicler, "how false, how unstable, is the good of this world. He who had been a powerful king and the lord of many territories, possessed not then, of all his lands, more than seven feet of ground."

In accordance with the Conqueror's will, his eldest son

Norman England. 57

Robert succeeded him in Normandy, William, the second son, became king of England, while to Henry Beauclerc, the scholar of the family, was left a sum of £5,000 and some private estates.

William II. had inherited the worst traits of his father with none of the good. His greed was restrained by no sense of justice, his impetuous will was guided by no statesmanlike fore-sight. He regarded his kingship only as an opportunity for indulging to the full his fierce and unbridled passions. Ranulf, the justiciar, was his able accomplice. This man, nicknamed Flambard, "the firebrand," had won the favor of his royal patron by his ingenuity in devising new pretexts for wringing money from the reluctant purses of the vassals. In accordance with the continental version of the relations between lord and vassal, the king had control of the estates of a minor and might pocket the income. On coming of age the heir must pay a large sum of money (relief) for the privilege of entering upon his inheritance. If the heir were a woman, the king could marry her to whomsoever he would. Choice of a husband was only conceded to the woman or her relatives on payment of a heavy fine. If there were no heirs or in case a vassal were convicted of felony, the estate lapsed (escheated) to the crown. Certain extraordinary "aids" might be demanded on the marriage of the king's eldest daughter or the knighting of his eldest son or, in case he was taken captive,

William Rufus. 1087-1100.

William Rufus.

Justiciar, vice-gerent or prime minister.

Feudal exactions.

for his ransom. All these services may be justified as medieval forms of rent, and they were in turn required by the king's vassals of their subtenants. Under a just administration they were not exorbitant, but the Red King and Ranulf, ignoring all right and precedent, set no bounds to their merciless greed. Of the second William, the Chronicle says: "He was very rigorous and stern over his land and his men and towards all his neighbors, and very formidable; and thro' the counsels of evil men, that were always grateful to him, and through his own covetousness, he was ever tormenting this nation with an army and with unjust exactions; because in his days every right fell and every wrong in the sight of God and of the world rose up." These exactions were felt most heavily, of course, by the Norman barons, and were promptly resented. Under the lead of Odo, Bishop of Bayeux, they revolted and declared for Robert, Duke of Normandy, the elder brother.

Female Costume of the reign of Rufus and Henry I.

Revolt of the Barons. The king in his extremity turned to his English subjects. "He then sent after Englishmen and told to them his need and desired their support and promised them the best laws that ever were before in this land, and every unjust impost he forbade and granted to men their woods and liberty of the chase; but," adds the chronicler dejectedly, "it stood no while." The revolt once suppressed, the king renewed his cruel practices.

In 1100 William Rufus was killed while hunting in the

New Forest and Henry was chosen king. This wise prince had shown himself an able ruler in his little Norman province, and his accession brought a much needed peace to England. The king desired, first of all, to be on good terms with his English subjects. With this in view he married Edgyth, the niece of Edgar the Atheling, "of the right royal race of England." Her name, which was impossible to a French tongue, was changed to Matilda. The Norman courtiers gave to the Saxon princess but a grudging welcome; they mocked the popular sympathies of the king and queen by giving them the homely English names, Goodrich and Godiva. But King Henry recked nothing of their merriment. He had "promised God and all the people to put down all the injustices that were in his brother's time, and to maintain the best laws that stood in any king's day before him." The Red King's justiciar Ranulf was thrown into the Tower of London and such officers were appointed as would rightly administer the government. The king's agents made regular circuits through the shires executing justice and collecting the royal revenues. Law and order were so far maintained that King Henry was called the Lion of Justice. Yet the imposts levied in the name of the king fell heavily upon the people, and the Chronicle bitterly complains of the sore oppression of the land. The malcontent nobles leagued against him. Flambard, escaped from the Tower, and Robert of Bellême concerted with Robert of Normandy an attack on England, purposing to place Duke Robert on the throne. Rallying to his aid the English and the lesser vassals, Henry worsted his foes. In the decisive battle of Tinchebrai, the two Roberts were taken prisoners and Normandy came into the possession of the English king. Duke Robert lingered out his days a captive in Cardiff Castle, and the Norman nobles, deprived of pretext for revolt, never again lifted hand

Henry I. 1100–1135.

The charter granted at his accession was the model for all subsequent guarantees of good government.

Revolt of the Barons.

Conquest of Normandy. 1106.

against Henry. In 1135 this good king died. "Then there was tribulation soon in the land, for every man that could, forthwith robbed another. . . . A good man he was and there was great awe of him. No man durst misdo against another in his time. He made peace for man and beast."

The barons had promised the dying king to place his daughter Matilda on the throne; but the kingdom was a

Vision of Henry I. An ancient Drawing, showing the Costume of the Clergy.

Stephen.
1135-1154.

turbulent one to be ruled by a woman. There was a rival claimant, Stephen of Blois, son of the Conqueror's daughter Adela. His cause was championed by the citizens of London, who hoped that he would maintain the peace and good order so essential to commercial prosperity. The support of the city of London has again and again in English history determined a doubtful contest. Stephen was chosen king by the barons and was soon after crowned at Winchester. But the hope of the Londoners was doomed to disappointment. Matilda urged her claims. Her cause was supported by divers of the great nobles who were, however, less concerned to maintain her right than to defy the royal authority. The weak, unstable character of Stephen gave them favorable opportunity to assert their independence. "When the traitors perceived that he was a mild man and soft and good and did no justice, then did they all wonder. . . . Every powerful man built himself castles and held them against the king and they filled the land full of castles. They cruelly oppressed the wretched men of the land with castle-works. When the castles were made they filled them with devils and evil men. Then took they those men that they imagined had any property, both by night and by day, peasant men and women, and put them in prison for their gold and their silver, and tortured them with unutterable torture. . . . Many thousands they killed with hunger; and that lasted the nineteen years while Stephen was king, and ever it was worse and worse. They laid imposts on the towns continually and called it 'censerie'; when the wretched men had no more to give, they robbed and burned all the towns, so that thou mightest well go all a day's journey and thou shouldst never find a man sitting in a town or the land tilled. . . . Men said openly that Christ and his saints slept." Better than such anarchy was the harsh rule of the Conqueror.

Stephen did not seek the support of the English as Henry had done. He foolishly spent his treasure in hiring foreign mercenaries, who were even more cruel than the barons and alienated the people from their once-loved king. Still Matilda could not win the kingdom. In the battle of Lincoln, Stephen was taken prisoner and for a few months Matilda reigned; but she proved to be a harsh and vengeful mistress. London revolted and the great barons renewed their allegiance to Stephen. The Angevin cause seemed lost when it was taken up and brought to a

Civil War.

1141.

triumphant issue by Matilda's son, the young Henry. Though but nineteen years of age, this prince was already lord of Normandy, Maine, Anjou, and Aquitaine, and ruled these restless provinces with a strong hand. He arrived in England in 1153 and, rallying Matilda's adherents about him, made such headway that Stephen was fain to treat for peace. A compromise was negotiated by the Archbishop of Canterbury. The king had just lost his only son, Eustace. He agreed, on condition that he might retain the crown during his life, to recognize Henry as his son and heir. So the long strife came to an end. When Stephen died in the next year, Henry was beyond sea; "but no man durst do other than good for the great awe of him." On his return he was crowned king and entered into undisputed possession of his inheritance.

Treaty of Wallingford. 1153.

RESULTS OF THE CONQUEST.

During the eighty-eight years since the Norman invasion, the aspect of England had undergone great changes. The Norman race had succeeded in establishing itself in possession not only of the crown but of every post of power and profit throughout the kingdom. No English names are to be found among the tenants-in-chief until a century after the Conquest. Latin was the language of the Church and the law, French that of the court. The separation between the two races, the conquering and the conquered, was wide and deep. Contempt and tyranny on the one hand, fear and hate on the other, prolonged the antagonism to which the harsh methods of the Conquest had given rise. Yet Saxon and Norman were originally of the same stock. The case was not that of the English in India or the French in Algiers. It was evident that the two races must eventually come together and fuse into one.

The immediate effects of the Norman rule were pregnant

Norman England. 63

with result. First of all England was brought into close relations with the Continent. The Conqueror ruled Normandy and England as one kingdom. His great barons held estates on both sides the Channel and much journeying between the French and English territories became necessary. Under William Rufus, Normandy and England were independent realms, but Tinchebrai gave Normandy to Henry I., and the duchy and the kingdom remained united for a hundred years thereafter. This political connection brought about such relations with the Continent as had not existed since Britain was a Roman colony. Commerce revived; merchants ventured to undertake a European trade, carrying to France, Flanders, and Germany the agricultural products of England, wool and grain, fish and cattle. In exchange they brought back the fine cloths, furs, wines, and other luxuries required by the Norman gallants. Lead and tin were also exported, while the indispensable iron, not yet discovered in the barren Northumbrian hills, was fetched from the Baltic coast. The precious metals, too, especially silver, were imported in considerable quantity. Commercial enterprise carried Englishmen far abroad, to Paris, to Marseilles, to Venice, and the Orient. The high-priced dainties they brought back in their brave ships were not their most valuable cargo. Strange tales of foreign lands and customs, marvelous stories of romance and adventure, wisdom won by contact with a superior civilization, these were the imports that affected most deeply the life of the English people.

Renewed intercourse with the Continent.

Furthermore the Conquest brought England into touch with the learning of the Continent. From the Universities of Bologna and Paris, from the renowned Abbey of Bec, came Lanfranc and Anselm and many less famous scholars and ecclesiastics, who introduced the Latin tongue and the continental authors and inspired the English Church

Intellectual impulse.

with a new zeal for letters. Out of obscure beginnings rose the great University of Oxford "where the clergy in England chiefly flourished and excelled in clerkly lore." Thousands of English youths crowded its cloisters, taking upon themselves the monk's vows, not in religious devotion, but because the monastery afforded the only opportunity for the scholar's life. The intellectual labors of these devotees of learning were confined to the transcription of Latin manuscripts, ecclesiastical and classical, and the embellishment of the national annals. The wordly-minded ecclesiastic found at the court a more congenial employment. Since the clerics were the only learned men of the day, they were almost exclusively employed by the Norman kings in the administration of the government. Hence resulted a notable modification of political theory. The monastic training had instilled into the thought of these cowled chancellors those conceptions of law and government which were handed down by the Church as part of her heritage from imperial Rome. Doctrines of the king's supremacy and the subject's duty of obedience are not of English origin, but derived from the Continent. They were imported into England by Norman priests. Moreover the greedy misrule of the barons tended to foster respect for the king's authority. The supremacy of the king came to be regarded as the safeguard of the subject against political anarchy such as devastated England under Edward the Confessor and the feeble Stephen. From the king's officers might be expected a more uniform justice than was meted out in the local courts, and men were willing to pay dear for such protection. Neither the stern cruelty of William nor the heavy taxes imposed by the Henries could obliterate the remembrance of "the good peace they had made in the land." Throughout these centuries king and barons were engaged in a well-matched

Exaltation of the king's authority.

contest for mastery. The ambitious vassals maintained a prolonged resistance against the royal authority. Again and again the strife broke out,—in the revolt of Hereford and Norfolk against the Conqueror, in the opposition of the barons to the exactions of William Rufus, in the rising against Henry I., led by Flambard, in the contemptuous misrule of the great lords under Stephen. It was a veritable tug of war, and the kings were forced to fall back on the English who, having their own grievances against the arrogant Norman lords, were ready to lend aid to the royal cause.

In the long struggle between king and barons, the clergy as a rule cast their weight on the side of royalty, and yet, influenced by the mounting ambition of the popes, the Church asserted privileges which not infrequently brought her into antagonism with the throne. Rome had hoped from William's invasion of England a revival of the old-time relations between the papal see and the English Church, and these anticipations were in some degree realized. There followed close upon the Conquest a revival, if not of Christianity, at least of ecclesiasticism. The Norman clergy introduced into England the stricter discipline imposed upon the continental Church by Gregory VII. Celibacy was enforced among the superior clergy, although the parish priests were contemptuously left to keep their wives if they would. Monasticism received a new impulse with the incoming of the Cistercians, whose voluntary poverty and severe asceticism attracted the admiration and devotion of the people. William's attitude toward the Church was that of the able ruler who sees that the clergy may serve an important function in maintaining order and in rallying the people to the support of the king. He deposed the English prelates and appointed Normans in their stead, thus securing his own influence in all the superior

Relations of Church and State.

Ecclesiastical courts were established having jurisdiction over the moral offenses of clergy and laity.

offices; but the clerics so appointed were selected with an eye to their churchmanship as well as to their loyalty.

A Bishop of the close of the Eleventh Century.

Lanfranc, Archbishop of Canterbury, was one of the most learned and able ecclesiastics of his day. William further converted the Church hierarchy to his purpose by requiring from each bishop and abbot the oath of homage and such feudal service as would be due from a lay lord holding the same lands. The Church was thus feudalized, and every acre of monastery land and every parish glebe was made to render its quota to the royal treasury. The Conqueror was a faithful son of the Church, and yet the pretensions of Gregory VII. to supreme authority in ecclesiastical affairs were met by uncompromising denial. The wise and wary king won from the pope, whose will no other European monarch had been able to withstand, most important concessions. No excommunication was to be declared in England without the king's leave. No papal bull could be received or executed without his consent. Legislation in church synod was subject to his veto. Appointments to ecclesiastical office were to be made by the secular power. The questions thus settled by the friendly mediation of Lanfranc were, however, destined to be opened again and again, and to vex statesmen for centuries to come. For example, the right of appointment to ecclesiastical office, which had been readily conceded to the great William, was challenged in the reign of Henry I. Anselm, the saintly successor of Lanfranc, refused to consecrate the bishops who had received in-

Relations of king and pope.

Gregory VII., 1073-1085. Aimed to establish celibacy, to repress simony, to free Church from control of State.

vestiture from the king. The conflicting claims of king and pope were again compromised. Prelates were to be elected by the clergy, but in the king's presence. The ring and the crozier, symbols of the spiritual function, were to be bestowed by the pope, while the newly elected bishop or abbot was to render homage to the king for his estates.

Right of Investiture, i. e., appointing to a spiritual benefice; claimed by king since incumbent was a vassal, by the pope since incumbent was an ecclesiastic.

Upon the life of the common people the effect of the Conquest is not easily ascertained. The early chroniclers, like later historians, are so fully occupied in recounting the deeds of rich and powerful personages, that they tell little of the aspirations, the achievements, the failures of the humble men and women who till the fields and weave the cloth, and perform the thousand tasks, without which the projects of king and statesman would avail nothing for the welfare of the land. This people, whose deeds no chronicler records, no poet sings, and concerning whose life we can gather only the scantiest information, was the major part of the nation. The population of England in the eleventh century was about 1,500,000. Judging from data afforded by the Domesday Survey only three per cent belonged to the feudal nobility. The remaining ninety-seven per cent were small landed proprietors, serfs, and slaves. The feudal lords in the eleventh century were almost without exception Norman, while the lower orders were wholly English. Speaking the Saxon tongue, ministered to by Saxon priests, observing the social and political customs of their ancestors, they lived a life apart and were little affected by the change of masters. The principal Saxon landholders were, as has been seen, degraded by the Conquest, but the tillers of the soil were left in undisturbed possession. They lived on in the ancient rural communities (called manors in the Norman speech), and cultivated the land they had inherited from their fathers, rendering to the new lord the labor, money, or product service re-

Life of the people.

Census of adult males. Vassals of the crown, 600; subtenants, 7,871; ecclesiastics, 904; free proprietors, 33,109; serfs, 195,580; slaves, 25,156; burgesses, 7,968.

Rectitudines singularum personarum.

Serf (villein), agricultural laborer, bound to the soil, but personally free.

quired by local usage. A quaint document of the tenth century gives us detailed information as to the duties and privileges of the serf. His services are "various, in some places heavy, in others moderate." He is required to work on his lord's land two days a week throughout the year and three days a week through the spring plowing and planting and during harvest. Other special services (boon-work) must be rendered upon demand. " From Martinmas to Easter he shall lie at his lord's fold as often as he is bid." He may be asked to fetch and carry, but "if he do carrying he is not to work while his horse is out." The remaining time he is free to use on his own land. On the great church festivals, the characteristic marks of time in the medieval calendar, each villein must bring to the manor house a stipulated contribution in money or produce.

Feast of St. Michael, September 11.

Feast of St. Martin, November 11.

On Michaelmasday, he pays tenpence rent; on Martinmasday, thirty-three sesters of barley and two hens; at Easter, a young sheep or twopence. It is the duty of the serfs to feed the lord's hounds and provide for the village swineherd to whom each man gives six loaves " when he goes to mast." The lord, for his part, provides his serf with thirty acres of land and an "outfit", *i. e.*, two oxen, one cow, and six sheep, tools for his work, and utensils for his house. "Then when he dies his lord takes back what he leaves." " This land law holds on some lands, but here and there, as I have said, it is heavier or lighter, for all land services are not alike. On some lands the serf shall pay a tax in honey, on some in meat, on some in ale. Let him who is over the district take care that he knows what the old land customs are and what are the customs of the people." To secure the fulfillment of these numerous and complicated services required sedulous attention, and for this purpose the lord of the manor, often an absentee, employed a steward or bailiff. His was a hateful task and medieval literature abounds in sarcastic allusions to his greed and cunning. Serf labor seems to us a cumbersome method of getting work done, but it was the form of service most convenient in a feudal society because it did not require direct supervision. It was to every man's interest to cultivate his own plot of land to the best of his knowledge and ability. On the demesne land he gave but a grudging service. The Domesday Survey reports only twenty-five thousand slaves, and after the eleventh century the number rapidly decreased. This was in part a consequence of the edict against the slave-trade issued by the Conqueror, but was due even more to the prevalence of the feudal relation with which property in human beings was inconsistent. The free proprietors formed only twelve per cent of the population, and they were to be found for the most part in the north among the recent Danish settlements. In the south, the feudal tenure was well-nigh universal.

Demesne, that part of the estate which the lord held in exclusive possession. It was cultivated by serf or slave or (later) hired labor.

Life within the manor was rude and simple in the extreme. Communication with the outside world, even with the neighboring villages, was of rare occurrence. Each community was self-sustaining. Iron implements, millstones, salt, and spices must be brought from a distance, but food, shelter, and clothing were amply provided by local industries. The methods of agriculture were primitive and much of the land lay unreclaimed and waste. Perhaps not more than one fifth of the cultivable area of England was in use. The people naturally sought the fertile fields of the southeast, while the less hospitable regions of the west and north were but sparsely settled.

Fully three fourths of the population of medieval England was agricultural, the proportion between urban and rural inhabitants being about what it is in Ireland to-day. Mention is made in the Domesday Survey of eighty towns, but only six of these were other than large villages. As in

Serfs escaping to a town and remaining unclaimed a year and a day acquired freedom. Considerable additions were thus made to the town population.

Ireland, the most prosperous towns were seaports. London and Southampton controlled the trade between southern England and the Continent. Norwich brought the products of the eastern counties within reach of the sea, while the western districts found an outlet at Bristol. York, Lincoln, Winchester, and Oxford were ancient fortified places of great strategic importance. The Conquest tended to foster the growth of towns since it not only opened new commercial opportunities on the Continent, but, by bringing the warring sections of England under one strong administration, facilitated internal trade. There ensued a period of marked prosperity. Increasing by rapid strides in wealth, numbers, and influence, the townsmen were soon in position to buy from the king or their over-lord charters of liberty that secured to them, in return for an annual tax, freedom from further imposts and practical self-government. The affairs of the burgesses were apparently held quite beneath the notice of the royal court and its chroniclers. The towns were thought of only as a source of revenue. Yet in the silent, unheeded growth of these trading communities there was preparing a power destined to play a notable part in the nation's history.

CHAPTER IV.

FUSION OF RACES.

Illustrative Readings.
Becket; Tennyson.
Henry the Second; Green.
Ivanhoe; Scott.
The Talisman; Scott.

Important Dates.
Reign of Henry II., 1154-1189.
  1164. Constitutions of Clarendon.
  1172. Death of Archbishop Thomas.
  1174. Rising of the Barons.
Reign of Richard I., 1189-1199.
  1194. Richard's return from the Crusade.

HENRY II.

Henry of Anjou was only twenty-one when he came to the throne but already men had learned "to bear him great love and fear." Born of two remarkable races, he inherited the strong qualities of each. His instinct of government, his laborious industry, and his practical wisdom were Norman, but he was Angevin in his patience, his tenacity, and his craftiness. The contrasts of his character were as marked as its power. In his passions he was half a savage; the results of long patient scheming were often marred by a moment's ungovernable rage, and his irreverence was only equaled by his superstition; he scoffed at God one instant, and groveled at the feet of a priest the next. All Henry's force and power and untiring activity were needed for the task before him. Order was to be restored, a rebellious baronage, grown more unruly during the disorder of Stephen's reign, was to be curbed, and the Church, dangerously strong and conscious of its strength, was to be brought within bounds. There were, moreover, new problems to be faced. Beneath the anarchy of the preceding years, the forces of modern civilization were at work, and in spite of misrule England shared in the great

Condition of England.

industrial and intellectual movement of the twelfth century. While rulers and barons were contending for the mastery, towns were growing in size and importance, new enterprises were started, and trade and commerce received a strong impetus. Outside the towns, Benedictine and Cistercian monks, the great farmers of the age, were at work changing the face of the country; they drained swamps, built roads, and reclaimed new soil, they were even accused in their greed of encroaching on the churchyards. Under their influence England was fast becoming the chief wool-growing center of the world. It was an age of eager living, of breathless activity, an age that outgrew rapidly the forms and systems of the past, that pressed forward to the new order of the future.

Henry II.

Henry's first work was to carry out the provisions of the Treaty of Wallingford. The Flemish mercenaries were sent home, the adulterine castles were destroyed, the courts of justice reëstablished. In rapid journeyings north and west he brought the rebellious border chieftains to terms, and wrung submission from the Welsh and Scots. By 1158 outward order was restored, and he could turn his attention to his possessions on the Continent. It is a mistake to look upon Henry's interests as bounded by England; he was a European ruler before he was an English king, and almost to the last he subordinated England to the interests of his continental domains. The ruling note in the policy of the early part of his reign was his desire to found a great Anglo-Angevin empire, but his position in France as well as in England was full of difficulties. To

Henry and the Continent.

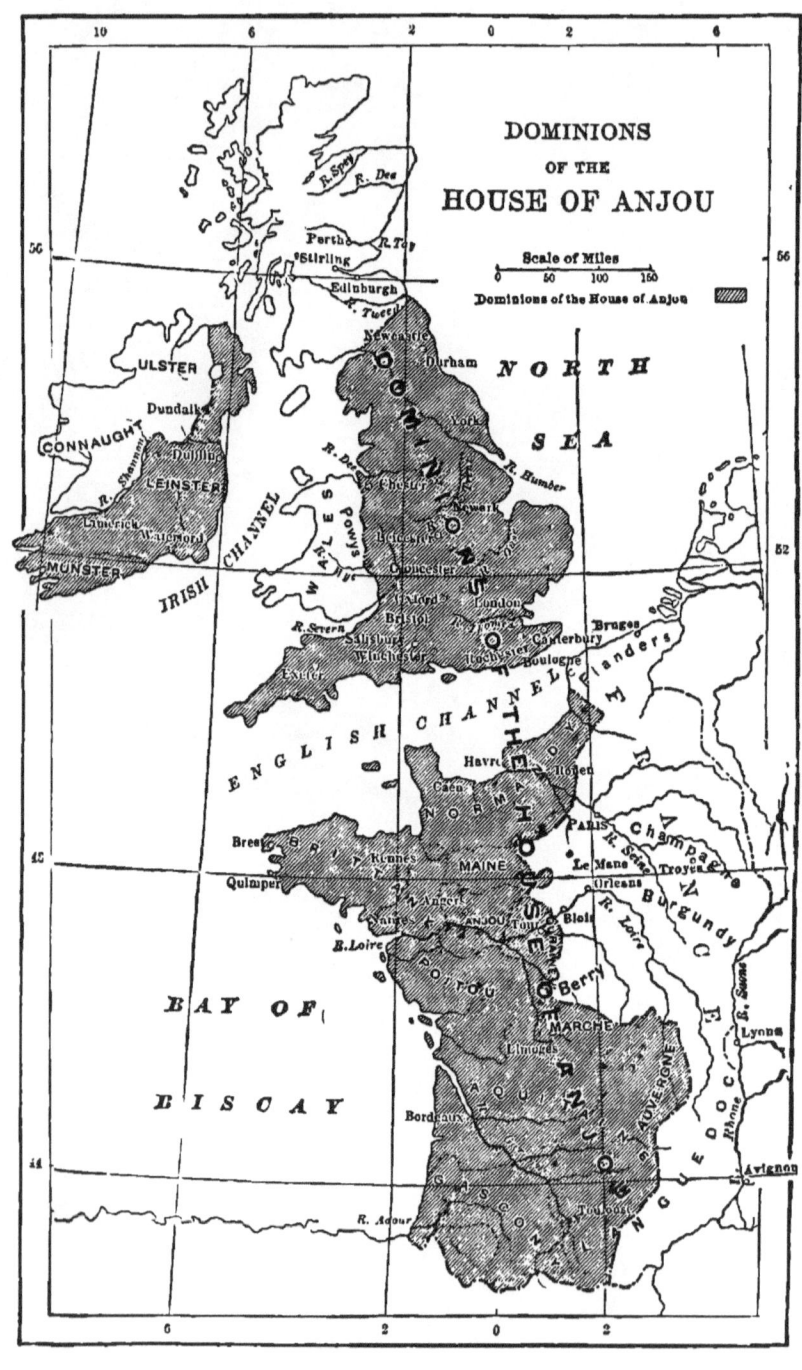

Fusion of Races.

the lands, inherited from his father and mother, he had added the duchy of Aquitaine, the dowry of Queen Eleanor, and his rule extended from the Orkneys to the Pyrenees; but his vast possessions were held together by no common interest, no common tie except that of subjection to himself, and in each his title was disputed. Moreover, he stood between two foes; on the one hand were his vassals, jealous of the interference of one who was to them almost a foreigner, on the other was his suzerain lord, the king of France, eagerly watching for a chance to stir up revolt against him.

For the time being, however, he was able through force and diplomacy to secure himself against all danger.

Henry II. saw plainly how much assistance England might be in carrying out his policy, and it was to strengthen his hold on the people as well as to increase the royal revenue that he began the reorganization of the administrative machinery. The need for reform was crying. Five or six different legal systems were administered in as many different courts. The men that gave judgment spoke a language unknown to the judged. Old cumbersome forms of procedure, handed down from a time when society was stationary, were still retained and the result of a trial was more often injustice than justice. To remedy these evils men were wont to look to the king; he was the fountain of justice, his will was law. It was Henry's great merit that he replaced the personal, irregular interference of the crown by a well understood

A Friar.

Legal reforms.

and uniform system of administration. He reorganized the central courts of justice, the Exchequer and Curia Regis, and to make their great powers more effectual, he sent itinerant justices from these courts into each shire to try all important civil and criminal cases. At the same time, by the decrees of the Grand Assize and the Assize of Clarendon, the Norman principle of recognition or inquest on oath was applied to all suits. If it were a question of the title to land, twelve sworn men of the district chosen indirectly by the sheriff were to decide the matter on their own knowledge or on information obtained from others.

Queen Eleanor.

If they could not agree in their judgment, other men were added until twelve were found of one mind. A similar method was used in criminal cases. Jurors, sworn men of the hundred, were to accuse before the shire court all whom they thought guilty of crime. They were sworn to speak the truth, hence their accusation was called a verdict (veré dicta), and there was no appeal from it except to the ordeal. Even if a man stood that test, he was bound to abjure the realm as one of evil repute. It is from these juries of recognition and presentment that by a long series of changes our modern jury system has been evolved. The results of Henry's reforms were of far-reaching importance. The royal exchequer was enriched and the royal authority strengthened by the increased business of the king's courts; at the same time the hold of the barons on their vassals was weakened, for the revival of the shire courts was at the expense of the private jurisdictions. Moreover through their enforced activity on the local juries, Englishmen received a training in public work that fitted them as nothing else could have done for the part they were to play at a later day in the government of the nation.

It was but as a part of his scheme for the ordering of his realm that Henry on his return to England in 1163 took up the question of the relations of State and Church. His aim was to establish one law for all, but a great body of his subjects stood wholly outside the secular law, beyond the reach of the royal courts. The clerical order, which at this time included all of the educated and professional classes, had, by a wide interpretation of the Conqueror's plan of separate ecclesiastical courts, freed itself entirely from the secular jurisdiction. But the Church could not inflict bodily punishment, hence no matter how serious his offense, a clerk convicted of crime needed to fear nothing worse than fine or imprisonment. As a result, holy orders had become a refuge for the lawless, and crime and disorder were on the increase. Henry had already prepared for his work of reform by forcing the primacy, made vacant by the death of Theobald, upon his friend and chancellor, Thomas Becket. Although an ecclesiastic, Thomas had shown himself so zealous a servant of the crown in the work of restoring order and administering the realm, that men had mocked at the haste with which he "put off the deacon"; but now he hung back declaring he could not "serve two masters." Henry insisted, however, and the election took place, but Thomas at once resigned the chancellorship, and it was plain that a breach between the two would not long be deferred.

It was over the trial of a clerk accused of murder that they first crossed swords. Henry would have the offender brought before the royal courts, but Thomas declared that the case belonged to the Church. Both appealed to the "customs" of the realm, and to settle what those customs

The Church.

Archbishop Thomas.

The Constitutions of Clarendon.

were a great council was held at Clarendon in 1164. There the ancient usages, collected and written down by some of the older nobles, were read before the assembled bishops and baronage. They were in the main the provisions established by the Conqueror and Henry I., and these passed unchallenged, but over the clauses relating to the jurisdiction of the ecclesiastical courts dispute arose. The Church was allowed to retain its control of all questions relating to marriages or wills or involving an oath, but in case of doubt the Curia Regis was to decide where the suit belonged. A clerk accused of crime was to be tried in the secular courts, and if convicted the Church should not interfere to protect him. Moreover all appeal to Rome without the consent of the king was forbidden. Thomas passionately refused to sign the Constitutions, as they were called, and withdrew from the council. A little later, fearing for his life, he fled to France.

For ten years the struggle continued between the two men, once friends, now bitter foes. Henry was contending for the supremacy of the State, Thomas for the independence of the Church. Each was sincere in his purpose, even though the king had an eye to his own authority as well as the good of the realm, and the archbishop never forgot personal ambition in the interests of his order. The king was perhaps in advance of his time, the priest did not realize that certain privileges of the Church were no longer necessary to her usefulnesss.

Death of Thomas, 1172.

All attempts at compromise between the two were rendered vain by the king's unreasoning violence and by the stubbornness with which Thomas held to the limiting clause "Saving the honor of my order." Excommunication of the churchmen who supported the king was answered by outlawry of all the archbishop's relatives, and when the pope threatened to lay the kingdom under an interdict, Henry decreed that anyone bringing the interdict to England should be punished as a traitor. At last, in 1170, a half reconciliation was brought about, and both men agreed to let the past go, but no sooner had the archbishop returned to England than he renewed the attack on the king by excommunicating those bishops who had taken part in the recent coronation of the king's eldest son. Henry, beside himself with rage at the news, uttered the hasty wish that he were freed from his stubborn foe. A few days later the archbishop was struck down in his own cathedral of Canterbury by four knights, roused to the bloody deed by the king's wrathful words. Thomas had won the crown of martyrdom to which he had so long aspired, and Henry was called to face the indignant horror of all Christendom. In vain he disowned the act and promised to punish the murderers; threatened with excommunication, he withdrew hastily to Ireland, hoping to appease the papal wrath by carrying out the long mooted conquest of that country.

Henry's work in Ireland was still incomplete when he was recalled by the rebellious attitude of his son Henry, whom he had caused to be crowned king that the succession might be secured, and who now wished to set his father aside. The danger from the young king was the greater because to him the discontented on both sides the Channel looked as a leader; Philip of France was always on the alert to stir up revolt, and, as a writer of that day says, "there were few barons in England not wavering in their allegiance to the king and ready to desert him at any time." From the beginning of his reign Henry had borne with heavy hand upon the strong feudal barons. He destroyed their castles, sent his justices into their courts, and forbade private coinage. In the Great Council, he diminished their importance by compelling the attendance of the lesser tenants-in-chief, and in 1170 he struck a blow

Rising of the Baronage.

at their political power by withdrawing the office of sheriff from them, giving it to men of lesser rank trained in his courts and more dependent upon his will. Moreover, Henry's plan of taking scutage or shield money in lieu of service in the field, although apparently in the interest of the baronage, told against their military superiority, for it took from their bodies of armed retainers the chance of acquiring skill in war, while it enabled the king to hire foreign mercenaries upon whom he could rely. These acts were viewed with alarm by the nobles, and the outbreak on the Continent brought matters to a crisis. In July, 1173, Normandy took up arms for the young king, and in a few months half England was in revolt. Ireland had risen against the English rule, and the king of Scotland at the head of an army was advancing into the northern counties. Henry was in Normandy when the news of the rising reached him, but he at once hastened home; he had learned the worth of his English possessions, and "he preferred that his lands beyond the sea should be in peril rather than his own realm of England." By a series of hard-won victories he succeeded in breaking down all resistance both in England and on the Continent, and in a few months the revolt was crushed and his foes were suing for mercy.

During the next few years Henry's power was at its height; by a compromise with the papal legate he secured the points at issue in his quarrel with Thomas, and with the aid of his able officials he worked out an administrative system through which he could make his will felt from one end of the kingdom to the other.

Henry's Death. The close of his reign was disturbed by the rebellion of his sons whom he loved and trusted in spite of repeated treachery. The young king was dead, but Richard, the heir apparent, fearing the favor with which Henry regarded his youngest child, John, allied himself with Philip of France and rose against his father. Defeated on all sides and ill of a mortal disease, Henry submitted to the hard terms forced upon him and turned to Chinon to die. They brought him from Philip a list of those who had conspired against him, and first on the list stood the name of his favorite son John. Turning his face to the wall he said, "Now let things go as they will—I care no more for myself or for the world." A little later he died, murmuring, "Shame, shame on a conquered king."

Of an alien race, speaking a foreign tongue, and spending but thirteen of the thirty-five years of his reign in England, Henry of Anjou has nevertheless left an indelible mark on English history. His ambition to figure as a continental ruler was a mistake, his Anglo-Angevin empire hardly outlived the century, but his policy determined England's foreign relations for centuries to come. The effect can be felt still in the traditional hostility between the English and the French people. It was chiefly, however, through his work at home that he impressed his personality on the national life.

Results of Henry's reign.

Seal of Henry II.

He destroyed feudalism as a system of government, brought the Church under the control of the State, and established a strong centralized administrative system. In doing this he raised the power of the crown to a dangerous height, but at the same time, in nationalizing the Church, in destroying the feudal traditions of the baronage, and in reviving the activity of the local courts, he nourished the forces which in the next century were to bring that power within bounds.

RICHARD I.

In 1189 Richard, the third son of Henry II., succeeded his father on the throne. There is little likeness between Richard, the brilliant knight-errant, and Henry, the hard-working man of business, but in the elements of constitutional progress and national growth one reign is but the continuation of the other. Abroad, Henry's policy was followed by his son, and at home the administrative system was developed along lines already laid down.

Richard I. Cœur de Lion.

Though born in England, Richard was even more truly than his father a foreign king. But twice during his reign of ten years did he spend a few months in England, and he touched the national life only through his demands for money. Soon after taking possession of his English kingdom he started on a crusade to the Holy Land, leaving the realm in the hands of his justiciar, William Longchamp. Called back in 1192 by news of trouble at home, he fell into the power of his enemy, the emperor of Germany, and for two years was held a prisoner. Released at last on the promise of paying a heavy ransom, he made his way to England only to find his brother John in open revolt. But John was far too unpopular to be dangerous, and order was soon restored. There were greater dangers to be met elsewhere, however, and the rest of his reign was spent in the effort to secure Normandy against the attacks of the French king. In 1199 his short troubled career came

Fusion of Races. 81

to a close; he was struck down by a shot from a castle he was besieging in Limousin, and he lived only long enough to declare John his heir, and to cause the barons to take the oath of allegiance.

Richard's share in the constitutional achievements of his reign was only indirect. Known in history and romance as the Lion-Hearted, the chivalrous soldier, the valiant crusader, to his English subjects he must have appeared a needy and rather greedy ruler who never thought of England except when in want of money. Probably, however, he conferred on the country the greatest benefit in his power by absenting himself on foreign wars. Richard was a warrior, not a statesman; he could not have understood his father's methods, and had he remained in England he would only have interfered in the development of the political system so carefully elaborated in the previous reign. In his absence the government was in the hands of such men as Longchamp and the Archbishop Hubert Walter, men trained under the eye of the late king and governed by the traditions of his reign. They were loyal servants of the crown, but their task was a difficult one, for the nation was becoming restive under the increasingly heavy burden of taxation, and John, as faithless to his brother as he was to his father, was at hand to take advantage of any discontent. To meet the demand

Richard I.

The work of Richard's ministers.

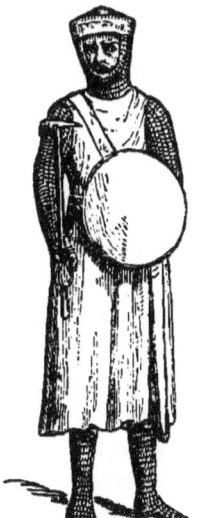

A Crusader.

of the king for money, the ministers were obliged to resort to every expedient. Personal property, taxed for the first time in the reign of Henry the Second, was now regularly assessed, and in 1194, when the nation was called upon to pay the king's ransom, old forms of taxes were revived and new ones were invented; no class of persons, no kind of property, was allowed to escape. It was in part because of the difficulty of assessing personal property, and partly from a wish to conciliate the people that the assessment of taxes was placed in the hands of juries elected by the freeholders of the shire. To the same body was intrusted at about this time the election of the juries of presentment. Thus the principles of election and representation were making their way in the administrative system, and at the same time the nation was receiving in matters of finance and justice a training in self-government—the necessary preparation for parliamentary rule.

Richard's Ransom. Aid on the knights' fee. Tallage on towns. Hideage and carucage on land taking place of Danegeld. A quarter of the movables of every person in the realm.

SOCIAL PROGRESS.

The England which Richard passed on to his worthless brother John was not the England of Norman time. During the half century that had elapsed since the Treaty of Wallingford a new nation had sprung into existence, a nation conscious of itself, having its own literature, knowing its common interest. Under the rule of the Angevin the differences between Norman and Englishman had well-nigh disappeared. The Great Charter, granted in the next reign, takes no note of race distinctions. The court still used French, but the Norman nobles had begun to learn the language of the subject race, and by the beginning of the thirteenth century English was the generally spoken tongue. Robert of Gloucester, writing at a later time, voices the prevailing sentiment in favor of the native language, in his indignant protest against the practices of the previous period:

State of the country.

Literature.

"And thus could the Normans speak but their own speech,
They spake French, as at home, and their children so did teach.
So that the high men of this land, who wear the Norman look,
Hold all to that speech, that they from their fathers took.
For save a man know French, small store by him men set.
But low men hold to English, and to their own speech yet.
I ween in all the world that there be countries none,
That hold not to their own speech, save England alone."

The new impulses which were stirring the life of the people found expression in the fresh, vigorous literary outburst that marked the close of the century. The growing national feeling was reflected in the work of Henry of Huntington and William of Malmesbury, who brought together the ballads and war songs embodying the traditions of early English history. In their writings the fire and color lent by Norman influence transformed the meager records of the Saxon chroniclers into a full and entertaining narrative. Even more marked was the secular tone of the new literature. It smacks of the court rather than of the cloister, both in freedom of treatment and greater fullness of information. Gerald de Barri, writing the history of Wales and Ireland, proposed to tell "the doings of the common people," and in half scornful apology for his disregard of old forms adds, " new times require new fashions; it is better to be dumb than not to be understood." There is something more than revolt against narrow ecclesiastical tradition in the attitude of Geoffrey of Monmouth who, in his "History of the Britons," the basis of the legend of the Table Round, sets before the world an ideal of manhood far removed from the clerical type. Walter de Map goes a step further in hostility to priestly dominion when, in the "Confessions of Bishop Goliath," he holds up the medieval church to the scorn of his age.

But even more truly than the literature did the universities represent the stirring, vigorous spirit of the

The Universities, Oxford and Cambridge.

time. Oxford, emancipated from the narrow traditions of the cloister, was now a school of European fame. The dark lecture rooms were crowded with students who flocked hither from all corners of the kingdom. Here every movement that stirred the political and ecclesiastical world first found expression, and in the narrow streets were fought out the questions of the day. "When Oxford draws knife, England's soon at strife," ran a popular saying. It was Oxford that led in the revolt against the intellectual tyranny and the spiritual corruptness of the Church. That wider sympathy, which overleaped the bounds set by narrow provincial jealousy, and included the whole world in its view, was the outgrowth of this intercourse between men of all classes and all nations; and it was in the atmosphere of the schools, where intellect, not birth, was the measure of each man's position, that a free democratic spirit first manifested itself.

It is stated that the students at Oxford numbered 30,000.

Seal of Richard I.

The Towns.

Town and university were widely separated in ideals and interests, but the one no less than the other furthered the growth of a spirit of freedom and of sturdy self-dependence. Throughout the twelfth century the towns were moving steadily toward municipal freedom, London always in the lead, and the lesser towns making the rights which it had secured the goal of their efforts. By the close of the century the struggle for self-government was practically complete. Most of the towns had gained charters which gave them their own courts of justice, and the right of controlling local trade. They were also permitted to pay their taxes in a lump sum into the royal treasury, assessing and collecting their dues themselves. The larger towns, moreover, were beginning to acquire the right of choosing their own chief officer, the mayor or reeve, until now nominated by the crown. The commercial privileges granted were usually very extensive. By the ordinary form of charter, trade was to be "quit and free from all tolls, dues, and customs at fairs or otherwise, in all harbors throughout all my dominions, both by the hither side and the further side of the sea, by land and by strand."

In their efforts to gain the privilege of self-government, the towns were aided by the necessities of the king and nobles, who were often in sore straits to meet the expense of their crusading enterprises, and were glad to yield some liberty or exemption in return for ready money. Each right gained was a matter of bargain. Rye and Winchelsey secured their charters from Richard by supplying him with two ships for one of his expeditions, and, a little later, Portsmouth obtained the same much-coveted possession by paying part of the royal ransom.

A Mounted Knight.

A more important factor in the emancipation of the towns than the Crusades was the influence of the merchant gilds. With the development of commerce and industry under Henry and Richard, trade had become the ruling interest in the towns, and the merchant classes the most powerful element in the life of the community. Their associations were originally formed merely to control the trade of the

The Merchant Gild.

place or to secure purely commercial privileges, such as the right of holding a fair or exemption from paying toll, but, including as they did the influential men of the community, and strong through effective organization, they naturally took the lead in wringing from the crown judicial immunity or political power. Almost every town and even village possessed a gild, and it was here that the stirring, vigorous life of the community centered. Each gild had its hall where meetings were held to make rules by which honest trade might be secured, and non-gildsmen kept from sharing in the traffic of the place. Moreover the gild was in truth a brotherhood, concerning itself with the whole life of its members, caring for those who were sick, and admonishing those who had fallen on evil ways.

As yet there was little freedom of commercial intercourse, protection and monopoly were the watchwords of the merchant world of the Middle Ages, and trade was shackled by many fetters. Business honor forbade methods now looked upon as entirely legitimate, for example, *forestalling*, or buying up at a distance in order to sell at a higher price in the home market, and *engrossing*, or buying at a season of plenty to hold over until a time when the goods were dear.

The Fairs granted by charter.

The great event in the life of the town was the yearly fair, and the right of holding it was dearly prized. The great fair of Stourbridge, a few miles from Cambridge, was known throughout Europe. It was held in September and, for days before it opened, the roads were blocked by wagons laden with wares from every part of the world. In the crowded ways of the improvised market, merchants from Genoa, bringing rich silks and jewelry, jostled the Flemish manufacturers with their treasures of holland and fine linen, and the home traders displayed with pride their stores of wool, side by side with the fur and amber from the Hanse towns of the Baltic. The narrow ways were thronged with men of all classes and every clime, tradesman and noble, soldier and priest, each intent on displaying his wares or laying in his winter stores. For three weeks the fair went on, and daily the mayor sat at his court "of the dusty feet" to give justice between disputing wayfarers, and on Sunday some monk from the neighboring priory said mass in the chapel that still stands near the spot where the fair was held. Between the chaffering, men discussed the questions of the hour, gave voice to the prevailing discontent, and laid plans which sometimes ripened into revolutionary action.

CHAPTER V.

STRUGGLE FOR THE CHARTER.

Illustrative Readings.
  King John; Shakespeare.
  Stephen Langton; Maurice.
  Simon de Montfort; Pauli.
  Edward the First; Tout.
Important Dates.
  Reign of John, 1199–1216.
    1204, Loss of Normandy.
    1206, Election of Stephen Langton.
    1215, The Great Charter.
  Reign of Henry III., 1216–1272.
    1232, Personal Rule of Henry.
    1258, Provisions of Oxford.
    1265, Battle of Evesham.
  Reign of Edward I., 1272–1307.
    1282, Conquest of Wales.
    1295, The Model Parliament.
    1297, Confirmation of the Charters.
    1305, Temporary Submission of Scotland.

JOHN.

"Foul as it is, hell itself is defiled by the fouler presence of John." This was the judgment of his own time on the disloyal youngest son of Henry II. Faithless to every trust, stained with every crime, John stands out as the most vicious and worthless of all the English kings. From first to last his life offers not one redeeming trait, not one saving act. And yet he had much of the ability of his house, together with an extraordinary power of winning the love of men. But he used his power over others only to their undoing, and the achievements of his undoubted force and talent were rendered vain by the baseness of his nature.

The reign of John falls naturally into three periods, each ending in crushing defeat and humiliation; in the first, interest centered in the wars with Philip of France; during the second, the king was carrying on his unequal contest with Rome, and the last was occupied with the events that turned upon the granting of Magna Charta.

Struggle for the Charter.

John's claim to succeed his brother met with no opposition in England, but on the Continent he was confronted with a dangerous rival in his nephew Arthur of Brittany, who found a ready supporter in the French king. However, Philip and Arthur soon quarreled. In Eleanor, his mother, John had a wise and experienced counselor, and within a few months he was master of all his continental possessions. But he misused his good fortune. Accused, and probably with justice, of the murder of his nephew Arthur, he gave Philip a chance to interfere, and Normandy was invaded by a French army. The barons, outraged and insulted by John, refused to rise in his behalf; town after town opened its doors to Philip, and by 1203 he was in possession of the province. A year later John's rule was limited to the lands south of the Garonne. That the work of Henry II. on the Continent was so soon undone was due largely to John's utter worthlessness, but the ease with which Normandy and Maine became a part of France showed how impossible was the idea of an Anglo-Angevin empire. To England the loss of the French provinces was an event of far-reaching importance. The barons were compelled to choose between Normandy and England, and in choosing England they became for the first time wholly English in sympathy and in interest. For the first time, too, since the Conquest, king and people were brought face to face. It was well perhaps for English freedom that just at the hour when the power of the crown was becoming dangerous, the throne should be occupied by a man whose crimes would make that power hateful to the people.

The death of Queen Eleanor, John's wise and shrewd

Loss of Normandy.

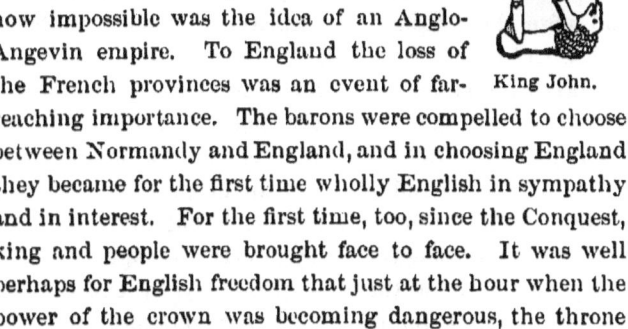

King John.

Normandy, Maine, Anjou, Touraine, and a part of Poitou.

The quarrel with the Church.

counselor, was followed by defeat in France, and when in 1205 the king lost in Hubert Walter, Archbishop of Canterbury, his most faithful and fearless servant, he at once plunged into a quarrel with Rome, which ended in complete humiliation. The difficulty arose out of the question of choosing Walter's successor, both king and chapter claiming it as their privilege. John was probably in the right, the power of the crown to nominate to the see of Canterbury had been conceded even by Anselm, but he spoilt his cause by his unreasoning violence. Unable to come to an agreement among themselves, all parties at length concluded to carry the matter before the Roman Curia. Pope Innocent decided the question by rejecting both candidates and causing his own man to be chosen. In this he probably thought chiefly of advancing the interests of Rome, but, by nominating Stephen Langton, he gave to England an able and disinterested leader in the coming struggle for freedom. The pope's decision was resisted by John, and he refused to admit the new archbishop to his see. Threat he met by counter threat; if Innocent should lay the realm under an interdict, he would banish the clergy and seize their goods. But Innocent did not draw back, and in 1208 the interdict fell. "All worship save that of a few privileged orders, all administration of sacraments save that of baptism, ceased over the length and breadth of the country; the church bells were silent, the dead lay unburied on the ground, many of the bishops fled from the country." Still John did not yield, but made good his threats by subjecting the clergy to every outrage. In 1209, the pope struck at the king personally by excommunicating him, but John met the excommunication with scorn. He feared only men, and, hated as he was, he was still too strong to be openly defied. There was but one weapon left the pope, and the time was come to use it, un-

Struggle for the Charter.

less he was to confess himself beaten. In 1212, he issued a bull deposing the king, absolving his subjects from their allegiance and calling upon the French king to execute the decree. Even yet, John might have proved a match for the greatest of the popes had he not suddenly found himself confronted by a more formidable danger close at hand.

Throughout his reign John had defied and oppressed the baronage. He had seized their castles and held their children as hostages. Illegal and burdensome enactions had been followed by repeated demands for service and scutage. Moreover, there was scarcely one among them but had some personal grounds for complaint. Their long endurance of John's tyranny bears witness to the strength which Henry's reforms had given the crown, but in secret the barons were united against the king, and it was the discovery of their conspiracies with Philip at this juncture that forced him to yield. His decision was quickly made. His present position was hopeless, but with the pope as an ally he could defy the rest of his foes. On the 15th of May he knelt before the papal legate at Ewell, and, surrendering his realm to the pope, received it back to hold as a vassal of the see of Rome.

Submission to Rome.

John and the pope were friends, but the English Church still stood aloof, and, for the first time since the Conquest, the crown was without the support of the clergy. The moment was critical, for the ecclesiastical quarrel was followed at once by an outbreak of the barons. The smouldering resentment had at last burst into open revolt. To the accumulation of long-standing grievances was added a new one in John's demand that his vassals should follow him in the expedition he was planning for the recovery of France. On all sides he met with determined opposition. They would serve him within the four seas, they said, but

Rising of the Baronage.

they would not cross the Channel. The baronage had hitherto lacked a leader, but the pope had unwittingly given them one in Stephen Langton who, ever since his arrival in England, had been untiring in his efforts to restrain the king from despotic measures. Now, with true statesmanship, he came forward to give the nation the necessary basis for action. In a meeting of the barons, held at St. Paul's, he displayed the half forgotten charter of Henry I., and proposed that it should be presented to the king as expressing the terms which he had promised to keep. John met the claim with delay. He was about to start on the expedition to France, from which he hoped much. During the next few months the fate of England trembled in the balance; had John returned victorious the rebellious barons would have had no chance; his overwhelming defeat at Bouvines gave the signal for the triumph of English freedom. Matters at once came to a crisis at home. The northern barons took the lead in resistance, but one by one the others deserted the losing cause of the crown, until when they appeared before him in January, 1215, to present their demands, only his ministers and a few princes of royal blood still remained faithful to John. Nevertheless he met their demand for the old liberties with obstinate refusal. "Why do they not ask me for my kingdom?" he cried. "I will never grant such liberties as will make me a slave," and he strove to divide opposition by detaching the Church from the constitutional party with offers of privilege and freedom. But in vain; the nation stood firm and John was forced to bow to necessity. On June

Military Costume.

15, 1215, he met his outraged vassals at Runnymede by the Thames, and made full submission in setting his seal to the charter of liberties which they laid before him.

The first step in the struggle for popular liberty was won. "The maintenance of the charter becomes henceforth the watchword of English freedom." In form it is a royal grant; in reality it is a formal statement of liberties wrung from the king by his bishops and barons. It contains little that is absolutely new, but it expresses with exactness what before was undefined. Thoroughly English in spirit, there is no statement of abstract rights; everything is thrown into a concrete, practical form. Some of the provisions limit the power of the king over his vassals, others protect the villein against his lord. To the Church are secured its ancient liberties; to the towns, their newly bought privileges. The care with which the interests of the merchants are protected shows the increasing importance of trade. In words which underlie our whole judicial system the right of justice is secured. "We will not go against any man, nor send against him save by the legal judgment of his peers, or by the law of the land. To none will we sell or deny or delay right or justice." Among the most important articles are the two which limit the power of the king in matters of taxation. "No scutage or aid shall be imposed in our kingdom unless by the general council of our kingdom," and just below, "For the holding the general council of the kingdom we shall cause to be summoned the bishops and greater barons, singly, and all others who hold of us in chief by our sheriffs generally." No interest, no class, was overlooked. In terms, the provisions by which freedom was to be secured were ample, but how ensure their fulfillment, how control a king whom no oath could bind? By the charter itself it was decreed that a council of twenty-five barons should be

The Great Charter. For text of Charter see Old South Leaflets, general series, No. 5.

chosen to enforce its provisions. "They have given me
five-and-twenty over-kings," cried John in rage, and he
at once turned to seek a way of evasion.

The Pope annuls the Charter.

The next four months were a period of anarchy. The
pope with little comprehension of the question at issue absolved
John from his oath, and recalled Langton to Rome.
The barons again took up arms. Without a leader and divided
among themselves, they could do little, and for a time
John swept all before him. But Philip's opportunity had
come. He renewed his intrigues with the English barons
and finally at their request sent his son at the head of an
army into the country. At once the tide turned, the
French mercenaries refused to fight against their king, and
John's cause was already lost when he died suddenly, worn
out in mind and body.

HENRY III.

The death of John changed the whole aspect of affairs.
A large part of the country was in the hands of the insurgents,
but the one bond of union among them was
their common hatred of John; John dead, differences of
opinion became manifest, national pride reasserted itself,
and the coalition showed signs of breaking up. Nevertheless
England might yet have passed under the rule of the
foreigner had it not been for the patriotic action of the Earl
of Pembroke, the greatest of the barons. Aided by Gualo,
the papal legate, who rightly appreciated the situation, he
caused Henry, the young son of John, to be crowned king,
reissued the charter, thus detaching many of the barons
from the French party, and by his vigorous efforts succeeded
in obliging Louis to withdraw his forces.

The minority of Henry.

The following years were occupied in reëstablishing the
government. In the minority of the young king, Pembroke
acted as regent until his death in 1219, when he was
succeeded by the justiciar, Hubert de Burgh, who continued

his work, carrying on the administration according to the principles of the Charter. De Burgh's efforts to give to England sound government were complicated by the presence of foreigners, the former supporters of John, and by the reappearance of the old feudal spirit of lawlessness among the barons, and also by one or two attempts of Rome to interfere. But the justiciar succeeded in expelling the foreigners, and, by reoccupying the royal castles, put a check on the barons, and Langton crowned his services to the cause of constitutional freedom by obtaining the papal promise that during his lifetime no Roman legate should be sent to England. These years of Henry's minority were a period of quiet national growth, of awakening political consciousness, of spiritual and moral regeneration; to priest and layman alike it was a time of training for the work to come.

In the thirteenth century the political power of the papacy was boundless, but secular interests had been secured at the expense of spiritual influence, and men were turning away from a Church controlled by worldly ambitions and considerations of material advantage. In England resistance to the authority of a political Church was strengthened by the national hostility to papal interference. "The pope has no part in secular matters," was the defiant answer of London to the interdict of Honorius. Nor was the condition of the English clergy more satisfactory. Despite the part they had taken in the struggle with John, they no longer commanded the respect of the people; political activity could not make amends for the lack of spirituality which marked both monk and priest. *The Church.*

To recall the clergy to its work, to bring men again into the fold of the Church, was the aim of the two great orders that suddenly sprang into existence at about the beginning *The Friars.*

of the century. Inspired with fiery zeal and tireless enthusiasm, the followers of the fierce Castilian Dominic and the saintly Francis d'Assisi wandered through Europe, attacking the corruptness of the clergy, combating the heresies of the age, seeking to reclaim the poor and outcast. They turned to the towns, neglected by the older orders, and there in the thick of the crowd, in market place and fair, they preached the way of life in words that the common people could understand, driving home each truth with apt anecdote and illustration drawn from the world of nature or from the daily lives of those to whom they spoke. The Black Friars, as the disciples of Dominic were called, reached England in 1221, and a few years later they were followed by the Gray Friars, or Franciscans. Their coming worked a revolution in the life of the nation. The indifference of the laity and the hostility of the clergy were not proof against their ardor and devotion; they aroused the Church to a new sense of its duties, and stirred the hearts of the people to a higher, more vigorous life. Grosseteste, bishop of Lincoln, writing of the friars to Pope Gregory, said: "O that your holiness could see how devoutly the people run to confess their sins, how much profit the clergy and monks take from imitation of them."

A Friar.

The Friars and the Universities. Less satisfactory were the results of their influence upon the intellectual life that centered in the universities. At first, with rigid interpretation of their vow of poverty, they denied themselves all books. "I am your breviary, I am your breviary," was the answer of Francis to a request for a psalter. But the tremendous interest aroused by their popular, dramatic preaching forced them to the study of theology, and within a short time they were firmly established at Oxford. Under the inspiration of their presence the schools were crowded with eager thousands, but the free spirit of the last century no longer ruled, the interest in science and literature died out before the irresistible bent of the time toward scholastic theology. Roger Bacon, first of English scientists, and last and greatest representative of the wider culture of the preceding century, bears witness in his writings to the changed temper of his University of Oxford. For forty years he labored to arouse men to an interest in the wide world of knowledge outside the narrow scholastic bounds, and in the end he was, as he himself wrote, "unheard, forgotten, buried."

Under the influence of the schoolmen, the intellectual life of the nation became narrow and unproductive, but the effect of their teachings on the political thought of the time was strong and invigorating. Their sympathies were with the people, and in lecture and open air sermon they developed a theory of government which made short work with the claims of the king to the unquestioning obedience of his subjects. "All things are lawful to the king for the government of his realm, but nothing is lawful to him for its destruction." "Let the community of the realm advise, and let it be known what the generality to whom their laws are best known, think on the matter." "It concerns the community to see what sort of men ought justly to be chosen for the weal of the realm." With such words as these they roused their hearers to a

Their political teachings.

Ancient Wrestling.

just sense of the duties of the king and the rights of the nation, and under their inspiration town and university stood firm in support of the cause of freedom in the coming struggle with the crown. The contest with royal misrule, which filled the later years of Henry's reign, is called the Barons' War, but it was the consciousness that behind them stood a nation that nerved the barons to rise against the king.

The misrule of Henry.

In 1227, Henry declared himself of age, and from this time his character tells upon the events of the period. Deeply religious, moral, refined, he had few of the vices of his father, but, on the other hand, he had little of the force and political capacity that had marked his house heretofore. Vacillating and weak, he showed himself throughout his reign incapable of either fulfilling the wishes of his subjects or carrying out a vigorous policy of his own. His rule was characterized by misgovernment at home and inefficiency abroad. To restore the absolute power of the crown he turned his ministers out of office, filling their places with clerks or men dependent upon himself. Again the nation groaned under the rule of foreigners, relatives or favorites of the king. In their hands were placed the royal castles and the high offices, the defense and administration of the realm, on them

Bowling. Thirteenth Century.

Struggle for the Charter.

was squandered one sixth the royal revenue. Extravagant and wasteful, the king was ever in need and ever demanding supplies, and his debts amounted to more than four times his annual income. Every expedient to fill the treasury was now used. Offices were sold, loans were wrung from the great nobles, clergy and laity alike were called upon for new and burdensome supplies. The weight of taxation was increased by the king's foreign expeditions. An attempt to recover Poitou ended only in failure and disgrace, and renewed demands for aid. The national pride was outraged, the national purse depleted.

But not by the king alone was the unhappy realm plundered and pillaged. Ever since the time of John, the pope had looked upon England as a vassal kingdom bound to supply the needs of the papal see. Large sums were exacted from the clergy, and many of the best livings of the Church were bestowed on Italians. In 1252, Grosseteste declared that the pope's nominees drew from the realm revenues three times as great as the royal income. Clergy and laity alike resisted the spoliations of Rome, and appealed to the king for protection, but in vain; both devoutness and personal gratitude bound Henry to the pope. Self-interest, too, led him to connive at the papal exactions in return for papal support in his dealings with his subjects.

The Pope and England.

Henry III.

Throughout the whole trying time the murmuring grew louder; the demand for supplies was sometimes met by angry expostulations. On one occasion the council de-

. L. cf C.

Discontent of the nation.

clared in words that sum up the long list of grievances "that it would be unworthy of them and injurious, to allow a king who was so easily led astray, who had never repulsed nor frightened even the least of the enemies of his kingdom, who had never extended the borders of his realm, but had contracted it and brought it under the rule of foreigners, to so often extort so much money from them, his natural subjects, as though they were slaves of the lowest degree." Over and over again they attempted to bind the king through renewals of the Charter purchased at a heavy price, but in vain. "The king breaks everything, the laws, his good faith, and his promises," wrote Matthew Paris, last of the monastic historians. The council, now beginning to be known as Parliament, acting in the spirit of the Charter, endeavored to put a check on royal exactions, and on one occasion refused the request for a subsidy. In 1244 an attempt was made to secure the appointment of officials to be held responsible to Parliament, and to act in all administrative matters. The innovation was too great to find ready acceptance, but it indicated the advance the nation was making in the conception of self-government. Still more important was the appearance in the great council in 1254 of knights of the shire, representative men, summoned to report on the amount of aid which the shires were willing to give. Little apparently was achieved, and yet throughout these dreary years, marked only by greed unsatisfied, by wrongs unredressed, the form and spirit of constitutional rule were taking shape. Slowly men were learning the identity of national interest, still more slowly the need of united national action. That action was so long delayed, was due in part to a certain apathy in the nation, but still more to lack of a leader.

Simon de Montfort.

Among the swarm of hated foreigners was a man who was soon to stand forth as the chief opponent of

Henry and his misrule. Simon de Montfort, Earl of Leicester and brother-in-law of the king, was Norman by birth and training. At first he was scarcely distinguishable among the foreign favorites at the court, but by 1244 he had ranged himself definitely on the side of the baronial party. During the years that followed he was much abroad on public business. In 1253 he returned to England and at once placed himself at the head of the English baronage. It is not easy to understand the true character of Simon de Montfort, nor to mark the steps by which the foreign favorite was transformed into the English patriot. Even to the men of his own time his character and career seemed full of contradictions. Generous and high-spirited, he was also overbearing and impatient of opposition. Firm and constant in his purpose and loyalty, it is yet difficult to free him from the reproach of ambition. But whatever his faults, he gave England the guidance and inspiration she needed, and advanced her far on the road toward constitutional freedom.

In 1258 matters came to a crisis. Misled by foolish ambition, Henry had consented to become the tool of the pope in his quarrels with the House of Hohenstaufen, and had pledged England to repay the sums necessary for carrying on the war. The patience of the country was at last exhausted, and the king's demands for aid were met by open revolt. Under the lead of Leicester, the barons appeared in arms before the king and demanded the appointment of a committee to carry out a work of reform. Unable to resist, Henry conceded all that was asked, and with his son Edward swore to observe the articles drawn up by the barons in the Parliament of Oxford. By the new scheme the government was taken out of the hands of the king and given to three committees made up of barons. It was an awkward and cumbersome device, sure to break down of its own weight.

The Provisions of Oxford.

The Barons' War.

For seven years longer the contest continued. A breach soon appeared between Leicester and the majority of the barons. They feared his ambition and he accused them of treachery, "With such feeble and faithless men I care not to have aught to do!" Henry was not slow to take advantage of the dissensions among his assailants, and in 1261 he induced the pope to absolve him from his oath. His defiance of their control at once led the barons to put aside their differences, and against their united front the king could make no stand. But with success the old distrust of Simon revived, and at last, in utter weariness, all agreed to refer the question to St. Louis of France. Just and wise as he was, Louis was yet a king and human, and his decision given in 1264 was entirely in favor of the crown. The barons at once rose in resistance, the towns and universities came to their aid, and the clergy were on their side. At Lewes the two forces met, Henry and Edward were taken prisoners, and the royalists were completely defeated. During the next year Leicester ruled in the king's name, but his path was beset with difficulties, since there were few among the baronage on whom he could rely. To strengthen his position he took the step that has brought lasting honor upon his name. Turning to the people, he summoned two knights of every shire and with them two burgesses from every borough. Knights and burgesses had long met in the county court to consider their common interests; now for the first time they sat side by side with barons and bishops in the national council. It was the last despairing effort of the great earl. Already his government was giving way; the hostility of the pope, the jealousy of the baronage, the loyalty of the nation, had united to undermine his power. Within a few weeks the country was again at war. At Evesham on the Welsh border the rival forces met. Simon watched the advance of

The Parliament of 1265.

Struggle for the Charter.

the loyalists under the lead of Prince Edward. "By the arm of St. James they come on cunningly. Yet have they not taught themselves that order of battle, but have learnt it of me." The end was not slow to come; one by one the comrades of the great earl were shot down. "If he died they had no will to live." At last he, too, fell, fighting bravely. For a moment it seemed as though the cause of freedom was lost, as though all that Simon de Montfort had struggled for was of no avail. But another stood ready to carry on his work. Something more than the art of war Simon had taught to the man who conquered him at Evesham. What he had failed to do, another, acting from the vantage ground of the throne, was to carry through to a glorious fulfillment.

EDWARD I.

With the death of Henry III. ended the days of foreign kingship. English in name and English at heart, Edward I. stands out as a truly national king. A man of action, thoroughly in earnest, and convinced of the righteousness of his purpose, he was often high-handed and impatient of opposition, but he was generous and conscientious, and not without reason were the words "Keep troth" inscribed upon his tomb.

Coronation of Edward I. From an Initial Letter.

Edward, like Henry II., came to the throne with a clear understanding of the task before him. Creative work was accomplished, the time for definition had begun. Edward originated little that was new, but he worked out and

New legislation.

adapted the materials that lay ready at hand. It was an age of lawyers and law-making, and Edward in this typified his time. He developed the judicial system along the lines laid down by Henry II., dividing the Court of the King's Bench into three separate tribunals, each with its own judges. By the Statute of Winchester he revived and reorganized the old institutions of national police and national defense. Every man was forced to hold himself ready to serve the king at home, and every district was made responsible for crimes committed within its bounds. "If any will not obey the arrest," so runs the statute, "the officers shall levy the hue and cry upon them, and such as keep the watch shall follow with hue and cry with all the town and the towns near and so hue and cry shall

Sword Play. Thirteenth Century.

be made from town to town until that they be taken and delivered to the sheriff." Another provision throws light on the state of the country: "And further it is commanded that highways leading from one market town to another shall be enlarged so that there be neither dyke, tree, nor bush whereby a man may lurk to do hurt within two hundred foot of the one side and two hundred foot on the other side of the way."

Conquest of Wales.

From his congenial task of legislation Edward was drawn by the revolt of Wales in 1282. Into the mountain fastnesses of the Welsh country, English arms and English influence had never penetrated. Divided into clans, the national spirit appeared only in resistance to the English rule, the love of freedom showed itself only in hatred of law and order. Lawless and unsubdued, the Welsh were a constant menace to the peace of England. Every outbreak was sure of their assistance, every rebel found a refuge among them. It was plain there could be no hope of tranquillity until the country was subdued and incorporated with England. The conquest was a national act, and Edward accomplished it in a national way, appealing to the people for support in two provincial councils called at York and Northampton. The war was successful, Llewellyn, the Celtic leader, fell on the banks of the Wye and with him ended Welsh independence.

Heralds.

Less defensible was Edward's action with regard to another question to which he now turned his attention. For centuries the relations between England and Scotland had been a subject of dispute. Relying on some vague tradition of the tenth century, the southern kingdom had always asserted its claim to overlordship, but the northern kingdom had as steadily denied it. Since the time of Henry I. the question had dropped out of sight, but in 1290 the matter was revived by the death of the Maid of Norway, the last of the direct royal line. At once a horde of claimants appeared. Perplexed, the Scotch barons turned to Edward for advice, but he refused to act unless

The Scotch succession.

his overlordship was recognized. To this the barons finally agreed, though the Scotch commons refused their assent. His claims once accepted, Edward acted with fairness and wisdom, giving his decision finally in favor of John Balliol.

The Model Parliament.

In 1293, Edward's greatness was at its height, his supremacy was acknowledged throughout the island, the country was at peace at home and abroad. Nowhere was there a sign that the crisis of his reign was impending. And yet within a few years the people had risen against the king, Wales and Scotland were in open revolt, and Gascony, the last of Henry the Second's continental possessions, was in the hands of the French. Philip of France, on the alert to seize any advantage, saw in the smouldering disaffection of the Scotch the chance of embarrassing Edward. By assurances of aid he precipitated the inevitable outbreak in the northern kingdom. Edward at once prepared to defend his rights and turned to the nation for aid. Anxious to avoid the arbitrary measures of his father's rule, he had repeatedly consulted his subjects in time of need, and now in his distress he called together men of every class, recognizing their right to act in words drawn from the Roman law, "What touches all must be agreed to by all." Bishops and barons were summoned to meet with representatives of the people, knights from the shires, and burgesses from the boroughs; the lower clergy also were represented. The calling of the Parliament of 1295 marks a turning-point in English history. From that day to this the form of the national council has remained practically unchanged, its place in the government scarcely questioned. "It was the greatest work of Edward's life to make a permanent and ordinary part of the machinery of the English government what in his father's time had been but the temporary expedient of a needy tax-gatherer, or the last despairing effort of a revolutionary partisan."

Two knights from each of 37 shires; two burgesses from each of 162 chartered boroughs.

The lower clergy soon ceased to send representatives.

The next two years were full of difficulties that tested to the utmost the constancy of the king and the forbearance of his subjects. Across the Channel the French were gaining ground, and at home discontent was rife. The burden of taxation was great, Edward's measures bore heavily on the barons, even his efforts to enforce order met with opposition. The Church especially had suffered from his exactions. "The royal officers spared neither monk nor priest: they broke open every money-chest: they even ransacked the towers and belfries of the churches." In 1296 the Church relying on papal support refused an aid demanded by the king. In retaliation, Edward at once outlawed the clergy, and soon brought them to terms; but the delay had led him to a step which at once put him in the wrong. On more than one occasion the king had evaded the demands of the barons by making terms with the merchants. Now in his need he raised the export duty on wool to six times its former amount. The barons at once prepared to resist, and occasion was given them in Edward's demand that they should lead the force to Flanders. This they refused to do. "By God, Sir Earl," stormed Edward to one of the leaders, "you shall either go or hang." "By that same oath, Sir King, I will neither go nor hang," was the defiant answer. The meeting broke up in disorder, and Edward found that he had gone too far; townsfolk and barons, laity and clergy, were united against him, and with what grace he could muster he yielded to the demand of the barons that he should

Confirmation of the Charters.

Civil Costume of the Reign of Edward I.

sign the Charter with additional articles limiting still more the royal power of taxation. By this act the king bound himself never again to take "aids, tasks, and prizes, but by the common assent of the realm," nor to impose on wool a heavy custom or "maletot" without the same consent. The confirmation of the Charter stands as a landmark in constitutional history; in Edward's concessions was summed up all that had been gained since the time of John.

War with Scotland.

The remaining years of Edward's reign were filled with the struggle with Scotland. Under the inspiration of Wallace, an outlaw knight, national feeling found expression in open revolt. In 1304 Wallace was captured and put to death, and for the moment it seemed as though Scotland was to share the fortune of Wales; but though defeated, the Scotch were yet unconquered, and under the lead of Robert Bruce again took up arms. The issue was still unsettled when in 1307 Edward died near Carlisle on his way northward. For a few years longer the struggle went on, but where Edward I. had failed, little could be hoped from his son; step by step the English lost ground, and at last, in 1314, in the hard-fought battle of Bannockburn, the invading army met with complete defeat, and Scotch independence was achieved.

Slings of Warfare.

CHAPTER VI.

RISE OF THE COMMONS.

Illustrative Readings.
  The Boy's Froissart.
  John Wyclif; Sergeant. Heroes of the Nation Series.
  Canterbury Tales; Chaucer.
  Dream of John Ball; Morris.
  Edward II.; Marlowe.
  Richard II.; Shakespeare.
  The King's Tragedy; Rossetti.
  The Fair Maid of Perth; Scott.

Important Dates.
  Reign of Edward II., 1307-1327.
   1311, The Ordinances.
   1314, Battle of Bannockburn. Loss of Scotland.
   1322, Downfall of Lancaster.
   1327, Deposition of Edward II.
  Reign of Edward III., 1327-1377.
   1336, Outbreak of the Hundred Years' War, 1336-1347; 1354-1360; 1368-1375; 1378-1389.
   1349, The Black Death.
   1351, The first Statute of Laborers.
   1376, The Good Parliament.
  Reign of Richard II., 1377-1399.
   1381, The Peasant Revolt.
   1384, Death of Wyclif.
   1386, The Commission of Reform.
   1397, The King's *coup d'etat*.
   1399, Deposition of Richard II.

Genealogical Table.

HENRY III.
  ├── Edward I., 1274-1307.
  │   Edward II., 1307-1327.
  │   Edward III., 1327-1377.
  │   ├── Edward, the Black Prince.
  │   │   Richard II., 1377-1399.
  │   ├── Lionel, Duke of Clarence.
  │   │   Philippa.
  │   │   Roger Mortimer, Earl of March.
  │   ├── John of Gaunt, Duke of Lancaster.
  │   │   Henry IV., 1399-1413.
  │   ├── Edmund, Duke of York.
  │   └── Thomas, Duke of Gloucester.
  └── Edmund, Earl of Lancaster.
        Thomas, Earl of Lancaster, beheaded 1322.

DURING the course of the fourteenth century, great and momentous changes were wrought out in the character and constitution of the English nation. The elements of progress which were gathering force during the thirteenth century reached a climax of development in the fourteenth. A marked invigoration of the national character, in which the whole people, high and low, rich and poor, had part, distinguishes the period. Roused to a consciousness of opportunity, the nation sought to attain a larger and freer life. The cruelties of the Conquest, the miseries of civil war, were forgotten in that glad sense of renewed strength which makes the fourteenth century seem the springtime of the English race. The buoyant aspiration of the people found expression in diverse ways. Thought and language responded to its call and a national literature arose. The religious instinct was awakened and a purer faith rejected the authority of a degenerate Church. Restless under restraint, men strove to cast aside the burdens imposed by lord and king, seeking to win industrial advancement and political freedom. In comparison with these mighty aspirations of the people, the enterprises of kings, whether in war or in court intrigue, seem but petty affairs and of slight consequence; nevertheless, the sovereign was an influential personage. His arbitrary will might do much to further or hinder the welfare of the nation.

CONSTITUTIONAL PROGRESS.

Taxation.

The remarkable progress toward constitutional government during this period is a direct consequence of the financial necessities of the crown. Military expenses constituted the most serious item in the royal debit account. The French wars dragged their weary length through the century and the burden imposed upon the nation became well-nigh unendurable. The cost of the several expeditions to France was defrayed by grants voted in Parliament with little grumbling, for the people were ready to pay taxes where the glory of the English name was at stake; but the expenses of the royal household were not so cheerfully met. Men argued that the king should "live of his own," that his court should be maintained out of the revenue

Rise of the Commons. 111

from the royal demesnes. Now the royal estates had been considerably reduced by sale and gift since the Conqueror's day, so that the private revenue of the crown had fallen off at the same time that the habits of the sovereign had waxed more luxurious. The ordinary income of the king, that from the royal demesnes and legitimate aids and customs, was probably at this time about £65,000. Of this sum, from £10,000 to £15,000 was spent upon the royal household, the rest being devoted to the maintenance of the king's castles, the army, the navy, and the civil service. Fifteen thousand pounds was perhaps not an extravagant sum to allow for keeping up an establishment that must compare favorably with the courts of continental monarchs, but the people fretted under the burden, and a number of clumsy efforts were made to control the royal expenditure. The Charter confirmed in 1297 bound the king to levy no extraordinary taxes "without the common consent of the realm and to the common profit thereof." Edward I. loyally observed the limitations so imposed, but his successors were less scrupulous. The king's lawyers were not slow to find means of evading the Charter, and the Parliamentary records of the period abound in protests against illegal taxation. Exorbitant sums were exacted from the royal demesnes, where the people, being immediate dependents of the crown, could make no effective resistance; new customs duties were imposed by special arrangement with the merchants (export duties on wool and import duties on wine and other luxuries); but the favorite device of a needy monarch was to borrow the money he could not raise by taxation. There was no lack of opportunity. The Jewish money-lenders, the never-failing resource of preceding kings, had been banished from England in 1290; but there were Italian bankers and Flemish merchants who might always be relied on to

Until the sixteenth century all money values must be multiplied by ten to estimate the equivalent in money of to-day.

accommodate a royal spendthrift, and the pope himself was not averse to loaning money on good security. These debts were of course a charge on future revenue and must eventually be paid by the nation. Money was not unfrequently extorted from wealthy English prelates and the prosperous towns of the realm, on the pretense of repayment, but subjects gave with a bad grace since the royal creditor had a poor memory for such obligations and could not safely be pressed. The most vexatious resource, and that which roused deepest animosity among the people, was the so-called right of purveyance. On the magnificent royal progresses through the realm, the king's officers provided for the needs of his household at the expense of the inhabitants. Food and shelter were demanded at the lowest prices and with no security for payment. The carts and horses, even the personal services of the peasants, were called into requisition, not merely for the king's use,

Purveyance.

Effigy of Edward II.

Edward II. 1307-1327.

but at the convenience of any one of the royal officers who dared ask them in the king's name. This abuse of power was frequently protested, and reform was no less frequently promised, but it was a privilege dear to the heart of royalty and was not readily relinquished. The practice was well calculated to bring home to the understanding of the common people the inconveniences of tyranny.

These questionable prerogatives of the crown were enlarged to dangerous proportions by the foolish and incompetent son of the great Edward. Edward II. was not so much despotic as self-willed and indulgent. He looked upon his realm as a fair pasture wherein he and his friends might fatten at their will. The prime favorite was Piers

Gaveston, a needy French courtier, brilliant and lovable even at this distance of time and space, a loyal friend but a dangerous adviser. For this petted gallant, great estates were carved from the royal demesne. He was made Earl of Cornwall, and when the king went over sea to bring home his French bride, Gaveston was appointed regent of the realm. The gay Gascon waxed fat and kicked. He flung jibes at the great English lords, reckless of their sullen wrath. In 1310 a convention of the barons, under the lead of Thomas of Lancaster, the king's cousin, presented a solemn protest. They complained that the people were burdened by heavy and illegal taxes, while the kingdom lay undefended, the money that should have been devoted to the Scotch war being wasted on unworthy favorites. The government was placed in commission for a year, twenty-one Lords Ordainers being appointed to act for the king, and a series of ordinances was drawn up which Edward was forced to confirm. Gaveston was banished from the realm, together with the Italian bankers who had lent their aid to the royal extravagance. The king was forbidden to alienate the royal demesne and was told that he must hereafter "live of his own." No unusual taxes were to be levied, nor could the king raise an army, go to war, or quit the realm without consent of the barons. Parliament was to be convened at least once a year to consider such requests from the king. The Ordinances gave the barons effective control of the government, but the untrammeled rule of the great lords proved to be no less despotic than that of the crown. When, a few years later, the king, under the guidance of his new favorites, the Dispensers, was able to accomplish the ruin of Lan-

Female Costume. Time of Edward II.

The Lords Ordainers. 1310.

In 1315, the king was put on an allowance of £10 a day.

caster, England rejoiced at his fall. The Dispensers had the good sense to see that the king's best security against any future effort of the barons was the support of the people. The Parliament of 1322, which repealed the Ordinances, decreed that all matters concerning the king and the realm must be enacted in full Parliament with the consent of the "prelates, earls, and barons, and the commonalty of the realm."

Such a declaration, if accepted in its full import by the king, might have furnished the basis of a successful reign; but Edward's foolish fondness for his favorites had raised up foes in his own household. His Queen, Isabel, resolving to avenge the slights put upon her, fled with her paramour, Roger Mortimer, to France. Prince Edward joined her there, and the three concerted rebellion. Landing on the English coast in 1326, they were joined by the leading barons. London declared for the prince, the Dispensers were hanged, and a full Parliament was convened at Westminster where the helpless king was forced to abdicate, young Edward being proclaimed king in his stead. The principal actors in this poor tragedy were, it is true, inspired by selfish and unworthy motives, and hardly deserved the success they achieved; but they wrought better than they knew. In summoning the nation to their aid, in appealing to Parliament to displace an unworthy king, they acknowledged in the national assembly an authority superior to monarchy. From this time Parliament was recognized as the dominant power in the realm. Without the consent of the assembled estates, no tax could be levied, no law passed. Kings and courtiers might terrify or cajole

Deposition of Edward II. 1327.

Female Costume. Time of Edward II.

Rise of the Commons.

the people's representatives into compliance with their will, but they must secure at least the show of popular sanction.

Coming to the throne under such conditions, Edward III. could not consistently dispute the authority of the national Parliament. Indeed he was not the man to enter into a constitutional contest. The third Edward was by instinct a general, not a statesman, and his energies were absorbed in the long war with France. So long as Parliament sanctioned his military enterprises and voted supplies for his army, he was ready to make any concessions required of him. Of the continental dominions of Henry II., Aquitaine only remained, and this fair province was wavering in her allegiance and inclined to admit the suzerainty of the French king. Edward III. was ambitious to restore the military prestige of his race and entered thoughtlessly into the project of conquest which ultimately cost England dear. Grounds of quarrel were not lacking. The aggressions of Philip VI. in Aquitaine, his interference in Scotland, his demand that Edward should make good the damage done to French merchants by English sailors in the Channel—all these were serious grievances, but they did not justify Edward's pretensions to the French crown. His claim* was based on the fact that he was, through his

Edward III. 1327-1377.

The French wars.

---

*Claim of Edward III. to the French crown.

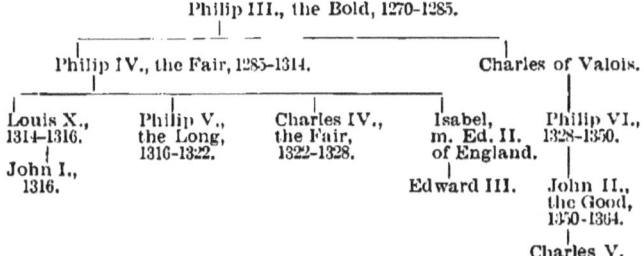

mother, Isabel, the only surviving grandchild of Philip the
Fair, while Philip VI. was but the son of a younger
branch. The French court repudiated the claim, citing the
Salic law to prove that the succession could not be claimed
through a woman. But this was a mere quibble of the
lawyers. The essential right of Philip, and that which
Joan of Arc urged for his successor one hundred years later,
was that the French people should be ruled by a French
king. In contrast to this fundamental right of a nation to
its own, the arguments of jurists, pro and con, are mere
"sound and fury, signifying nothing."

Victory was at first on the side of England. Edward

commanded a loyal army be-
cause he had a united people
and a well-filled treasury at his
back. Philip VI., on the other
hand, was but feudal lord of
France. His force was made
up of mounted knights, the unruly retainers of his great vas-
sals. Discipline, generalship, was out of the question.
The battlefield of Crecy bears witness to the weakness
of a feudal force when brought face to face with national
troops. The bulk of the English army was made up of
foot-soldiers, stout yeoman archers, who steadily stood
their ground, while the bad management and disorder
of the French were indescribable. The hero of the French
wars was the eldest son of King Edward, "the Black
Prince." Nothing more clearly indicates how distorted
were the moral ideals of the age than this universal
admiration of Prince Edward. That he was a brilliant
and daring warrior was abundantly proved at Crecy and
Poitiers; but personal courage was offset by a cruelty and
greed that rendered him the prince of plunderers. Rich

booty was wrung from the unhappy people only to be spent in wasteful revel. The fairest districts of France were devastated to no military end, and the country reduced to a state of anarchy. It was the vice of the times. Medieval chivalry imposed a high code of honor upon its devotees, but their superfine courtesy did not extend beyond their own class. Peasants and burghers were thought creatures of another clay. Froissart lauds the generosity of the Black Prince when, after Poitiers, he rewards the

Cannon used at Crecy.

valiant knight who led the fray with a pension of six hundred marks, and serves the captured King John at a sumptuous supper, standing by his side with deferential solicitude. The princely chronicler ignores the fact that the treasure dispensed in such royal fashion was wrested from starving peasants.

After years of this wasteful and inhuman warfare, Prince Edward returned home laden with booty, but broken in body and spirit. The best blood of England had been spilled on the fields of France, but the country was no nearer submission than when the war began. By the Peace of Bretigny, the king surrendered his claim to the French crown, and, in 1375, a truce was agreed upon which left the English in possession of no French territory but the seaports Calais, Cherbourg, Brest, Bordeaux, and Bayonne.

The long and costly war was not merely fruitless ; it was demoralizing. It is true that bravery and knightly honor were fostered by these years of desperate adventure, but the same conditions bred brutality and avarice. Princes and barons returned to England to spend in reckless extravagance the wealth amassed in the French campaigns.

Constitutional results of the French wars.

Disastrous as were the French wars, they yet served one useful purpose. They furnished the opportunity for constitutional progress. Great armies could not be maintained without frequent appeals for money, and the Parliaments of this period were not slow to utilize such occasions for extorting concessions from the king. Grants were only voted in return for redress of grievances, and the king was forced to surrender, one after another, the most cherished prerogatives of the crown. Exclusive right of taxation was accorded to Parliament, together with the power to specify the object to which the supply should be devoted. The royal accounts were examined by auditors appointed by Parliament, and the king's ministers were held responsible to the representatives of the people. These were great and important concessions. They secured to the Parliament of the fourteenth century authority almost coextensive with that exercised by the House of Commons to-day.

A Mounted Knight.

Organization of Parliament.

Forty-eight Parliaments were convened in the fifty years of Edward III.'s reign, and the mass of business considered rendered effective organization necessary. The methods of procedure then determined upon are still observed, curious and antiquated though many of them seem. By 1343 the representatives of the several estates had established the custom of meeting in two distinct assemblies, the House of Lords and the House of Commons. In the House of Lords, the lineal descendant of the Great Council, sat some fifty barons and as many great ecclesiastics who together represented the interests of a small fraction of the English nation, the privileged orders. Knights and burgesses originally sat apart as representing distinct estates and separate interests, but they gradually learned how much might be gained by alliance. The knight spoke for his shire, and the burgess for his borough, but both stood for the interests of the middle classes as opposed to those of the barons and clergy. Their union in the House of Commons was a gain to the cause of con-

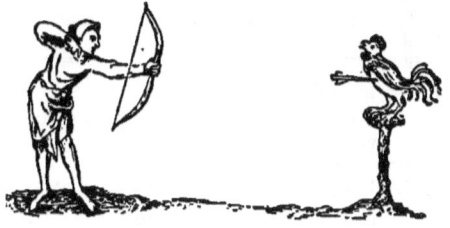

Archery. Fourteenth Century.

stitutional development. Jointly they gathered courage to undertake reforms that neither estate would have ventured alone.

The reign of Edward III., held to be so brilliant by contemporary annalists, drew to a close in grief and gloom. The last expedition to France had been a pitiful failure, and England was forced to sue for peace. The Prince of Wales, his splendid energy exhausted, had come home to die. The old king was in his dotage. Ruled by his greedy, unscrupulous mistress, Alice Perrers, he weakly yielded to the clamors of the cunning parasites who fattened on the life-blood of the nation. Bribery, peculation, fraud, every form of corruption, was rife at court. The ostentatious extravagance of the upper classes showed in startling contrast to the misery of the people. Moreover, the Black Death, a mysterious pestilence that visited England in 1348 to return again and again before the close

The Black Death.

of the century, had swept away half the population and left the nation terrified and spent. The government had

Effigy of Edward III. in Westminster Abbey.

fallen into the hands of John of Gaunt, a younger son of Edward III., and the ablest of his house. He made but selfish use of his great power. Allying himself in political trickery with Alice Perrers, he winked at the malpractices of the court. When Parliament at last set about the work of reform, the great Duke of Lancaster was recognized as a most dangerous opponent. The grievances of the people were voiced by the House of Commons. Encouraged by the support of Prince Edward, they presented a remonstrance, boldly complaining of the extravagance and corruption of the court and denouncing the king's ministers as evil counselors. At first the reformers carried everything before them. Lyons and Latimer, officers of the king, were accused of gigantic financial frauds, and

The Good Parliament. 1376.

solemnly impeached. Heavy fines were imposed on Alice Perrers and others convicted of receiving bribes. A Council of Government was chosen, composed of men who could be trusted to regard the interests of the nation. Petitions were presented, 140 in number, protesting against the maladministration of the government. They enumerated the grievances that had been accumulating since the beginning of the reign. The old king bent his head before this storm of indignation and granted all that was asked of him, but Lancaster bided his time. The death of Prince

Female Costume. Time of Edward III.

Edward that same year struck the ground from under the feet of the reform party. His son Richard was but a child

of ten years and John of Gaunt aspired to the succession.
Hardly was the Good Parliament dissolved when its acts
were arbitrarily revoked; Alice Perrers, Latimer, and
Lyons were recalled, and the Parliamentary leaders punished. Lancaster convened a Parliament the following
spring, having first looked well to it that the representatives sent to the House of Commons should be such as
would serve his purpose. From an assembly so packed, no
resistance was to be feared, and the necessary supplies were
granted without remonstrance. So the work of the Good
Parliament was undone because there was not in the Lower
House sufficient staying power for persistent opposition.

Throughout the reign of Richard II., the Commons played but a minor part in the government. A council of regency was immediately appointed with John of Gaunt at its head. His administration was far from brilliant. The war with France was renewed, but carried on with so little energy that Ghent and Flanders passed into French control, and the Flemish trade, a rich source of profit, was lost to England. The French grew so bold as to undertake invasion in their turn. A force was landed in the Isle of Wight and with difficulty repulsed. The formidable insurrection of the people, which broke out in 1381, was in its political aspects a protest against the misgovernment of Lancaster.

Richard II. 1377-1399.

The inconstant Gaunt withdrew in 1386, to follow a wild goose chase in pursuit of the Spanish crown, and the government came into the hands of the youngest of the king's uncles, the Duke of Gloucester. Hitherto Richard had been allowed to choose his own ministers and waste the royal revenues unmolested. Inquiry was now made into the abuses of the court, and a council of reform was intrusted with the government. The king's effort to free himself was successfully withstood by the Lords Appellant, and the "Merciless Parliament," acting at the instance of Glouces-

> The Lords Apellant, the five great nobles who brought accusation of treason against the king's counselors.

ter, impeached the friends and ministers of Richard and condemned them to death. Thus far the young king had seemed a submissive tool in the hands of the party in power; but, in 1389, he suddenly shook off the restraint of the Council, announced himself of age, and took possession of the government. For eight years Richard reigned in accordance with constitutional forms, but, in 1397, this policy was sharply reversed. Having secured a long, truce with France by his marriage with the daughter of Charles VI., the king, relieved of the embarrassment of foreign war, found his hands free to strike the long delayed blow at the Lords Appellant. One after another they were seized and thrown into prison. A packed Parliament voted their condemnation, declared the acts of the Merciless Parliament void, and vested the legislative power in a permanent committee made up of twelve peers and six commoners. Richard now seemed absolute. Taxes were levied

> Absolutism of the king.

without regard to right or usage. Men were even compelled to put their seals to blank promises to pay, which the king could fill up with any sum he pleased. Richard's enemies were thrown into prison or sent into exile without show of right. But the work of two centuries could not be so easily undone. The party of resistance found a leader in Henry, Duke of Hereford, son and heir of John of Gaunt. This prince, exiled by arbitrary decree of the king, returned in 1399 to claim not only his confiscated ancestral estates, but the crown itself. All elements of the opposition flocked to his standard—outraged nobles no less than rebellious commons. Richard, betrayed into the hands of his foes, was forced to resign the throne. "Your people, my Lord," said Lancaster, "complain that for the space of twenty years you have ruled them harshly; however, if it please God, I will help you to rule them better." "Fair cousin," responded the helpless Richard, "since it pleases you, it pleases me well." The king was tried in full Parliament and declared to be "useless, incompetent, and altogether insufficient and unworthy." The grounds for deposition were faithlessness toward divers of the great lords, transgression of the constitutional rights of the nation, and the assertion of absolute sovereignty. It was the tragic failure of Edward II. repeated, but with a deeper significance. We may see a Piers Gaveston in Robert de Vere and a Thomas of Lancaster in the Duke of Gloucester; but Richard was a stronger man than Edward II. It is difficult to discern his real character and purposes in the partisan report given us by the friends of the rival dynasty. It is, however, evident that he definitely projected an absolute sovereignty. The victory of Lancaster may thus be justly regarded as the triumph of constitutional government.

Parliament assembled for the Deposition of Richard II. From an Illustration in the Harleian MS., No. 1319.

Deposition of Richard II. 1399.

INTELLECTUAL REVIVAL.

In the realm of thought even more than in that of action, the reinvigoration of national life made itself felt. The barren controversies of the scholastics were cast aside. Men turned from the contemplation of abstruse problems of theology to the more vital questions of social and political life. Human passions, human needs, the effort to realize happiness in this present life—these were the absorbing interests of literature and polemic. Under the influence of this new humanism, writers for the first time gave adequate expression to the play of thought and feeling in the world about them, and there appears for the first time in England a literature to which we return with something more than curiosity—with a vivid interest in the men and women portrayed.

Address from the throne given in English for the first time in 1365.

It is most natural that this sympathetic literary impulse should express itself in the speech of the people. The fourteenth century, indeed, witnessed the final triumph of the English language. Though Latin continued for some time yet to be spoken in the universities, English was by the reign of Richard II. commonly used in the lower schools. In the latter part of the century, the English speech was adopted in Parliament and in the Courts of Law. French was still affected by the aristocracy; but Chaucer and Langland and Wyclif, the great writers of the age, made noble use of the native tongue. In Chaucer, the day-star of English poets, the effect of Norman blood and continental culture makes itself felt by a lightness and grace, foreign to the Saxon genius; but in a certain simplicity and sincerity of expression, in the frank realism of his thought, in a wholesome aversion to the transcendental, he is wholly English. Chaucer's life was spent at court and in the king's service at home and abroad. Scholar, courtier, soldier, ambassador, and man of business—his was a many-sided experience, and his knowledge of men was wide and varied. That catholic sympathy which was an inherent quality of his genius was never chilled by the pride of worldly success nor embittered by disappointment. And yet the picture Chaucer gives us of the England that he knew is colored by the "gracious worldliness" of the prosperous man of affairs who finds life much to his liking. His Canterbury pilgrims ride gayly through blooming lanes to the music of song and bagpipe, shortening the way with merry tales. All is vivid light and color, buoyant mirth and badinage, with never a somber touch. The characteristic

Geoffrey Chaucer. 1340(?)-1400. "Dethe of the Duchesse." "Parliament of Foules." "Troilus and Cressida." "Legende of Good Women." "Canterbury Tales."

figures of medieval English society ride in this picturesque cavalcade. First of the merry company appears the courteous knight who has proved his valor on many an oriental battlefield. Well he loves "truth and honor, freedom and courtesy." He and the blithe young squire who holds pace at his side, "a lover and a lusty bachelor," represent the best fruit of medieval chivalry. The attendant yeoman, "clad in coat and hood of green," bearing in hand a "mighty bow," may well be one of those who fought at Crecy and Poitiers. Worthy to ride among the gentry, in his own estimation at least, is the merchant with forked beard and foreign dress, "boasting always the increase of his winning." Of the gentry, too, are the sergeant of law, "wary and wise," a consequential body who ever "seemed busier than he was," and the doctor of physic who has grown rich on the Pestilence and is dressed in scarlet and sky-blue silk like a great gentleman. The penniless clerk of Oxenford bestrides a horse as lean "as is a rake." Hollow-eyed and sober, clad in threadbare coat, it is clear at a glance that like his great predecessor, Roger Bacon, he has spent all he could beg or borrow "on books and on learning." Neither office nor preferment awaits his unworldly service, but his eagerness to find and to teach the truth is better than a patent of nobility. A very different character is the fresh and ruddy franklin (free-holder) of excellent appetite, in whose hospitable hall it "snowed of meat and drink." The worthy vassal of a great lord, he has many times represented his shire in Parliament and has even served as sheriff of the county court. Several holy personages adorn this worshipful company, the fat monk with bald head "that shines as any glass," an unlettered prelate, who delights in hunt-

A Youth of Noble Birth.

ing and a good table and rejects his order's discipline as
out of date.

> "Full many a dainty horse had he in stable,
> And when he rode, men might his bridle hear
> Jingling in a whistling wind as clear,
> And eke as loud as doth the chapel bell."

No less worldly is the prioress with her simpering smile
and affected airs and graces, the sentimental Madame
Eglantine, who wears a love-motto on her brooch and
manages to give a hint of coquetry to the severe black garb
of her order. A more arrant hypocrite than either of these
is the friar, "wanton and merry," who sells absolution to
his well-to-do patrons, holding that genuine penitence is
evinced less by tears and prayers than by "giving silver
to the poor friars." Humbler characters join in this Canterbury pilgrimage; several craftsmen dressed each in the
spruce livery of his fraternity, thriving fellows these, good
gild-brethren and honest
burgesses; a pirate with
sunbrowned visage and
viking beard, who sits his
nag with a sailor's awk-
wardness—a hard drinker
and a hard fighter he; a
reeve (bailiff), "a slender colerik man," shrewd and
thrifty, the dread of the tenants, who fear him as they fear
the Pestilence; and his fellow extortioner, the miller, a
short, stout rascal with cunning, brutal face, from whose
foul mouth, "as wide as is a great furnace," low jests and
obscene tales reek forth. Their jovial peer in ribaldry is
the good wife of Bath, a buxom dame of florid countenance,
who ambles easily along in broad hat and scarlet hose, gar-
rulous and grotesque. Among these lesser folk rides the
"good man of religion," a parish priest, lowly but learned,
and "rich in holy thought and work." He is a true shep-

Practicing with the Crossbow.

herd, stinting himself that he may give to the needy, and sparing no pains or labor in the tending of his flock.

> "This noble example to his sheep he gave,
> That first he wrought and afterwards he taught."

His brother, the plowman, is a "peasant saint" who does his whole duty by God and his neighbor.

> "An honest workman and a good was he,
> Living in peace and perfect charity."

It is a marvelously vivid picture, a panorama of medieval society, which teaches more of actual conditions than many a learned volume ; but it is after all a superficial view that Chaucer gives us. He does not adequately represent the forces at work in fourteenth century England. His is the eye of an artist, delighting in the play of light and shade, and overlooking the deeper aspects of life, the strife, the aspiration, the defeat, that make up the tragedy of human existence. He does not trouble himself with the why and the wherefore of folly and sin, with the problems of evil and loss, but laughs at human foibles and takes pleasure in human graces with the delicate discrimination of the connoisseur.

Lady in Hunting Garb.

Not so Langland ; the rugged inartistic lines of this poor village priest bear witness to the grim life battle waged by the men of humble birth. The world was to him no gay show where a man might look on at the play, a disinterested spectator. Life was a stern reality where the powers of evil well-nigh overmastered the power that makes for righteousness. Chaucer could jest at the corruption of the clergy, the venality of the courts, the arrogance of the upper classes, the servile vices of the poor ; for, well-fed gentleman

William Langland. 1332(?)-1399(?). "Vision of Piers Plowman."

that he was, his individual happiness and that of his social order was not at stake, but to Langland, born and bred among the people, making their struggle and sorrow his own, the misery of a world out of joint was a matter of galling personal experience.

In the Vision of Piers Plowman, we are shown, not a jocund cavalcade riding through April sunshine, but a panorama of busy toil. Wandering on Malvern Hills, bathing a troubled spirit in the beauty of a May morning, the poet sinks down in weariness by a brookside and falls asleep. He dreams that the world lies before him, "a fair field full of folk." Toward the east, standing out clear against the sunlight, rises a tower, which is the habitation of Truth, the Father and Redeemer of men. On the other hand the ground sinks to a deep vale where lies a dungeon, "the castle of care." Wrong dwells therein, the Father of Falsehood, the Tempter. In the plain between, all manner of men, the mean and the rich, are "working and wandering as the world asketh," unconscious of the influences that play upon them, moving them for evil or for good. Serfs toil at the plow, with rare intervals for pastime, painfully winning what their glutton lords will soon waste in revelry. Merchants buy and sell, making snug fortunes in thriving trade. Barons are here, and their bondsmen, burgesses and city rabble, side by side. All manner of artisans, men and women, ply their trades, bakers and brewers and butchers, tailors and tinkers and weavers of woolen and linen cloth. These are hardy craftsmen and well able to earn their own living; but one sees others, lazy louts, good for nothing but spading and ditching, who while away the tedium of the day's labor with ribald songs. Some there are who manage to live without work. These wander through the land singing gay glees in rich men's halls, or, feigning folly, earn many a good penny by tumbling and jesting. Stout beggars, too, with whining lies, entreat the alms that will be spent in drunken riot. Here and there in the motley throng run cooks and their serving boys crying "Hot pies, hot! Nice roast pigs and geese! Come and dine, come!" while taverners stand at the inn-door calling out the merits of their choice drinks, the red wine of Gascony and the white wine of Alsace. Some, turning their backs upon such fleshly delights, give themselves to prayer and penance, hoping to "win heaven's bliss." A hundred or more sly fellows are hanging about, law sergeants, "who plead a case but for pence and pounds, never for love of our Lord." "Thou mightest easier measure the mist on Malvern Hills than get a mumble from their mouths till they see the glint of silver." This picture of the world, as it looked to an honest priest, would be incomplete without the pious rout of monks and friars, pilgrims and palmers, that go to Rome, to do honor to the saints, and return with "leave to lie all their life after"; wanton hermits, long-legged lubbers, who, being too lazy to work, wear the celibate's habit and live at their ease; friars in plenty—all the four orders—preaching to the people for their own profit, interpreting the Scriptures to suit their own purposes. In the midst stands a pardoner, armed with a papal bull, and professing to have power to absolve men from falsehoods and broken vows. The ignorant people believe him and throng to his feet, bringing rings and brooches and hard-earned pennies to pay for the pope's indulgence. Langland pours out the vials of his wrath upon the monks and friars. Toward the secular clergy he is somewhat less severe, but he says that the parish priests complain that their people are too poor to support them "since the Pestilence time," and depicts them begging leave to go up to London, where they may win silver by singing masses for the rich in sculptured chantries. The superior clergy, too, desert their rural charges and flock to London with the rest, hoping for some fat office in the king's employ.

The Vision of Piers Plowman was one of the most popular books of its day. Written in the rough vernacular, its alliterative verse caught the ear of the people and fixed itself in peasant memory. Reading was still a rare accomplishment, but this poet of democracy had disciples and interpre-

Balloon Ball. Fourteenth Century.

ters who carried his message far and wide. Gathered about a tavern table or lounging on the village green, the group of rustics listened with short, gruff laugh while some gaunt clerk of Oxenford read the story of the humble Plowman, the Christ returned to earth, who so gently teaches knight and cleric their duty, guiding wandering pilgrims to the well-nigh forgotten shrine of Truth. The seed so sown bore fruit in the Lollard movement and the Peasant Revolt.

WICLIF AND THE REFORM IN RELIGION.

This is the degenerate period of the English Church. Wealth and power had so far contaminated the upper ranks of the hierarchy that the superior clergy regarded themselves rather as privileged recipients of the contributions of the faithful, than as the servants of the Church of Christ. The ambitious and the lazy both found holy orders much to their liking, and crowded into the Church and the monastic establishments, until they far outnumbered the religious requirements of the nation. This involved a heavy tax on the resources of the country. The Church

Wealth and corruption of the Church

held fully one third of the landed property in England, while the income from the offerings of the people amounted to twice the royal revenue.

The regular clergy were even more corrupt than the seculars. Contemporary literature gives abundant evidence that they were held in less reverence by the people. The friars, so zealous for reform on their first coming into England, had degenerated in their turn and become mere servile bigots and shameless mendicants. The popes, to whom the friars were immediately responsible, far from calling them to account for breach of their vows, set them a demoralizing example. When the spiritual Franciscans, endeavoring to reform their order, taught that the possession of wealth was inconsistent with Apostolic Christianity, they were denounced by John XXII. as heretics. *and monastic orders.*

The influence of the Church over the minds and hearts of the people was not strong enough to enable her to hold her own against the protest raised by the wakened thought of England. Chaucer's polished sarcasm and Langland's fierce denunciation were echoed by many lesser observers. Jests and jibes against the clergy found ready listeners in the hut of the peasant and at the court of the king. Yet the spirit of religion was not dead in England. Men knew and loved righteousness and pure devotion. "When all treasures are tested, Truth is the best," says Langland in the person of Holy Church, and Chaucer reverences the good priest who practiced even better than he preached.

Protest against the pretensions of the Church found expression in deed as well as in word. A series of Parliamentary enactments undertook to restrain the power of the pope and to check the worldly ambitions of the English clergy. The Statute of Praemunire forbade the reception or execution of bulls from the pope, together with any appeal to the papal court. The Statute of Provisors forced *Statutes of Praemunire (1353) and Provisors (1351).*

the pope to surrender the practice of appointing foreigners to English benefices. In 1366, the tribute of 1,000 marks, which John had promised to the Holy See, but which had not been paid for thirty years, was refused once for all. The Good Parliament protested against other papal exactions. "The pope's revenue from England alone is larger than that of any prince in Christendom. God gave his sheep to be pastured, not to be shaven and shorn." The Parliament of 1377 mooted the question whether, in view of the impoverished state of the country, Peter's pence might not properly be withheld. Such bold defiance of the Holy See was justified in the minds of contemporary Englishmen by the degenerate state of the papacy. These are the years of the "Babylonish captivity." The popes dwelt in exile at Avignon, an isolated bit of papal domain which lay so near the territories of the king of France that it could hardly escape his influence. The English people scoffed at "the French pope" and suspected him of being but a puppet in the hands of their foe. In 1378 came the Great Schism; and for fifty years the rival popes of Rome and Avignon contested the powers and privileges of the Holy See. This "uncouth dissension" further alienated the loyalty of all thinking men till it became evident that the reform could not long be delayed. The attack on the English clergy was led by John of Gaunt. The political honors of the great churchmen were intolerable to this ambitious prince, and he set about curbing their pretensions. A statute passed in 1371 declared the clergy unfit to hold office, and a tax was levied on church lands acquired since 1292.

On the part of Lancaster and the lords, this assault on the power and wealth of the Church was not disinterested, but they found a champion whose single-hearted zeal for reform cannot be called in question. John Wiclif,

Twenty thousand marks a year were sent to the papal treasury.

1305–1378.

1378–1439.

the first great Protestant, was a learned doctor of Oxford, whose fame had secured him the honorable post of chaplain to the king. His views on the relation of Church and State had attracted the attention of John of Gaunt, and that crafty politician had conferred upon him the doubtful favor of his patronage. Wiclif had ably seconded the endeavor of Parliament to restrict the privileges of the pope and the English clergy, arguing that such power and wealth were inconsistent with the teachings of Christ. The essential feature of Wiclif's reform was the endeavor to recall the Church to Apostolic Christianity. Since God had revealed himself as the Redeemer of men, each human soul might have access to the divine life and was responsible to God alone. The mediation of the priest was unnecessary, and the ecclesiastical hierarchy with its pride and its greed for power was a fungous growth upon the Church of Christ. The claim of a sinful pope to act as vicegerent of Christ was blasphemous. No authority could be legitimate that was not sanctioned by God. Ruler and priest alike held of him. Obedience need not be rendered nor tribute paid to an unrighteous lord, though he were the king himself. _{John Wiclif. 1320-1384.}

Such doctrines quickly called down upon Wiclif the condemnation of the ecclesiastical authorities. The Friars raised the first cry of alarm. Their hypocrisy and immorality had excited the indignation of Wiclif, and they had writhed under many a scathing denunciation at his hands. Now his bold utterances against the papal supremacy gave them opportunity for revenge. Courtenay, Bishop of London, the champion of clerical privilege and sworn foe of John of Gaunt, summoned Wiclif to defend himself against the charge of heresy. Lancaster maintained his cause, and the citizens of London made a demonstration in his behalf; but the attack was renewed _{Opposition of the Friars.}

Persecution of Wiclif.

and he was finally condemned by a synod of the clergy. The last eight years of Wiclif's life were overshadowed by persecution so persistent, so formidable, that a feebler spirit would have quailed before it, but he maintained undaunted confidence in God and in the truth as he saw it. The faith he defended grew clearer while he argued. Pardons, indulgences, pilgrimages, were one after another declared of no avail. The climax was reached when he boldly denied the doctrine of transubstantiation, the corner stone of priestly authority. At this his friends wavered. John of Gaunt protested and withdrew his support. The Peasant Revolt, which broke out at this inopportune moment, was attributed to Wiclif's subversive doctrines. The condemnation of the synod was at last accepted by the university, and the great teacher was obliged to withdraw to his parish church at Lutterworth. Here, as if despairing to accomplish reform by the aid of princes and learned men, he devoted his energies to translating the Bible into the speech of the people and training disciples—his "poor priests"—who should perpetuate his message. In 1384 he was summoned to Rome to defend his doctrines before the pope, but a stroke of paralysis rendered the journey a physical impossibility. He sent a written statement of his faith, saying, "I joyfully admit myself bound to tell to all true men the belief that I hold, and especially to the pope; for I suppose that if my faith be rightful and given of God, the pope will gladly confirm it, and if my faith be error, the pope will wisely amend it." These were bold words to address to the tribunal where heresy was more hateful than sin. The Vicar of Christ immediately recognized in the advocate of poverty and righteousness an arch-enemy of the Church of God. Wiclif died before the pope's anathema could reach him, but the sentence was executed without delay. His doctrine was denounced as

Papal condemnation.

heresy, his writings were condemned, and his poor body,* exhumed from Lutterworth churchyard, was burned by the common hangman. [1415.]

Not so, however, was the work of the great reformer undone. The students of Oxford cherished his memory and the people secretly revered the valiant advocate of the rights of man against iniquitous privilege. His "poor priests" became most zealous evangelists. They are described in a contemporary statute as "going from county to county and from town to town, in certain habits, under dissimulation of great holiness, preaching daily not only in churches and churchyards, but also in markets, fairs, and other open places where a great congregation of people is." The writings burned in accordance with papal decree were reproduced with marvelous rapidity and copies of Wiclif's Bible † were furtively read in the houses of the nobility, in the court of the king. Knighton says, doubtless with some exaggeration, that every second man one met was a Wiclifite.

Statute against preachers of heresy (1382) never assented to by House of Commons.

PROGRESS OF THE PEOPLE.

A reform movement of even greater significance than that of Wiclif and the Lollards was agitating the people during this vital century. The laboring population—the ignored nine tenths of the nation—were waking to self-consciousness and were striving to free themselves from the fetters of feudal dependence and to better their lot in life. This upward movement had its origin in the industrial prosperity of the period. England was sufficiently removed

---

*Tradition says that the ashes were scattered in a stream near by, a branch of the Avon. Hence the popular rhyme.
"The Avon to the Severn runs,
The Severn to the sea;
And Wiclif's dust shall spread abroad,
Wide as the waters be."

†Anne of Bohemia, first queen of Richard II., possessed a copy of Wiclif's Bible. Through her the works of the English reformer found their way to Bohemia, and there inspired the ill-fated protest of Huss and Jerome.

from the imbroglios of the Continent to escape the devastating wars that checked productive enterprise. The quarrels in which the country was involved by the ambitious projects of her kings, were fought out on foreign soil. They did not directly interfere with England's industrial development. In the reign of Edward III., an effort was made to advance the commercial interests, and, hence, the tax-paying power of the kingdom. Foreign merchants were admitted to full trade privileges within the realm, and when they encountered the jealous opposition of the English traders, were taken under the special protection of the king. Manufacturers, moreover, were systematically encouraged. England had been, hitherto, an agricultural country, and the wool cut from the backs of English sheep had been sent to Flanders to be woven and dyed. Only the coarsest cloths were manufactured at home, for skill and implements were still of the rudest. With a view to developing this "infant industry," Edward III. offered the king's protection to Flemish artisans, who, driven from their own land by civil strife, gladly availed themselves of the royal favor. They settled in London, Norwich, and the eastern counties, and gradually taught English workmen better methods of manufacture. The same policy was carried out in this and later centuries by heavy duties imposed on the importation of foreign cloths and the exportation of wool. By 1600 woolen cloth had become one of the most important articles of export.

This development of the woolen industry was accompanied by a marked increase in the numbers, wealth, and influence of the artisan class. The medieval workman occupied a very different position from that of the modern factory operative. Machinery had not yet superseded skill, and labor, not capital, was the *sine qua non* of industry. The artisan was trained for his craft by several years' appren-

Commercial prosperity.

*Exports of woolen cloth.
1354, 5,000 pieces.
1509, 80,000 pieces.
1547, 120,000 pieces.*

Artisan class.

ticeship, and might spend several years more in the trade as a journeyman laborer before his education was regarded as complete. The fully accredited workman who had saved enough money to buy an outfit and hire a shop could set up for himself as a master craftsman. As such, he bought his raw material, and made it up with as much excellence and beauty as his skill allowed. The finished article was frequently displayed in his shop window for sale.

Bandy Ball. Fourteenth Century.

With the accumulation of means, he added to the number of his looms, and hired journeymen or took on apprentices as they were needed. He was capitalist, employer, and workman combined. The artisans of any particular town who followed one craft soon saw the advantage of uniting for the furtherance of their common interests. Artisan associations arose spontaneously wherever there was a considerable body of men engaged in the same trade, and were called "craft-gilds" or "fellowships." Several such gilds trace their origin back to the twelfth and thirteenth centuries, but the political and economic conditions of the period under consideration were especially favorable to the extension of the system. By the close of the fourteenth century there was hardly a trade or occupation that was not so organized.* A monopoly of its particular industry was accorded to the gild, and it was held responsible by the town authorities for the honest conduct of that trade. Fraudulent sales, dishonest or bungling

Craft-gild.

e. g., the weavers' gild of London. 1093.

Shuttlecock. Fourteenth Century.

---

* There were some eighty chartered craft-gilds in London. Twelve of these still exist, viz.: Mercers, Grocers, Drapers, Fishmongers, Goldsmiths, Skinners, Merchant Tailors, Haberdashers, Salters, Ironmongers, Vintners, and Cloth-makers.

workmanship, were punished by fine or withdrawal of the gild privileges. Unruly members were tried by the officers of the gild and then handed over to the town authorities for punishment. The craft, no less than the merchant gild, undertook the relief of sick or disabled members. Hospitals were provided and charitable funds, from which accidental losses might be made good, and widows and orphans pensioned. These artisan associations acquired wealth and influence hardly inferior to that of the older trade gilds. They had a co-ordinate part in the town government and in the election of the two burgesses who represented the interests of the municipality in Parliament. During this and the succeeding century, the burgess members of the House of Commons probably played but a shamefaced part in the presence of the knights and court lawyers who constituted the aristocratic element in that composite assembly; but they were gaining confidence with experience, and bade fair to become in time the bold and progressive party.

The serfs.

In manor as well as in town, new forces were coming into action, and the restricted conditions of medieval life were giving way before the augmenting vitality of the people. The serf population, ignored and despised by lord and townsman alike, with no voice in the local or national government and no recourse against oppression, was waking to a sense of its wrongs, making ready to assert its right to "life, liberty, and the pursuit of happiness." Here, as in the town community, economic influences were at work that, by bettering the material condition of the people, inspired them with courage to demand freedom. Throughout the fourteenth century there was a general and increasing tendency to commute labor for money service. Just as the king had been ready to convert military service into scutage, so the lord found it convenient to receive a payment of silver in lieu of the labor hitherto extorted with so much difficulty from the reluctant cultivators of his manor lands. Wherever this was accomplished, the demesne was henceforth tilled by hired laborers, and the serfs were left free to care for their own holdings, for which they still paid rent in money and produce. The thrifty serf was now in a fair way to become a small peasant proprietor, while his less industrious or less fortunate fellow might lose his claim to the land and drift into the class of free laborers. In any case a long stride was taken toward complete emancipation when a man rid himself of the old degrading services.

From the two great disasters of the century, the famine (1313 and '15) and the Black Death, the working classes reaped an incidental advantage. The great falling off in the number of laborers, especially after the Black Death, occasioned a rise of wages which was sufficient distinctly to advance the material well-being of the surviving population. Langland grumbles at the preposterous demands of the aspiring hind :

"Laborers that have no land to live on but their hands
Deign not to dine to-day on yesterday's victuals.
No penny ale will pay them nor yet a piece of bacon
Unless it be fresh flesh or fish fried or baked ;
And it must be "hot and still hotter" lest their stomachs be chilled
And unless he be well-paid, he will chide at fate
And bewail the time that he was born a workman."

Alarmed by the exorbitant demands of their former bondmen, the landlords appealed to the king, who, without waiting to convene Parliament, issued an ordinance decreeing that the former rates of wages should be enforced. "Because a great part of the people and especially of the workmen have lately died of the Pestilence, many, seeing the necessity of masters and the great scarcity of servants, will not serve unless they may receive excessive wages," and considering the "grievous incommodities" which from

Statute of Laborers.

the lack especially of plowmen and such laborers may hereafter come "the king ordains that every man and woman of whatsoever condition he be, bond or free, able in body and within the age of three-score years, not living in merchandise, not exercising any craft, nor having property of his own whereof he may live, nor land of his own to till," shall be bound to serve the lord who shall require his labor and to take only such wages as were customarily paid in his parish before the Pestilence. Laborers refusing to work on these terms were liable to imprisonment, and masters offering more than the legal rate of wages should forfeit double the sum so paid. The artificers and workmen of the towns were made subject to like restrictions and penalties. Ten statutes to the same import were enacted within the next fifty years, each imposing heavier penalties than the last, but in vain. Wages rose steadily*

Rise of wages.

The Unearthing of a Fox.

from an average of threepence a day, in the beginning of the century, to sixpence at its close. The several Statutes of Laborers were so many attempts to dam an incoming tide. The workmen had the vantage-ground, and were able to enforce their claims. There is evidence that they combined to resist any return to the old rates, and formed organizations quite comparable to the modern trades unions. Violent outbreaks were not infrequent. The employing class took alarm, and, being all-influential in Parliament, passed, in 1360, the statute against "covin and conspiracy," which declared alliances of workmen against their masters illegal.

---

* From three pence in 1300 to four pence in 1330; five pence in 1370, and six pence in 1400.

Legislation could not, however, prevent combination among men who suffered the same wrongs and hoped for a common remedy. Secret associations were formed, with recognized leaders and passwords. It is altogether probable that the more radical of the Lollard priests aided the movement and served as messengers between the different sections of the country. Wiclif's saying, that obedience was not due to an unrighteous lord, was interpreted to give license for revolt. Matters came to a crisis in 1381 when the people rose in insurrection. Adequate cause for the revolt may be found in the discontent of the laborers and the protests of the villeins against the ignoble services still exacted by their lords; but the immediate occasion was the imposition of a poll tax in 1380. An attempt had been made to distribute the burden according to wealth and station; the rich merchant or landowner was to pay sixty groats, the poorest workman no less than one. For every child above fifteen years the tax was exacted. To the aggrieved peasant, the tax was exorbitant, and its ruthless collection seemed the last unendurable straw. The revolt broke out simultaneously in Kent, Essex, and Hertfordshire, and spread with marvelous rapidity into all the southeastern counties. There were similar risings in districts as remote as York and Lancashire and Devon. All accounts of the insurrection are written from the landowner's point of view. Froissart's account sounds like the report of a labor riot given by the "capitalist press" of to-day. "There happened in England great commotions among the lower ranks of the people, by which England was near ruined without resource. Never was a country in such jeopardy as this was at that period, and all through the too great comfort of the commonalty. It is marvelous from what a trifle this pestilence arose. . . . It is customary in England, as well as in several other countries,

The Peasant Revolt. 1381.

A groat=4d., or 4s. in money of to-day.

for the nobility to have great privileges over the commonalty whom they keep in bondage; that is to say, they are bound by law and custom to plow the lands of gentlemen, to harvest the grain, to carry it home to the barn, to thresh and winnow it; they are also bound to harvest the hay and carry it home. . . . In the counties of Kent, Essex, Sussex, and Bedford, these services are more oppressive than in all the rest of the kingdom. The evil-disposed in these districts began to rise, saying that they were too severely oppressed. . . . This they would no longer bear, but had determined to be free; and if they labored or did any other works for their lords, they would be paid for it. A crazy priest in the county of Kent, called John Ball, who, for his absurd preaching, had been thrice confined in the prison of the Archbishop of Canterbury, was greatly instrumental in inflaming them with those ideas. He was accustomed every Sunday after mass, as the people were coming out of the church, to preach to them in the marketplace, and assemble a crowd around him to whom he would say: 'My good friends, things cannot go on well in England, nor ever will, until everything shall be in common; when there shall be neither vassal nor lord, and all distinctions leveled; when the lords shall be no more masters than ourselves. How ill they have used us! And for what reason do they thus hold us in bondage? Are we not all descended from the same parents, Adam and Eve? . . .

Spearing a Boar. Fourteenth Century.

They are clothed in velvets and rich stuffs, ornamented with ermine and other furs, while we are forced to wear poor cloth; they have wine, spices, and fine bread, when we have only the refuse of straw, and, if we drink, it must be water; they have handsome seats and manors, when we must brave the wind and rain in our labors in the field; but it is from our labor they have wherewith to support their pomp. We are called slaves, and if we do not perform our services we are beaten; and we have not an overlord to whom we can complain, or who wishes to hear us and do us justice. Let us go to the king, who is young, and remonstrate with him on our servitude; telling him that we must have it otherwise, or that we shall find a remedy for it ourselves.'" The insurgents first attacked the manor houses, and committed considerable violence, being bent on destroying the court-rolls which recorded their ancient servile dues. Then they set out for London, marching in scattered detachments, village by village. Their leader, Wat Tyler, whom Froissart describes as "a bad man and a great enemy to the nobility," had learned something of generalship in the French wars. Arrived at London, a rabble of some 100,000 men, not one in twenty armed, they found the gates closed and the government prepared for resistance. The common people of London, however, sympathized with the revolt. In response to their protests, the gates were opened and the insurgents entered the city. Some violence was inevitable. Savoy Palace, the residence of John of Gaunt, was burned. The Archbishop of Canterbury, who, as king's chancellor, had proposed the poll tax, was beheaded, together with many lawyers and some unfortunate Flemings and Lombards. Meanwhile, the king and his counselors, safely ensconced in the Tower, debated what might be done. Should they gather the nobles and their retainers, and, falling upon the rebels in the night, kill them "like flies"? This they dared not do for fear of the sympathetic populace. "Sir," said the king's counselors, "if you can appease them by fair

Wat Tyler.

words, it will be so much the better, and good humoredly grant them what they ask; for should we begin what we cannot go through, we shall never be able to recover it; it will be all over with us and our heirs, and England will be a desert." It was determined to treat with the enemy, and the king sent orders that they should retire to "a handsome meadow at Mile-end, where, in the summer, people go to amuse themselves." Arrived at the place, the young king rode forward bravely enough, saying: "My good people, I am your king and your lord; what is it that you want, and what do you wish to say to me?" Those who heard him answered: "We wish thou wouldst make us free forever, us, our heirs, and our lands, and that we should be no longer called slaves nor held in bondage." The king replied: "I grant your wish; now, therefore, return to your homes, leaving two or three men from each village . . . to whom I will order letters to be given, sealed with my seal . . . with every demand you have made fully granted." Thirty secretaries were immediately set to work to draw up the charters of manumission, and the greater part of the people departed for their homes, saying: "It is well said; we do not wish for more." Then the king's party threw off the mask of courtesy and good humor. Wat Tyler was foully murdered. Jack Straw, John Ball, and other ringleaders were seized and executed without form of trial. Many serfs suffered death at the hands of their outraged masters. The villeins had no resource, since the landowners were all-influential in both Houses of Parliament. The charters of manumission were revoked on the ground that they were granted by "compulsion, duress, and menace," and an act of pardon was passed, exempting from blame and penalty any lords and gentlemen who, in the emergency, had taken the law into their own hands and inflicted bodily injury on their bondmen.

Seven thousand are said to have perished.

So were the people outwitted and the insurrection crushed in blood. The dominant classes were, as yet, too strong to be withstood. It is quite probable that fear of another rising induced many a lord to abate his claims somewhat, but he would still enforce what he could, and there is abundant evidence that certain forms of serf-labor persisted into the sixteenth century. The eventual emancipation of the serfs was due, not to insurrection or legislation, but to the gradual operation of economic forces. *e. g.,* Elizabeth enfranchised the bondmen on the royal estates, 1574.

A Lady Hunting. Fourteenth Century.

CHAPTER VII.

Struggle for the Crown.

Illustrative Readings.
Henry IV.; Shakespeare.
Henry V.;   "
Henry VI.;   "
Richard III.;   "
The Last of the Barons; Lord Lytton.
Warwick; C. W. Oman.

Important Dates.
Reign of Henry IV., 1399-1413.
1401, Statute for the burning of Heretics.
1400, Revolt of Wales; 1403, of the Percies; 1405, of Archbishop Scrope.
Reign of Henry V., 1413-1422.
1414, Lollard conspiracy.
1415, Battle of Agincourt.
1417, Conquest of Normandy.
1420, Treaty of Troyes.
Reign of Henry VI., 1422-1461.
1429, Siege of Orleans.
1450, Cade's insurrection.
1451, Loss of Normandy and Guienne.
1455, Battle of St. Albans.
1461, Battle of Towton.
1471, Battle of Barnet.
Reign of Edward V., 1483.
Reign of Richard III., 1483-1485.
1485, Battle of Bosworth Field.

Genealogical table.   The rival dynasties.

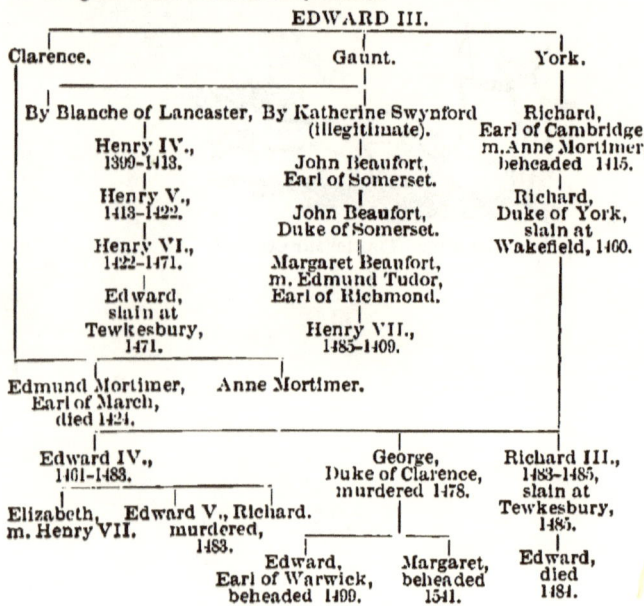

146

THE brilliant promise of the fourteenth century was destined to fail of fulfilment. The hopes and aspirations awakened in the good times of Edward I. were undone by the great calamities which fell upon the land in the reign of his successors. War, pestilence, and famine wrought their hideous work, sapping the energies that should have gone into progress and expansion. The forward movement toward political, religious, and industrial freedom proved premature and abortive. In the succeeding age the best achievements of the fourteenth century were rendered void. Degeneration and decay characterized every aspect of the national life. Politics dwindled into mere strife of faction, worship passed into formalism, the literary impulse ebbed, and social relations became demoralized even to brutality.

THE DYNASTIC WARS.

Henry IV., like Edward III., came to the throne pledged to respect the constitutional rights of the nation. His usurpation was a protest against the misgovernment of Richard II., and success was achieved by the support of the Lords Appellant. At his coronation, he confirmed the ancient laws and charters, and promised to govern not according to his own arbitrary pleasure, but by advice of the estates assembled in Parliament, and loyally did the king keep his word. Constitutional forms were scrupulously observed. Taxes and legislation were determined by the will of the people. "Never before and never again for two hundred years were the Commons so strong as they were under Henry IV." But the first Lancastrian came to the throne under obligation to the great lords and prelates who had combined to depose Richard. Their zeal was rewarded by rich booty in titles and estates. Arundel was made Archbishop of Canterbury, while the Percies and the Nevilles were given ample assurance of the king's favor. The obligation to the Church was redeemed by prompt legisla-

Henry IV. 1399-1413.

Statute against heretics. 1401. tion against Lollardry. All previous measures had been ineffective. The doctrine of Wiclif was preached through the length and breadth of the land, and the reformed faith was being accepted not only by peasants and artisans, but by learned doctors and court nobility. The clergy, in alarm, appealed to the king to reinforce ecclesiastical sentence by civil penalty. Henry had inherited nothing of his father's quarrel with the Church, and looked upon the Lollards as dangerous adherents of Richard. He readily lent his influence to the petition which resulted in the first act against heretics inscribed among English statutes. The confirmed heretic was to be burned to ashes in some high place before the eyes of the people, in order to strike fear to the hearts of any who might be wavering in the approved creed. When the commons petitioned that the wealth of the clergy should be confiscated to the uses of the State, the king sent answer that "from thenceforth they should not presume to study about any such matters."

Effigy of Henry IV. and his Queen, Joan of Navarre.

1410.

Revolts in favor of Richard. Such efforts to reinforce his position could not guard the new-made king against rebellion. Richard's friends soon gathered courage to assert his right to the throne. The unhappy prince was secretly murdered the year after his deposition, but his partisans did not despair. Rumors that Richard was alive, that he had been seen in Scotland, that he was rallying his forces at Chester, were rife in the land, and stirred the latent discontent of the people. Henry was deep in debt and the heavy requisitions he made upon the nation's wealth soon quenched the loyalty called forth by his regard for constitutional forms. Divers plots were undertaken against the king's life. Wales revolted and the Percies, whose allegiance Henry had thought secure, joined the Welsh in proclaiming the young Earl of March rightful heir to the throne. Northumberland rose at their call, and the insurrection was with difficulty suppressed. The king of France, whose daughter was Richard's queen, protested against the usurpation and sent aid to the Welsh insurgents. The Gascon cities that had remained loyal to the English mistrusted the new dynasty and lent ear to the overtures of France. One by one all obstacles were overcome, all enemies were outwitted, reconciled, or destroyed, and the people won over to the House of Lancaster. But the task wore out the king's life. Haunted by secret doubts as to his right to the crown, weighed down by a disease which his superstitious contemporaries believed to be the judgment of God, he grew jealous and suspicious, fearing to be displaced in his turn by the popular heir-apparent. "He reigned thirteen years," says Holinshed, "with great perplexity and little pleasure," but he left a well-founded inheritance to his successors.

Henry V. was a man of different temper; able, upright, and generous, a brilliant warrior and a wise ruler, he was the best product of his age. Prince Hal, the gay and mischievous youth whom Shakespeare depicts as Falstaff's boon companion, was suddenly sobered by the responsibility of kingship. "He was changed into another man," says Walsingham, "studying to be honest, grave, and modest." Disturbing questions as to dynastic right died into silence before the popularity of the brave, self-confident young king. The Earl of March was received into royal favor, and the conspiracy undertaken in his name by the Earl of Cambridge was readily brought to naught. The king's championship of orthodoxy doubtless added greatly

Henry V. 1413-1422.

The execution of Cambridge (1415) occasioned the blood-feud between the houses of Lancaster and York.

Obscure Lollard rising under Jack Sharp crushed 1431.

to the security of his administration. The statute against heretics was reinforced in 1414, and a formidable Lollard rising under Sir John Oldcastle was quashed by Henry's prompt interference. The leaders were put to death, and the movement so discredited, that Lollardry never again figured as a menace to the established order. Religious discontent smoldered in secret until the Reformation.

The French Wars.

The renewal of the French wars was another popular measure. Henry's claim to the French throne was slighter than that of Edward III. and had even less chance of success; but its assertion was eagerly applauded by Englishmen of the day. The war with France had become an ancestral feud that must be prosecuted without regard to consequences. The barons welcomed the opportunity to win fame and plunder, while the clergy were glad to divert attention from a second proposal to confiscate ecclesiastical revenues, by voting taxes for the French campaigns.

Military Costume of the Reign of Henry V.

The war, so cordially undertaken, was carried to a brilliant conclusion. The battle of Agincourt was a repetition of Crécy. Once again English yeomen overthrew French knights with well-directed shots from skilful long-bows, and once again the English army, invincible in battle, was destroyed by famine and disease. Good fortune, rather than valor, gave Henry the ultimate victory. France was demoralized by civil strife. The king, Charles VI., was imbecile, and the kingdom was divided between hostile factions. The Burgundians held the north and west, while the partisans of the Dauphin were in control south of the Loire. The country lay waste and desolate; the cities were reduced

Struggle for the Crown.

to anarchic misrule. A land so distraught was not difficult to conquer. The assassination of the Duke of Burgundy ruined the cause of the Dauphin. A treaty of peace was concluded, the hand of the Princess Catherine being given in pledge of fulfilment. The rights of the Dauphin were set aside, and it was agreed that Henry was to succeed to the throne on the death of Charles VI. In 1421 Henry returned to England, accompanied by his fair French bride. He was joyfully greeted by a people intoxicated with triumph, but a sinister fate awaited the warrior king. Returning to France to pursue the conquest of the south, "he fell sick of the great heat," and died only two months before the mad monarch whom he had expected to succeed. Henry V. had dreamed of reducing France, not merely to submission, but to order and renewed prosperity—of carrying the terror of the English name to the far east—of conquering the Turks and restoring the Holy Sepulcher to Christian keeping; but all these great projects came to nothing, for the king was cut off in the first flush of success before his initial conquests could be secured.

Treaty of Troyes. 1420.

Female Costume of the Reign of Henry V. From the MS. Royal, 15, D. 3.

England was undone by his death. The Prince of Wales was but nine months old, and the realm was exposed to all the difficulties and dangers of a long minority. Parliament vested sovereign authority in a council of regency, appointing the late king's brothers, the Dukes of Bedford and Gloucester, to the government of France and England respectively. Gloucester was a vain, ambitious prince who did not hesitate to sacrifice the peace of the country to his own advancement. He was soon engaged in a fierce quar-

Henry VI. 1422–1471.

rel with Bishop Beaufort, his rival in the government. The feud, ceasing only with the death of the principals, continued through the first twenty-five years of this unhappy reign, and involved the council, the court, and ultimately the dynasty in its fatal toils.

French victories under Joan of Arc.

In the meantime, Bedford was spending his splendid energy and sorely needed wisdom in the vain endeavor to retain the French conquests. The fortunes of France had touched lowest ebb in the Treaty of Troyes. With the death of the mad king, courage revived, and loyal Frenchmen turned to the Dauphin as the hope of the nation. Awakened patriotism found expression in the self-forgetting zeal of Joan of Arc, the marvelous peasant girl of Domremi, who inspired the dejected forces of the Dauphin with such enthusiasm as enabled them once more to win victories from the English. A besieging force was driven back from Orleans, the strong city of the loyal south ; the Dauphin was carried to Rheims, and there triumphantly crowned in the heart of the enemy's country, while one after another the fortified cities were recovered from the English garrisons. Not even the capture and barbarous execution of the Maid of Orleans could daunt the renewed courage of the French, but the death of the Duke of Bedford removed the single element of strength in the English resistance. In 1436 Paris was lost and England's possessions rapidly narrowed down to the limits attained by Henry II.

At home, meanwhile, matters were going badly. The little king, a delicate but precocious child, was being carefully educated, and he showed himself an apt and submissive pupil. In happier times he might have become a good, even a great sovereign ; but the storm and stress of civil strife forced upon him responsibilities far beyond his strength. He was crowned king of England when only seven years of age, and king of France at ten. Again and again, while still a mere child, he was called upon to mediate between the great barons of the council. The death of Bedford bereft him of his only wise and disinterested minister. The fragile body and overwrought brain of the boy king broke under the strain. He was still a young man when the curse of his house fell upon him and he became a helpless imbecile. The condition of England was pitiable. The people groaned under the burden of taxes imposed for the prosecution of the French war. The heavy drafts required to fill up the ranks of the depleted army, coupled with frequent recurrences of the plague, had sensibly reduced the population. The strength of the nation was nearly exhausted, and yet Parliament was unwilling to treat for peace. Race pride revolted against a humiliating conclusion to the war so brilliantly inaugurated. The counselors of the king, however, seeing that failure was inevitable, negotiated a truce. A marriage was arranged between the young king and Margaret of Anjou, Maine and Anjou being ceded as the price of peace. Normandy was lost in 1450, and the coast cities, Bordeaux and Bayonne, in 1451. The remnant of Guienne thus passed into the hands of the French king, and Calais alone remained to England.

John Talbot, Earl of Shrewsbury, in the Habit of the Order of the Garter, presenting a Book to King Henry VI. and his Queen, Margaret. From an illustration in the volume so presented, marked Royal, 15, E. 6.

Loss of French territories.

With the close of the war, a crowd of disappointed knights and ragged soldiers returned from over-seas, seeking to better their desperate fortunes. They found the country well-nigh ruined, the king impotent, the queen generally hated because of the humiliating marriage treaty, and the princes

Civil dissension.

of the blood-royal engaged in a life and death struggle for control of the government. Edmund Beaufort, Duke of Somerset, head of the illegitimate branch of the Lancastrian House, had the confidence of the court and the queen; but he was unpopular with the people, and was charged with every disaster at home and abroad. His rival, Richard of York, had, on the contrary, proved himself an able ruler, both in France and in Ireland. He was not only heir-apparent to the childless king, but, being descended through his mother, Anne Mortimer, from Lionel, Duke of Clarence, elder brother to John of Gaunt, he might advance a better claim to the throne than the reigning dynasty. Distrusted by the queen's party and driven from court, his name was caught up by the malcontents as the guarantee of efficient government. Jack Cade, who incited the fruitless peasant insurrection in 1451, assumed the name of Mortimer. The "Complaint of the Commons of Kent" protested against the misgovernment of unworthy favorites, and demanded that the king recall to court "that high and mighty prince, the Duke of York." The Kentish rising, far from inducing the king to summon York to his council, only heightened the antagonism between that great lord and the court party.

Civil Costume of the Reign of Henry VI.

In 1453, Henry fell into a state of imbecility which endured, with brief intervals of sanity, through the remaining eighteen years of his life. The birth of Prince Edward in the same year gave at last an heir to the House of Lancaster. Relying on the support of powerful barons, notably the Earl of Warwick, York laid claim to the protectorate, and did not hesitate to maintain his right by

Struggle for the Crown.

force. Somerset was slain at St. Albans, and Queen Margaret was left alone to defend the interests of her feeble husband and infant son. The queen was justly unpopular, since there was reason to believe that she was soliciting the aid of France and Scotland against her English foes. Nevertheless she could count on the loyalty of the north and west. The Yorkist cause, on the other hand, was maintained in London and the rich and populous southeastern counties whose commercial and industrial interests were dependent on efficient government. Richard of York, as well as his successors, courted the alliance of the people. In 1459, the quarrel so long smoldering broke into flame. Parliament, acting under the influence of the queen, attainted York and his principal supporters. They armed in self-defense and the land was given over to civil war. Victory was at first with the Duke of York. At the battle of Northampton, Henry VI. was taken prisoner and York laid claim to the crown. A compromise was effected by the advocates of peace; Richard was to succeed Henry VI., the claim of Prince Edward being set aside. Queen Margaret, however, rejected the arrangement and fought like a lioness for the rights of her son. Richard fell at Wakefield, but his heir, young Edward of York, proved as strong a leader. Getting possession of London, he was proclaimed king by the citizens and crowned, before the sanction of Parliament was obtained, by a group of partisan lords. The bloody battle of Towton Field wrecked the hopes of the Lancastrians. The leading men of the party were slain, and the fierce queen was forced to flee to Scotland, carrying with her the husband and son for whom she waged this desperate contest. Thus was the work of 1399 undone, and the act of deposition reversed. The coronation of Edward IV. was a reassertion of hereditary right.

The cause of the White Rose had been staunchly main-

1445.

Wars of the Roses. Lancastrians wore the red rose, Yorkists, the white.

Coronation of Edward IV. 1461.

Warwick. tained by Richard Neville, Earl of Warwick, near kinsman to the house of York, and the most powerful lord in England. He held great estates in the midland counties and could gather an army of trusty vassals under his banner, the ragged staff. He was further so connected by blood and marriage with other great families that he could count on the support of the major part of the English nobility. It was said that "half England would rise at his word." An able politician, a man of genial manners and wide sympathies, he won the steadfast confidence of the people. "He ever had the good voice of the people," says the chronicler, "because he gave them fair words, showing himself easy and familiar." He, far more than the Duke of York, fought in the interest of good government, and the victory of the White Rose was due in great part to his valiant service. After the crown was won and Edward IV. established at Westminster, Warwick was sent to guard the north country against the raids undertaken by Margaret and the Scots. It was no easy task; the indomitable queen stirred the discontented of Northumberland to revolt, and rising after rising was attempted, tasking the skill of Warwick to the utmost.

Meanwhile King Edward at London was pursuing his own pleasure as gayly as if his tenure of the throne was indefeasible. In 1464 he married Lady Grey, rejecting the high-born brides proposed by Warwick, and proceeded to bestow titles and offices upon her numerous relatives, the Woodvilles, with slight regard to the advice of his former councilors. The people murmured that Lancastrian feebleness "was no worse than the reckless misrule of a York." The rebellious commons of Yorkshire, led by Robin of Redesdale, protested against burdensome taxation, the alienation of the royal estates to upstart favorites, and the exclusion from the king's council of the princes of the blood. Warwick began to repent him of his work and to plot resistance. It required but the weight of his influence on the Lancastrian side to turn the tables. A sharp reversal of fortune drove the over-confident Edward beyond seas and restored Henry VI. to the throne. For five months the frail old man held the scepter in his feeble grasp. He was but a shadow king, the real sovereign was the great Earl of Warwick. In the spring of 1471, Edward returned to England, protesting that he had come in all loyalty to King Henry, to recover but his ancestral estates. Encountering no resistance from the apathetic people, he gathered courage and reclaimed the throne. In the struggle that ensued, Warwick was slain, together with Prince Edward, the hope of the Lancastrians; Margaret was taken prisoner, and the old king, consigned to the Tower, died on the night of Edward's triumphant return to London. The House of Lancaster fell, overborne by force. Twenty years of civil strife had resulted in the triumph of a rival dynasty. It was not a constitutional struggle like that led by Simon de Montfort, by Thomas of Lancaster, by the Lords Appellant. Henry IV. and his successors had been most scrupulously observant of every constitutional form. They had neither attempted arbitrary rule nor sought to enrich themselves and their favorites at

Restoration of Henry VI. 1470.

Female Costume of the Reign of Edward IV.

Final defeat of the Lancastrians at Barnet. 1471.

the expense of the commonweal. Their failure was in "want of governance." The dynasty had failed to strike deep root in the loyalty of the nation, because it had furnished no able administrator. England needed above all things a strong and efficient government which should protect the weak and restore order to the disorganized State. The House of York did not meet this need. The government of Edward IV. was arbitrary rather than strong.

Tyranny of Edward IV.

Since John, no king had sat on the English throne so abandoned to vicious pleasure, so lacking in the sense of responsibility for his people. Edward had "a conspicuous talent for extortion." Money was wrung from his helpless subjects by new and ingenious devices. Heavy fines were imposed for fictitious offenses and "benevolences" were demanded on such terms as made this form of contribution to the king's necessities even more vexatious than the forced loans of Richard II. No class escaped the royal exactions. "The rich," says a contemporary, "were hanged by the purse and the poor by the neck." Parliament was summoned at rare intervals, and its principal business was the voting of forfeitures and bills of attainder against the Lancastrian lords. No reform legislation was attempted.

Civil Costume of the Reign of Edward IV.

Edward V. 1483.

Edward's sudden death left the succession ill-defended. His son, Prince Edward, was but thirteen years of age. The young king's uncle, Richard, Duke of Gloucester, deformed of body, brilliant of intellect, and of all the House of York most cruel and selfish, the man to whom tradition has attributed the worst crimes of this brutal age, had enjoyed the full trust of the late king. No sooner was Edward dead

Struggle for the Crown.

than Richard began his bloody march toward the throne. The Woodvilles were driven from court, some into exile, some to the block, and Gloucester was elected protector of the realm. The wily duke took the oath of allegiance to his young nephew; but before Edward could be crowned, his royal right was set aside and Richard was invited by a partisan gathering of lords and clergy, acting in the name of the three estates, to assume the crown. The boy king and his little brother were murdered in the Tower.

Richard III. was a man of sinister genius—the worst product of his age. The single Parliament of his reign passed a series of remedial statutes, and these are sometimes cited as evidence that the last York was maligned by his successors—that the real man might have become a great sovereign. Since, however, the king did not hesitate to set at naught the only statute of importance—that declaring benevolences illegal—he can hardly be regarded as the author of the reform movement. The two years of his reign were spent in the vain endeavor to defeat the rival claimant to the succession, Henry Tudor, Earl of Richmond, the last surviving heir of the House of Lancaster. At the decisive battle of Bosworth Field, Richard was slain, and Henry was proclaimed king.

Richard III. 1483-1485.

Female Costume, Reign of Richard III. From an illum. Royal MS.

Overthrow of the Yorkists at Bosworth Field. 1485.

THE STATE OF THE COUNTRY.

The misery of the people during these years of civil strife was such as England had not known since the evil days of Stephen. The land was laid waste by rival armies in pursuit of plunder or revenge. Crops were destroyed and cattle driven off, the very huts of the peasants were torn down, and their owners left to naked beggary. Villages

Devastation caused by the wars.

and towns were sacked and burned to the ground, and the countryside reduced to smoking ruins. More men died of want than were slain in battle. Famine and pestilence, the attendants of war, added their horror to the general distress. The fields lay untilled in many parts of the country. The price of wheat fluctuated with every harvest, but again and again during the century, it rose to famine rates. Pestilence followed close upon famine. The chroniclers record some twenty outbreaks of "the Death," with hardly a space of five years free. Not only was the growth of population checked, but the number of souls actually fell below what it was in the thirteenth century. Suffering and the failure of accustomed restraints demoralized the nation. Loyalty, honor, all sense of obligation, weakened in this age of social disintegration. Treachery, breach of vows, barbarous cruelty, characterized the party leaders. Their followers, not slow to imitate the evil example, robbed and murdered in their turn.

The Church had well-nigh lost its influence for good. Dogma once rendered secure by the suppression of the Lollards, little concern was felt for the well-being of the people. The superior clergy, younger sons of baronial families, took an active part in the civil strife, and proved themselves a shade more faithless than their non-tonsured allies.

The baronage was decimated in the course of the dynastic struggle.* Many old houses were extinguished, the men of the family having fallen in battle. Many more were impoverished. The wasteful expenses entailed in 120 years of public and private war, and the cost of maintaining the splendid establishments required by the fashion of the times, were a heavy charge, while the returns from landed

e. g., George Neville, Archbishop of York, surrendered London to King Edward as the price of safety. 1471.

---
* The loss of life was heaviest among the nobility. At the battle of Northampton, Warwick gave orders that none should slay the commons, but only the lords, with whom lay the responsibility for the war. But twenty-nine barons were summoned to the first Parliament of Henry VII.

property were diminishing. Wealth and influence were centered in a few great families. There were half a dozen peers whose power rivaled that of royalty itself. The Earl of Warwick boasted so large a following that six oxen were daily slaughtered to provide his breakfast table. The Duke of Buckingham's rental was estimated at £180,000 in money of to-day, while in his great hall of Thornbury 200 guests partook of his bounty. The Earl of Berkeley was accompanied on his journeys by a retinue of 150 retainers, dressed in his livery. A baron's strength was measured by the number of followers he could maintain. Such attendants were fed and clothed, armed and mounted by their lord, and were entitled to a share in the booty of war. In return for such "livery," the man bound himself to espouse his lord's quarrels, to answer his summons, and follow him to battle at home or abroad. It was just such a relation of mutual service and protection as existed between the Saxon earl and his thane. There was, in fact, in the disorganized state of society, a reversion to feudalism. Backed by their armed retainers, powerful nobles made war upon each other, in pursuit of personal ends. Fierce feuds and private wars, such as disgraced the reign of Stephen, were of frequent occurrence.

Liveried retainers. "Livery" (liberatio) was originally the allowance in clothing and provisions.

Preparing for a Joust.

There was no authority strong enough to cope with the turbulent gentry. The kings were but their creatures and the courts of justice could not withstand their influence. A powerful nobleman had only to appear before the justice with several thousand henchmen at his back to secure the reversal of a hostile sentence. The Parliamentary records of the period abound in complaints

Maintenance was the support given by lord to client, whether in a private quarrel or in the courts of justice.

of "the outrageous oppressions and maintenances made to the damage of the people in divers parts of the realm." From Edward III. to Henry VII. this was a growing evil. No less than twelve statutes were enacted against the giving of liveries and the maintaining of false quarrels; but legislation could effect nothing when there was no strong central authority to put the law into execution. In the ignoble strife for possession of the crown, the royal authority was discredited. The institutions of government, local as well as central, were demoralized, and the kingdom lapsed into anarchy. Parliament, formerly the staunch defender of the people's liberties, had degenerated into the servile tool of dynastic faction. By neglecting to summon the hostile lords and by skilfully manipulating county elections, the party in power could at any time convene an assembly that would ratify its measures of attainder and restitution.

Anarchy.

Industrial progress.

Bad as were the political and social conditions of the age, there was still room for considerable industrial progress. The citizens of the towns and the lesser folk of the country had little to do with the civil wars. Yeomen and all below the rank of squire were forbidden by law to don a livery or to follow a lord to battle, while participation in the county elections was limited to persons possessed of land worth forty shillings a year.* The process of commuting personal for money service was virtually accomplished in the course of the fifteenth century and the former serfs became copyhold tenants. The demesne lands were rented on easy terms by their necessitous owners to thrifty yeomen who knew how to lay up money in spite of the turbulent times. Such a man is described in

---

*Statute of 1430, enacted in consequence of tumults made in the county courts "by great attendance of people of small substance and no value, whereof every one of them pretended a voice equivalent, as to such elections, with the most worthy knights and squires resident."

Latimer's sermon before Edward VI. "My father was a yeoman and had no lands of his own, only he had a farm of three or four hundred pounds (rent) by year at the uttermost, and hereupon he tilled so much as kept half a dozen men. He had walk for a hundred sheep, and my mother milked thirty kine. . . . He kept me to school, or else I had not been able to preach before the king's majesty now. He married my sisters with five pounds apiece. . . He kept hospitality for his poor neighbors and some alms he gave to the poor, and all this he did of the same farm." Such a man, too, was Clement Paston, the ancestor of the Pastons of Norfolk, whose son became a prominent judge and whose grandson married the heiress of a good county family

The fifteenth century has been called "the golden age of English labor," and it is true that the period is marked by a steady rise of wages; but prices rose no less steadily and the irregularity of employment (all labor was suspended on the frequent Church holidays) reduced the earning power of the workman to the mere cost of subsistence. The oft-enacted statutes of laborers empowered justices of the peace to fix the rate of wages and forbade the laborers to move about in search of better pay. Lamenting the degraded lot of the farm servants, Sir Thomas More says: "The state and condition of the laboring beasts may seem much better and wealthier; for they be not put to so continual labor, nor their living is not much worse, yea to them much pleasanter, taking no thought in the

Misery of the people.

Lord Rivers and Caxton, his Printer, presenting a Book to Edward IV.

mean season for the time to come. But these seely poor wretches be presently tormented with barren and unfruitful labor, and the remembrance of their poor, indigent, and beggarly old age killeth them up. For their daily wages is so little that it will not suffice for the same day, much less it yieldeth any surplus that may daily be laid up for the relief of old age." The food and shelter that might be procured with such meager earnings was so poor and unwholesome that the laboring classes fell an easy prey to the pestilence. Leprosy, typhoid, and other filth diseases ran riot.

Prosperity of the towns.
The citizens of the towns were far more prosperous. It was the policy of the burgesses to shirk all responsibility for the dynastic strife. Neither White Rose nor Red was worth the cost of a siege and the city gates flew open to the first comer. The wars, foreign and domestic, were a serious interference to commerce. Pirates infested the seas and the ports were not infrequently burned by French fleets that scoured the coasts. The victory of York, however, furnished opportunity for the revival of industrial prosperity. Edward IV., who earned the title of "Merchant Prince" by his successful trade speculations, did much to restore security to commerce. A typical burgher of the day was Sir Richard Whittington, a prosperous member of the worshipful Mercers Company, who built hospitals and colleges, loaned money to the king, and four times fulfilled the prophecy rung in his boyish ears by London's bells— "Turn again, Whittington, Lord Mayor of London."

The fifteenth century produced no statesmen and no poets. It was a brutal age, in which the ideas that had redeemed medieval society—patriotism, religion, chivalry— languished, overborne by selfish materialism. The literary impulse of the fourteenth century was prematurely checked. The ill-fated Henry VI. founded the grammar

school of Eton and built King's College Chapel, Caxton
set up his printing press at Westminster in the reign of
Edward IV., but with such rare exceptions, the age seemed
intellectually dead. There was a dearth of poetry and
romance. Even the chroniclers give evidence of the general mental apathy. Their meager records rival the Anglo-Saxon in dullness. Yet though the times admitted of no
individual eminence in culture or in art, the people at
large had their heart-stirring ballads, their quaint religious
dramas, played in the city streets on holy days, and faithful craftsmen wrought new beauty into church and gildhall and market-cross.

Mummers. Fourteenth Century.

CHAPTER VIII.

THE TUDORS AND THE REFORMATION.

Illustrative Readings.
Henry VIII.; Shakespeare.
Wolsey; Creighton.
Queen Mary; Tennyson.
Kenilworth; Scott.
Elizabeth; Beesley.
Westward Ho! Kingsley.

Important Dates.
Reign of Henry VII., 1485-1509.
1503, Alliance with Scotland.
Reign of Henry VIII., 1509-1547.
1512-1514, War with France.
1529, Fall of Wolsey.
1529, Reformation Parliament.
1533, Marriage of Anne Boleyn.
1534, Separation from Rome.
1539, The Six Articles.
Reign of Edward VI., 1547-1553.
1547-1548, Scotch war.
Reign of Mary, 1553-1558.
1554, Marriage with Philip.
1555, Beginning of persecution.
1558, Loss of Calais.
Reign of Elizabeth, 1558-1603.
1559, Acts of Supremacy and Uniformity.
1568, Overthrow of Mary.
1570, Papal Bull against Elizabeth.
1580, Arrival of Jesuits.
1587, Execution of Mary.
1588, Defeat of Armada.

Genealogical Table. The Tudor dynasty.

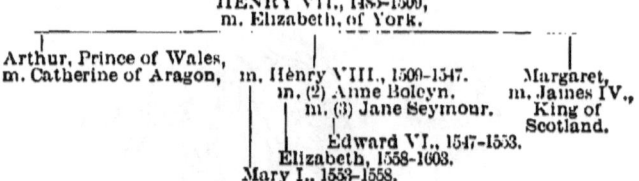

CHURCH AND STATE.

Character of the sixteenth century.

THE sixteenth century marks the change from medievalism to modern society. It was a time of transition, old landmarks were passing away to be replaced by a new world with different ideals, organized on a different basis. The temper of the times was favorable to experiments, eager for reforms. Rapid movement and restless activity characterized an age fruitful in large ideas and in epoch-making events. The old conception of Christendom as a great commonwealth ruled by pope and emperor disappeared with the fifteenth century, and for the next hundred years the fortunes of Europe were in the hands of the two strong centralized states of France and Spain. The sixteenth century saw the break-up of ecclesiastical unity with the revolt of half the Christian world against the spiritual dominion of the pope. Outside the realm of politics and religion, even vaster changes were taking place. To the material world of the fifteenth century a whole continent had been added, and the Atlantic, formerly a boundary, was now the highway between the Old World and the New. The deadened intelligence of Europe was stirred by the wonders suddenly revealed, the chains of medieval thought were thrown off, and the intellectual life of the age thrilled in response to the new vigor of the world of action.

England could not remain unaffected by the changes that were taking place. She had her Renaissance, her Reformation, and her future was linked more closely perhaps than any other to the newly discovered world beyond the seas. But at first she stood somewhat aloof, content to develop along the old well-trodden lines. Henry VII., the first of the Tudor line, was scarcely thirty when he ascended the throne. His tastes were literary and artistic, and he sympathized ardently with the intellectual revival of his time, but his reign was one continuous struggle to make secure the throne which treachery and a successful battle had given him. He had no claim to the crown upon which he could rely, even the Lancastrians were not united in his support. His security lay in the lack of any powerful rival and in the political exhaustion of the country. The nobility, diminished in number and still more in wealth and influence, was not strong enough to be formid-

Henry VII. 1485–1509.

able alone, and the Church, alarmed by attacks upon its doctrine and its property, clung to the throne for support, while the people, weary of bloodshed, turned eagerly from war to trade and commerce, and were ready to give their allegiance to any ruler who would establish order and maintain peace. In many ways Henry's reign may be looked upon as a continuation of that of Edward IV. To establish his rule and to make himself independent of Parliament, was the object of his policy. He bore heavily upon the nobility, exacting benevolences and reviving forgotten feudal dues. The statutes of maintenance and livery were rigorously enforced. To remedy the weakness of the ordinary courts in dealing with great offenders, he formed a new tribunal which could be neither bribed nor bullied. While thus holding the nobility in check, Henry courted the favor of the industrial classes by sparing their pockets, and by encouraging trade and commerce. To this end he furthered commercial intercourse with the Continent, but he carefully kept out of political complications. Peace at any price was his policy, and he strove to gain his ends by diplomacy and by judicious marriage alliances. He disarmed Scotland by marrying his oldest daughter Margaret to the Scotch king, and he strengthened the connection with Spain by obtaining as a bride for his son Prince Arthur, Catherine, the daughter of Ferdinand and Isabella. His work was crowned with success. The spirit of opposition was thoroughly cowed, and two risings in support of pretenders to the throne were easily quelled. Constitutional aspirations were checked, few Parliaments were called, and the personal rule of the king replaced the old limited monarchy. As a result of his

Court of the Star Chamber.

In 1496 a commercial treaty, the Great Intercourse, was concluded with the Netherlands.

A Knight of the Reign of Henry VII.

cautious if inglorious policy, Henry left to his son and heir a secure throne, a full treasury, and a prosperous people.

The accession of Henry VIII. marks an epoch in English history. Young, vigorous, conscious of power, and filled with ambition, he could not be content to play the unaggressive waiting part so well suited to his father's temper. The home and foreign policy of his reign was, however, not so much the conception of the king as of his great minister, Thomas Wolsey, who for a number of years held supreme power in Church and State, uniting in himself the functions of Chancellor and Cardinal. Wolsey's aim was to make the king absolute in England, England first in Europe. He felt that the royal authority was the only means of holding the country together, and that the time had come for England to take part in continental affairs if she would maintain her place among nations. Peace was his policy, however, and diplomacy his weapon. England was to make her influence felt not through conquest, but by holding the balance between the rival states of France and Spain now contending for mastery in Europe. For a time he was successful. Henry was popular among his subjects, and Parliament was usually subservient to his will, although on two occasions it offered a vigorous resistance to the royal demand for money. Abroad, English influence was slowly making itself felt even if her "threats were more efficacious than her performances," for her army and navy were ill-equipped, and her population was small as compared with other states.

Henry VIII. 1509-1547.

Wolsey's policy.

Female Costume of the Reign of Henry VII.

Wolsey, however, was not destined to complete his undertaking. Forces were at work which were to transform England and undo much that he had accomplished. On the Continent, the fierce passions of religious revolution were stirring. Men had long been ready for revolt against the misused authority of the papacy, and the attacks of Martin Luther, a Saxon friar, on the teachings and practices of the Church found a quick response. England was not slow to feel the impulse of the new movement. Lollardry had accustomed men to criticize the Church. The bold, vigorous, intellectual spirit of the age was impatient of the superstition and ignorance of the clergy. The very greatness of the resources of the Church made its misuse of them the more flagrant. Books and pamphlets from Germany flooded the country, Cambridge became a hotbed of heresy, associations were formed for the study and circulation of the Bible recently translated by Tyndale, and rendered accessible through the printing press. It was plain that the seeming strength and power of the Church was a mere shadow, wholly dependent upon royal support. As yet, Henry was unwavering in his loyalty, but his temper was too selfish, his love of popularity too great to afford any security for the future.

The immediate occasion for the crisis was, however, in appearance insignificant and far removed. In the beginning of his reign Henry, having first obtained the necessary papal dispensation, had married Catherine, the widow of his brother Arthur. For almost twenty years they had lived together, and she had borne him several children, of whom, however, only one, the Princess Mary, survived. At length the king's scruples were awakened as to the validity of the marriage. He began to doubt the pope's power to grant the dispensation. Henry was skilful in finding conscientious reasons for gratifying his selfish desires. It is probable that it was the bright eyes and merry wit of Anne Boleyn, one of Catherine's ladies-in-waiting, that aroused him to the sinfulness of his condition. Moreover, he realized the danger to the peace of the country in the lack of a male heir. As Catherine proudly spurned the suggestion that she should quietly submit to being set aside, Henry was forced to appeal to the pope for a divorce. But Clement was not free to act, for he was practically in the power of the emperor, Catherine's nephew. He agreed, however, to let the case be tried by a legatine commission in England. Cited before the court, the outraged queen pleaded her cause to the king in pathetic words: "Sir," she said, "I beseech you for all the loves that have been between us, and for the love of God, let me have justice and right, take of me some pity and compassion, for I am a poor woman and a stranger born out of your dominion, I have here no assured friend, and much less indifferent counsel; I flee to you as to the head of justice within this realm. Alas! Sir, wherein have I offended you? . . . I take God and all the world to witness, that I have been to you a true, humble, and obedient wife, ever conformable to your will and pleasure." Popular sympathy was with the queen, but Henry was unmoved. Nevertheless he could not gain his purpose, for the pope dared not annul the marriage, and the trial before the legates ended in nothing. The king's disappointment, however, led at once to the overthrow of Wolsey, on whom he most unreasonably threw the blame of defeat. With untiring zeal and personal devotion the Cardinal had labored in the interest of the king and for the

Henry VIII. From his Great Seal.

good of England. To Henry he had given the credit of every success. The odium of all unpopular measures he had taken upon himself. He had made the king absolute at home, and had raised England from a third rate power to the rank of a great state. But no memory of past services could impose a check on Henry's selfishness. Wolsey had failed to procure the divorce that he wished, and with royal ingratitude he threw the minister aside.

Thomas Cromwell, vicar-general.

Wolsey's fall prepared the way for momentous changes in Church and State. The aim of Thomas Cromwell, his successor in Henry's confidence, was, like Wolsey's, the concentration of all power in the hands of the king, but the methods used were different. Rapidity and boldness were the watchwords of his policy. During the next ten years every constitutional safeguard was swept away, every limitation on the royal will was removed, and the government became a despotism pure and simple. No man was too high, no interest too powerful to lead him to stay his hand. It was at his advice that Henry by the assertion of the royal supremacy freed himself from Catherine. Where Wolsey strove to rule without Parliament, Cromwell made it his tool. The first indication of the change from the conservative action of the Cardinal was shown in the work of the Parliament that met in 1529 and sat for seven years.

Long Parliament of the Reformation. 1529-1536.

Henry was willing to acknowledge the power of the pope so long as that power was used to further his will, but he now began to doubt the usefulness of an institution that stood in his way. The Church in England also had aroused his hostility by espousing the cause of Catherine, and he was ready to respond to the national demand for reform. The beginning once made, the advance was rapid; one abuse after another was attacked. The clergy were deprived of their privileges, the Church was made more dependent on the crown, and the connection with Rome was weakened by a statute forbidding all appeal. Finally in 1534 the last step was taken by the passing of the Act of Supremacy by which the king became "the only supreme head on earth of the Church of England."

As a whole the attack on the abuses of the Church and the changes in the ecclesiastical system met with popular approval. A few, among them Sir Thomas More, foremost of English scholars, refused to acknowledge the royal supremacy, and were put to death, but the majority of the nation went with Henry in his breach with the papacy. Even when Convocation at the instance of the king drew up the Ten Articles, a statement of doctrine which showed a decided advance toward Lutheranism, there was little opposition. Nevertheless the national temper was conservative, and the ancient Church still held men's hearts if not their minds. The excesses of some of those who had embraced the reformed doctrines, their attacks on shrines and holy relics, gave deep offense. Popular dissatisfaction was increased by the dissolution of the monasteries. This action had long been impending, the age of monasticism had passed, and as a rule the religious establishments had become mere landowning corporations, chiefly interested in adding to their own wealth. Henry and Cromwell, led by a desire to get at the revenues, caused Parliament to pass measures suppressing all monasteries and confiscating their property to the crown. Part of the wealth was used for national purposes, but the greater portion was squandered upon the nobles and courtiers about the king. That these measures were opposed by the people was shown by a rising in the north in 1536. Many of the gentry and nobility and the country people led by the parish priests joined the Pilgrimage of Grace, as the movement was called, and demanded the restoration of the monasteries, the extirpation of heresy, and the overthrow of Cromwell.

Attitude of the nation.

In 1536 the smaller monasteries were dissolved. All others were suppressed in 1539.

In the main, Henry was at one with the people. He would have been content with separation from Rome. At heart he was opposed to doctrinal change, and with the extravagances of the Protestants he had no sympathy whatever. He was ready to unite with a majority of the nation, and set a limit to the incoming flood of religious innovation. Parliament, as usual completely subservient to his will, passed in 1539 an act for "abolishing diversity of opinion in certain articles concerning Christian religion." The six articles* of the act contained the fundamental Catholic doctrines and closed the way to even moderate reform. Under the "whip with six strings," persecution of the Protestants followed, and many suffered for conscience' sake. Nevertheless, Henry abated nothing of his pretensions, and "at the very moment that heretics were suffering for denial of the mass, others were suffering by their side for denial of the supremacy." Throughout the remaining years of his reign he succeeded in maintaining an uncertain balance between the old and the new order, but it was plain that a tide of feeling was rising which would soon sweep away all compromises.

The six articles.

Political considerations strengthened Henry's natural conservatism. Cromwell's foreign policy was based on a union with the Protestant princes of North Germany, and it was in the interest of this plan that the king for a time connived at the progress of the Reformation in England. A marriage between Henry, who was now a widower for the third time, and a German princess was a part of Cromwell's scheme. But the grand alliance against the emperor came to naught in 1539, and the minister's doom was sealed by his failure to give the king a wife according to his taste.

---

* The Act of Six Articles asserted: (1) The truth of transubstantiation; (2) the sufficiency of communion in one kind; (3) clerical celibacy; (4) the obligation of vows of chastity; (5) the necessity of private masses; (6) that auricular confession should be retained.

Nothing could save Cromwell from the usual fate of Henry's instruments when no longer needed. Charged with treason, he was sent to the scaffold by bill of attainder without being heard in his own defense. Cromwell's overthrow was but the natural result of the system which he had built up. All power was concentrated in the hands of the king, the Church lay at his feet, Parliament simply registered his will. Nevertheless, Henry did not lose touch with the nation; he understood the temper of his subjects, and, unscrupulous and self-seeking though he was, he still won popular approval even while treading popular liberty under foot.

Fall of Cromwell, 1540.

Hènry VIII.

Edward VI. was a mere boy when he ascended the throne, and during his reign the government was in the hands of his ministers, chief of whom was his uncle, the Duke of Somerset. Personal feeling as well as self-interest led Somerset to oppose the old ecclesiastical order. In his policy he was supported by the young king, who was a Protestant by conviction, and who, with all the conceit of a precocious boy, was determined to force his views upon the country. The short reign was a period of religious revolution. By law or royal injunction, changes were introduced with bewildering rapidity. The sacred images were removed from the churches, the beautiful stained glass was broken, and the pictures painted on the walls were covered with whitewash. Of more permanent importance was the substitution of the vernacular for Latin in the church ritual. The mass was replaced by the communion service in

Edward VI. 1547-1553.

The English prayer-book was based mainly on the Roman Catholic missal and breviary.

English, and a book of common prayer, still in use almost unchanged, was substituted for the Latin missal and breviary. Upon the authority of the king, forty-two articles smacking strongly of Calvinism were promulgated as the national standard of faith. The confiscation of church property was carried to a length unthought of by Henry. Somerset leaned for support upon the "new men," the nobility enriched by the plunder of the monasteries, and it was necessary to satisfy his rapacious following. The chantries were despoiled. Gild property devoted to religious uses was appropriated, and the revenues of some of the bishoprics were seized. These revolutionary measures were hurried through with every aggravation of insult, and with small regard to popular feeling. A writer of the time says: "Also this same time was moche speking agayne the sacrament of the auter, that some callyd it Jacke of the Boxe, with divers other shamfulle names . . . and at this time was moche preching agayne the masse and the sacrament of the auter pullyd downe in divers placys." It soon became plain that the nation was not ready for such extreme action. The feeling of discontent was general. All opposition was, however, put down with a high hand. The opposing clergy were bridled by decrees that there should be no preaching except by a few licensed preachers; and some of the bishops who clung to the older doctrines were thrown into prison.

The political policy of the government was as ill-judged as its ecclesiastical reforms. The country was involved in causeless wars with Scotland and France, and the burden of taxation was heavy. At length the prevailing discontent found expression in a rising in Devon and Cornwall, followed by another in Norfolk. The only result was the overthrow of Somerset. He was succeeded by the Earl of Warwick who proved no wiser nor better. Nevertheless the country remained quiet, looking to the time when the young king would come of age and set things right. Had Edward lived, his fanatical temper would probably have brought matters to a crisis, but in 1553 he died, and, in spite of a conspiracy headed by Warwick to set her aside, Mary obtained the crown without striking a blow.

Warwick purposed to place on the throne Lady Jane Grey, granddaughter of a younger sister of Henry VIII.

The religious system which Edward and his advisers had built up rested solely on the will of the king, and at the accession of Mary a reaction at once set in. Without the interference of the government, mass was restored and the forms and practices of the reign of Henry VIII. were reëstablished. Mary, however, was not content with a return to the system of her father; she wished to restore the ancient order in all its completeness, to set up the monasteries again, to renew the connection with Rome. It was in part to further her religious scheme that she desired to marry her cousin Philip of Spain. At first Parliament showed itself, as usual, obedient to the royal will, but it soon became evident that there was a limit to its complaisance, and that in its opposition it was supported by the country. It was certain that reconciliation with Rome could never be brought about if it meant the restoration of the abbey lands in which forty thousand families were interested. Moreover, national feeling was aroused at the idea of the Spanish marriage which might bring not simply ecclesiastical subjection to Rome, but political dependence upon Spain. Parliament, however, was at length brought to the point of acknowledging the spiritual leadership of the pope, on condition that the monastic lands should be left undisturbed, and the Spanish marriage was finally consummated in spite of the opposition at home and abroad, and the lukewarmness of the bridegroom who, much as he prized the crown of England, cared little for its wearer.

Mary, 1553-1558.

Persecution.

Mary was not content, however; she believed that "she had been preserved by God in the succession of the crown for no other end save that He might make use of her above all else in the bringing back of the realm to the Catholic faith." In forcing her views upon the nation she showed all the self-will of the Tudors, united to the intemperate zeal of the fanatic. Her advisers hesitated; even Philip counseled moderation, but nothing could deter the queen from the work upon which she had set her heart. She forced from Parliament a renewal of Henry's laws against heresy, and at once pressed on their execution. From 1555 to 1558 persecution raged. Neither high nor low were spared. The Martyrs' Memorial at Oxford marks the place where Ridley, the deprived bishop of London, and Latimer, Henry the Eighth's favorite preacher, were burned side by side. "Play the man, Master Ridley," were Latimer's last words, "we shall this day light up such a candle by God's grace in England as I trust shall never be put out." Foremost of the martyrs stood Cranmer, primate of the Church. Of great learning, but of cautious temper, he had slowly come to take an advanced stand in opposition to the papal pretensions; but though his conviction was strong his heart was weak, and he shrank before the final test. Six successive times he recanted in the hope of purchasing pardon, but pardon was out of the question; he stood as a representative of English Protestantism, and, moreover, Mary was personally hostile to him as an active agent in her mother's divorce. When once his final doom was pronounced he regained his courage. "I have written many things untrue," he said, "and forasmuch as my hand offended in writing contrary to my heart, my hand therefore shall be the first burnt." Nearly three hundred, in all, suffered for the right of individual conscience—most of them in the towns and thickly settled districts, for there

Last Archbishop of Canterbury to receive the pall from Rome.

new opinions found more ready acceptance than in the country.

Darkened by bitter disappointment, the life of the unhappy queen drew to a close. A loving wife, she was forced to see that Philip had sought in her merely the instrument of his political schemes. Through the Spanish connection, England was involved in a useless war with France which had resulted in the loss of Calais. This was a heavy blow to the nation, and Mary was too much a Tudor not to feel the popular disapproval visited upon her. Moreover, all her efforts had brought England no nearer the old faith, nay, had rather frustrated her purpose. Men looked askance at a church that could maintain itself only through persecution.

1558.

"It is the Lord's doing, and it is marvelous in our eyes," was Elizabeth's exclamation when informed of her peaceful accession to the throne. The task before her was one to daunt a heart less strong. England stood almost alone in Europe, at war with France, the treasury empty, without army or navy. Her only security lay in the rivalry between France and Spain. The internal condition of the country was even more critical. Religious strife had passed beyond the point of reconciliation. The bulk of the nation longed for peace and might have agreed to a return to the system of Henry VIII., but that was impossible, for the Catholic party was bent on maintaining the connection with Rome, while persecution had made more fierce and uncompromising the temper of the Protestants. Elizabeth had little sympathy with either extreme. The Protestant contempt for authority and tradition was distasteful to her. Subjection to Rome was out of the question, for the pope refused to recognize her claim to the throne. But she approached all religious questions in the temper of the politician. She was not blind to the fact that the Protes-

Elizabeth. 1558–1603.

Elizabeth's religious policy.

tants were her surest support, that her cause was theirs. But, on the other hand, she knew that severe measures against the Catholics would open the way to foreign intrigue. To establish national unity in Church and State was the aim of her home policy, and to this end a religious settlement was to be devised which would win the support of the moderates and drive no one to extremes. In religious matters, Elizabeth was content to move slowly. The supremacy was restored, mass was abolished, and an Act of Uniformity decreed the use of King Edward's Prayer Book. But although the oath of supremacy was rigorously exacted from the bishops, all but one preferring deprivation to compliance, the majority of the clergy were left unmolested.

Queen Elizabeth.

Nor was the Act of Uniformity very severely enforced. The queen feared above all things the renewal of strife; she discouraged preaching, and she would gladly have abated the interest of her subjects in religious questions. There was no revolution; the changes were scarcely noticed, and yet, within a year after Elizabeth's accession, England had ranged herself once for all on the side of Protestantism.

The condition of affairs beyond the border was at this time a serious menace to Elizabeth's throne, and made religious contest more than ever to be feared. In 1558 the long-standing friendship between France and Scotland was cemented by the marriage of Mary, the young Scotch queen, to the Dauphin of France. Denying the right of Elizabeth on the ground of illegitimacy, Mary assumed the title and style of Queen of England. The danger of her claim lay in the certain support of France and the English Catholics. Left a widow by the sudden death of her husband, Mary returned home to find her kingdom rent by civil strife and religious dissension. She was a mere girl of nineteen, but in her were combined womanly beauty and grace with masculine vigor of body and mind. For a moment discord was silenced by her skilful diplomacy and personal fascination. She united the warring nobles in her support, and settled the religious question by acknowledging the Calvinist establishment. These measures were but the first steps toward the attainment of the real end of her policy, a Catholic combination which would place her on the English throne. Unfortunately for Mary's success, the achievements of her diplomacy were speedily undone by the ungoverned passion of her nature. In 1565 she made a political marriage with her cousin Lord Darnley. He was a miserable creature, ill-fitted for such a wife. Mary's contempt for her weakling husband was soon turned to hate by his cruel murder of her friend and secretary, Rizzio. "No more tears," she exclaimed at the news of the deed, "I will think upon revenge." A few months later Darnley was assassinated at Kirk o' Field, a lonely house near Edinburgh. Mary's part in the affair is doubtful, but at any rate she did not scruple to marry within three months the man generally held to be chiefly instrumental in the deed. Brutal and self-seeking as he

England and Mary Stuart.

Mary Stuart, daughter of James IV. of Scotland, and granddaughter of Margaret, elder sister of Henry VIII.

was, the Earl of Bothwell had succeeded in winning Mary's passionate devotion, and for his sake she threw away crown and reputation. Her subjects were filled with horror at her act, and within a month Bothwell had gone into exile, and the queen was a prisoner in Edinburgh. Before another year was past she had abdicated in favor of her son James, born of her marriage with Darnley, and had fled to England to throw herself on the mercy of Elizabeth. It was not an easy question for the English government to face. To replace Mary by force upon the Scotch throne was out of the question, nor did it seem wise to let her go free to stir up trouble among the Catholics. The difficulty was met by holding her virtually a prisoner in England.

During the following years, the country, under Elizabeth's cautious guidance, was quietly preparing for the crisis of the reign. Religious war raged on the Continent, but by skilfully balancing one party against another, while committing herself to none, Elizabeth kept England at peace. An ever present danger was the Catholic party. The hostile spirit of the pope and a rising of the Catholic nobility of the north in favor of Mary, led the government to severer measures of repression, and freedom of thought was interfered with as well as freedom of worship. The acceptance of thirty-nine of the Articles of Edward was demanded of the clergy, and by the Test Act, the first in a long series of penal statutes against the Catholics, the oath of abnegation was exacted from all officeholders. For the present, the adherents of Rome remained quiet, disheartened by the defeat of the Scotch intrigue and the inactivity of the Catholic rulers of the Continent. In the growing dissatisfaction of some of the Protestants there was a hint, however, of coming trouble. Many among the nation felt that the queen had not gone far enough in the settlement of the religious question. They

The Thirty-nine Articles, 1563.

Test Act passed in 1562, but not at first generally enforced.

The Puritans.

had no thought of separating from the Church as established, and they did not wish the abolition of Episcopacy, but they contended for greater purity of worship, for the rejection of certain practices and rites that suggested Rome. These Puritans, as they were called, scarcely represented the nation as a whole, but they were active and intelligent, and constituted a strong element in the House of Commons. More than once their independence and bold speech brought them into conflict with the queen, who had little patience with their religious aspirations or political views. They were desirous that England should commit herself to a decided Protestant policy by taking sides with the French Huguenots and the revolted Netherlands. Moreover, they felt that the safety of the nation depended upon the queen's marriage with a Protestant and the settlement of the succession. Both requests Elizabeth steadily refused. She felt that decided measures would drive the Catholics to extremes. Moreover, a diplomatic steering between two courses was a policy well suited to her temper, for she found nothing so difficult as making up her mind.

Costumes of the Reign of Elizabeth, about 1588.

However, events were soon to compel England to take an active part in the great struggle between the opposing forces of Calvinism and Rome. The pope had at length learned that the Protestants must be met with their own weapons, that revolution could be arrested only by reform. The chief instrument of the purified papacy in the task of winning back Christendom to the pale of the Romish Church was the Society of Jesus. Unquestioning obedience and untiring devotion were shown by the Jesuits in their work of combating heresy and heathenism, and under their inspiration the broken ranks of the Catholics were slowly closing up. In 1570 the pope issued a bull of excommunication against Elizabeth, and absolved her subjects from their allegiance. This was but preliminary to a well-organized plan for the reconquest of England. Jesuits from Douay wandered about the country in various disguises, striving to revive the zeal of the Catholic party. Their success was marked, and there seemed danger that they might undo all that had been gained by Elizabeth's policy of compromise. The Protestants and the government in their fear magnified the danger, and strove to meet it by a revival of persecution. The priests were driven from the country, liberty of opinion was crushed, and a policy of suspicion and repression adopted toward all Catholics, which but served to increase their devotion to the ancient Church.

English Catholic Seminary at Douay, in Flanders.

The fear of an impending religious crisis was intensified by the shadow of political danger. The power of Spain was steadily growing; in wealth and military strength she held the foremost place, and her great resources were controlled by one man whom national feeling as well as ardor in the cause of Rome made the implacable foe of England. Not only had Elizabeth interfered in Philip's political and religious schemes, but her subjects were waging a destructive if desultory war against Spanish commerce all over the world. The time was favorable for action. France was under the control of the Guises, in close alliance with Spain, and in the Netherlands Parma was gaining ground against the revolted Protestants. Everywhere the temper of the Catholics was rising. England was not slow to realize the situation, and the first result of her sense of danger was the death sentence of

Execution of Mary Stuart, 1587.

Mary Stuart. For eighteen years the Scotch queen, the center of Catholic intrigue, had remained a prisoner on English soil. Plans for the assassination of Elizabeth had been more than once discovered, and it was now felt that there was but one way of saving her life, and that was by taking the life of the woman whose existence alone gave rise to such plans.

<small>Ridolfi plot, 1572.</small>

<small>Babington plot, 1586.</small>

Mary's death left England free to meet Spanish hostility as a national question and forced Philip to conduct his attack in open day. An invasion of England had long been planned. In 1588 the preparations were complete and the "Invincible Armada," a fleet of over one hundred and twenty vessels, set sail for the English coast. With her usual parsimony and dilatoriness the queen had delayed taking measures for defense. The navy contained but thirty-eight ships all told, most of them small and ill-equipped. But private enterprise made good the royal shortcomings, and the merchants of every port sent their best ships well-manned to take a share in the national defense. Moreover, the English were fired with enthusiasm; they longed "to have a good, severe, open war with Spain, as the only road to an honorable settlement." But English seamanship united to English courage might have failed to win the day had the winds not done their part. A terrible storm arose, rendering unmanageable the unwieldy Spanish vessels. The enterprise ended in failure; of the great fleet but fifty-four ships returned to Spain.

<small>The Armada.</small>

The defeat of the Armada marked the crisis of Elizabeth's reign. One by one her difficulties had cleared away. There was no fear of a second attack from Spain; France was now ruled by Henry of Navarre, leader of the Huguenot party. All internal troubles had been vanquished by her moderation. At the time of the Armada, national feeling triumphed and the Catholics had re-

<small>Close of the reign of Elizabeth.</small>

mained quiet, taking no advantage of the difficulties of the government. By the close of the century many of them had found their way into the Anglican Church. The Puritan spirit was growing stronger, and a few persons declaring for independence had established a separate sect. But as a whole men were united in support of the national Church. In political matters there was a good understanding between the queen and her subjects. The administration had been economical, and as a rule Parliament had cheerfully granted the royal demands. A spirit of independence was becoming more manifest, but the queen never mistook the popular temper. She might "rate her Commons like school-boys," but she could yield gracefully. The welfare of the nation was ever her chief concern. With masculine intellect and womanly devotion she had labored in its service, sacrificing personal happiness and ambitions in its interest, and she spoke from the heart in her last words to the Commons, "Though you have had, and may have many princes, more mighty and wise, sitting in this seat, yet you never had, or ever shall have, any that will be more careful and loving."

Elizabeth.

THE ENGLAND OF THE TUDORS.

The England of to-day, a great maritime, commercial, and industrial power, began to take shape in the sixteenth century. Economic and social conditions were changing. The old medieval industrial system was breaking up, and trade and commerce, animated by a keener, bolder spirit, were seeking out new channels of enterprise. At the opening of the century England was still an agricultural country; wheat and wool were her staple crops, and she bore to Flanders the relation that Australia now bears to the mother country. At its close, wool was no longer sent abroad, but was woven and spun at home. When the first Tudor ascended the throne, England was without a navy, and much of her carrying trade was in the hands of foreigners. The defeat of the Armada in the reign of Elizabeth paved the way for the ultimate commercial supremacy of England.

Foremost among the causes for these changes was the discovery of the New World. Trade with America had become of importance, and England's position gave her at once a superiority over all rivals. The religious conflicts of the Continent, resulting as they did in the disturbance of trade and industry, redounded also to England's advantage. It was the destruction of Antwerp by Alva that made possible the development of London into the leading mart of Europe. Nor should the policy of the rulers be overlooked. The Tudor rule was despotic, but at least it was paternal, and the statute books of the century bear proof to the unwearying interest of the government in the welfare of the people and the development of national wealth. Not one detail of life and industry was overlooked. Exports and imports were regulated, prices were fixed, the time of sale was set, and the quality and character of goods to be manufactured decided; wages were established and the length of service decreed. Everywhere the State interfered, and, on the whole, with good results. *Statute of apprentices, 1562, regulated conditions of service.*

Such vast changes could not be brought about without serious disturbances in society. The effect of increasing industrial activity and the new money-getting spirit was shown in the agrarian revolution of the early part of the *Agriculture.*

century. Wool-growing was becoming more profitable. There was a tendency to the formation of great sheep farms, and land was being turned from tillage to pasture. As the land became increasingly valuable, the commons were enclosed, and the open fields, the arable lands tilled by the villagers, were not infrequently seized by the lord under a strained interpretation of his proprietary right. Evictions became frequent, houses, whole villages even, being torn down and the fields turned into sheep-walks. "All the houses of Burton Lazars in the same vill (Choysell) are laid waste, and the inhabitants have departed; and there belonged to the same houses three hundred acres of land, whereof forty are plowed, but the rest are in pasture; and by the downfall, the church has fallen into ruins." These changes entailed grievous suffering upon the cottagers and small farmers. Rents rose, and at the same time the rights of common pasture were cut off. Moreover, work became scarce, for one man was now employed where formerly the labor of many was required. "For whereas," wrote Latimer "have been a great many householders and inhabitants there is now but a shepherd and his dog." The small holders were ruined, many of them becoming homeless wanderers swelling the ranks of paupers and vagabonds. Sir Thomas More, in his Utopia, voices the popular grievance: "Sheep," he wrote, "become so great devourers and so wild that they eat up and swallow down the very men themselves. They consume, destroy, and devour whole fields, houses, and citizens." The government recognized the evil and strove to meet it by legislation. It decreed that no man should keep more than two thousand sheep, and at the dissolution of the monasteries it was enacted that the new owners should "occupy yearly as much of the same demesnes in plowing and tillage of husbandry . . . as hath been commonly used." Legisla-

Open field, the survival of the early communal lands, was divided into acre or half-acre strips. Each tenant cultivated a number of such strips, lying in diverse parts of the field belonging to the village.

tion availed little, however, and the evil continued until the close of Elizabeth's reign.

Side by side with laws which point to the miserable condition of the country people, are others that would seem to indicate the decay of industry and trade and the impoverishment of the towns. Many of the towns lost in population and wealth during this period. This was due chiefly to the ill-judged interference of the gilds which drove new enterprises into the country. The usefulness of the gild system was gone; it no longer served its original purpose, and the gilds themselves had become narrow corporations. Membership was restricted to the sons of members or to those who could pay heavily for the privilege, and it was no longer possible for the average journeyman to become a master craftsman. The antiquated regulations of the gilds were inconsistent with the increasing activity of trade, and the government tended more and more to transfer their functions to the municipal authorities. Freed from the jurisdiction of a system which was outgrown, manufactures took a vigorous start. The making of woolens became an important element of national wealth. The eastern counties were noted for their worsteds and fine cloths, and even the backward north felt the effect of the new interest, and developed its own special line of friezes and rough goods. The government endeavored in every way to promote a growth so favorable to national prosperity. The export of materials that might be manufactured at home was forbidden, and the consumption of English goods was decreed by statute. "On every Sunday and holy day every person of six years old and upwards,

Manufactures.

Civil Costume of the Reign of Henry VII.

with some few exceptions, was to wear on his head one cap of wool fully wrought in England." The manufacturing interest owed less, however, to legislation than to the steady hospitality which the government extended to the persecuted of other lands. In the latter part of the reign of Henry VIII. an immigration of religious refugees began which continued until after the revocation of the Edict of Nantes, a century and a half later. Most of those who came were skilled workmen, and they enriched the country with many new manufactures. As early as 1544 Flemings and Walloons swarmed into England and established at Norwich the silk industry, the source of its later prosperity. At the fall of Antwerp, one third of the merchants and manufacturers of the city came to London and laid the foundations of its commercial greatness. Sometimes the immigration was opposed by the jealousy of the natives, but as a rule its value was recognized, and towns are found petitioning to have strangers allotted them.

Commerce. The growth of manufactures, coupled with the protective policy of the government, might have resulted in isolation had it not been for the expansion of commerce which marked the close of the century. Under Henry VII. England had no navy, and but little commerce of her own. Her sea-going population showed nothing of a spirit of enterprise and adventure, and England's share in the discovery of the New World was but insignificant. Even a hundred years later a navy scarcely existed. It is true that Wolsey and Henry VIII. paid some attention to its development, and at the beginning of the reign of Elizabeth a statute was passed making the eating of flesh on Friday and Saturday a misdemeanor, for the "increase of fishermen and mariners." The government saw in the fisheries the best school for seamanship. Elizabeth, however, was content to commit the defense of the country to private enterprise, and of the vessels that went out to meet the Armada, only about thirty belonged to the State. Nor did legitimate commerce flourish. In 1573 the burden of all the ships engaged in ordinary trade was less than fifty thousand tons. It was in privateering that the love of adventure and the desire for gain, which marked the mariners of the Elizabethan period, found vent. Great as were the risks involved, the returns were even greater. Moreover, England's rival on the sea was Spain, and patriotism and religious fervor combined to give these buccaneering raids something of the character of a crusade. While the two governments were still formally at peace, Spanish and English sailors were fighting on every sea, and politic as might be Elizabeth's regrets for the depredations committed by her subjects, she was too wise to interfere with enterprises that increased the national wealth and insured the national defense. Unchecked, therefore, by the government, this irregular commerce flourished and became a favorite investment for capital. Still more directly supported by the crown were the merchant companies chartered to have exclusive control of the commerce of different lands. Monopolies of local trade were felt to be a serious grievance and were constantly protested against, but in foreign lands they were a necessary means of defense for the trader. The most important of these associations was the East India Company, which was incorporated in 1600 for the purpose of obtaining a share in the trade of the east. *The sea dogs.*

It was to be expected that the overturning of industrial conditions would for a time affect disastrously the working classes, and the marked increase in pauperism during the century is therefore not surprising. The main cause of the evil was to be found in the agricultural changes. The difficulty of the situation was aggravated, however, by the rise in prices, due to the influx of silver from America. *Pauperism*

Moreover, the decay of husbandry had resulted in scarcity of food. In words that call to mind our own times, More describes the condition of those evicted to make room for sheep. "By one means or other . . . they must needs depart away. . . . All their household stuff . . . being suddenly thrust out, they be constrained to sell it for a thing of naught. And when they have wandered abroad till that be spent, what can they else do but steal, or else go about a-begging?" Then as now, side by side with the helpless poor were found the worthless and lazy. Complaints were frequent of the "sturdy beggars," forerunners of the modern tramp, who swarmed over the country, terrorizing the rural districts. A contemporary wrote of them: "If they ask at a . . . farmer's house his charity, they will go strong as three or four in a company, where for fear more than good will they often have relief." At first there was no systematic attempt to face the situation. Relief of the poor was originally a function of the Church, especially of the monasteries, but with time the obligation was either lost sight of, or aid was so unwisely given that it was said "the abbeys did but maintain the poor they made." It was impossible, however, that a government so paternal as the Tudors should not endeavor to meet the growing evil, and step by step, by means of a long series of experiments, an elaborate system of poor relief was worked out. The obligation of the State in the care of the poor was fully recognized, and what was formerly a religious duty to be enforced by the Church came to be regarded as a public charge to be met by a regular assessment on property by the civil authorities. The principle of local responsibility was soon established, each parish being bound to care for its own poor. Gradually the proper distinction between paupers and vagabonds was worked out, houses of correction being erected for the lazy and vicious, while suitable relief was given to the helpless poor, children being usually apprenticed to a trade. Some effort was also made to provide work for able-bodied paupers, and the county authorities were empowered to lay in a stock of hemp, wool, iron, and other materials "to the intent that youth may be brought up in labor, . . . also that rogues may not have any just excuse in saying they cannot get any service or work, . . . and that other needy persons being willing to work may be set on work." In 1601 the long series of statutes culminated in the great poor law of Elizabeth, an elaboration of the principles and machinery already recognized. This in its main provisions remained the basis of the English system of poor relief until the eighteenth century.

Extremes met in the sixteenth century; the growth in luxury and extravagance was as marked as the increase in pauperism. Everywhere were visible new conceptions of comfort, increased attention to display. The gloomy, fortress-like dwellings of the nobility gave place to the Elizabethan manor house with its wide portals and long lines of windows. In the towns, the growing wealth of the merchant class was indicated in the appearance of much finer residences, and throughout the country generally wooden houses were replaced by dwellings of brick or stone. A contemporary writer in speaking of the changed manner of living notes "the multitude of chimnies latilie erected"; "the great amendment of lodging"; "the exchange of vessels, as of woodden platters into pewter, and woodden spoons into silver or tin." Increased gorgeousness of attire was

Social Progress.

Ladies of Quality.

as marked as the improvement in house furnishing. Men "wore a manor on their backs." The Englishmen's love of feasting had always been noticeable. A Spaniard, writing in the time of Mary, said of them, "they fare commonly as well as the king," but even in this regard there was increased expenditure. This spread of luxury was viewed by many with dismay. "England spendeth more on wines in one year than it did in ancient times in four years," was the complaint of a royal minister. One writer laments "the over quantity of unnecessary wares brought into the port of London." Numerous sumptuary laws were passed, with, however, but little effect.

Literature.
The vigorous life and restless activity which stirred the material world was reflected in the world of letters. The Renaissance, the great intellectual movement that originated in Italy in the fifteenth century, was slow in reaching England. While continental Europe was reading with avidity the stores of classic literature, brought to its shores by the Greek scholars driven from the East at the fall of Constantinople, England was torn asunder by the contending factions of the Roses. With the restoration of peace, however, Englishmen caught the impulse of the new movement, and turned with eager enthusiasm and untrammeled zeal to the study of classic lore, and the investigation of the wonders in the world of nature. The English Renaissance received its impulse from abroad, but it at once assumed a tone all its own, "less literary, less largely human, but more moral, more religious, more practical in its bearings both upon society and politics." In the life and work of three men, Colet, Erasmus, and More, its diverse aspects found expression. In Colet was typified the religious rationalism of the new movement; Erasmus reflected its more purely intellectual character; while in More all its freshness and audacity of thought were brought to

bear on the practical questions of the day. His famous work, Utopia, was a satire on the defects of English society brought out in a description of the condition of life in "Nowhere." In his views More was strangely at odds with the tendencies of his age; he anticipated, however, the most important social and political reforms of later times.

The promise of the Renaissance was great, but before it had reached fulfilment it was overwhelmed by the fierce tide of religious revolution. Reason and reform were trampled under foot by dogma and fanaticism. It was not until the settlement of the religious question under Elizabeth left men free to consider other things, that the earlier revival of letters bore fruit in the wonderful outburst of literary activity which marked the close of the century. The vigor of the national life was reflected in the originality of thought, the boldness of conception that characterized the world of letters. Its restless curiosity, the many-sidedness of its interests, found expression in a literature which in-included the "Novum Organum" of Bacon, and the "Ecclesiastical Polity" of Hooker, Spenser's "Faerie Queene," and Shakespeare's "Hamlet."

CHAPTER IX.

THE STUARTS AND PURITANISM.

Illustrative Readings.
Three English Statesmen ; Goldwin Smith.
Woodstock ; Scott.
Old Mortality ; Scott.
John Inglesant ; Shorthouse.
Lorna Doone ; Blackmore.

Important Dates.
Reign of James I., 1603-1625.
1604, Hampton Court Conference.
1621, Fall of Bacon.
Reign of Charles I., 1625-1649.
1626, Impeachment of Buckingham.
1628, Petition of Right.
1637, Ship money decision.
1639, War with Scotland.
1640, Short Parliament.
1640, Long Parliament.
1641, Execution of Strafford.
1641, Grand Remonstrance.
1643, League with Scotland.
1644, Marston Moor.
1645, Naseby.
1649, Execution of Charles.
Commonwealth, 1649-1660.
1653, Dissolution of Long Parliament.
1653, Barebone's Parliament.
1654, First Protectorate Parliament.
1656, Second Protectorate Parliament.
1658, Death of Cromwell.
Reign of Charles II., 1660-1685.
1661, Cavalier Parliament.
1665, Dutch War.
1667, Fall of Clarendon.
1670, Treaty of Dover.
1678, Popish Plot.
Reign of James II., 1685-1689.
1687, First Declaration of Indulgence.
1688, Acquittal of Seven Bishops.
1688, Landing of William.
1689, Crown accepted by William.

Genealogical Table.

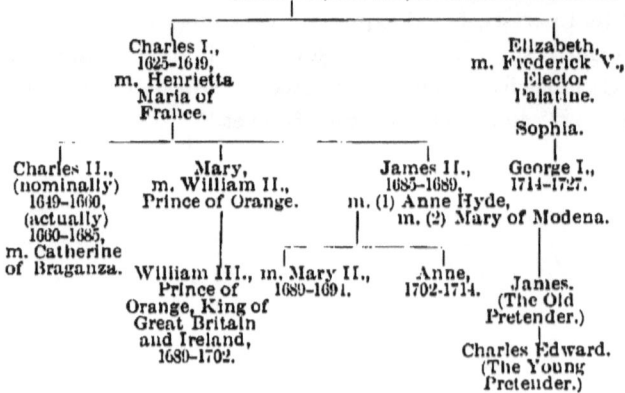

OPPRESSION AND REBELLION.

The accession of the House of Stuart marked the close of a century of personal rule based on public opinion, and the opening of a century of conflict between Crown and Parliament for supremacy. Under the Tudors, royal will and national interest were in the main identical, but the Stuarts, with complete disregard of popular feeling, strove to set their wishes against the nation. Moreover, as if to force a decision which Tudor tact had avoided, they were not content with the substance of power, but insisted upon its formal recognition, maintaining in all its boldness the doctrine of the divine right of kings. Popular temper could ill brook such assumptions. The nation had acquiesced in the Tudor despotism because it saw in the royal authority the only means for securing peace and for carrying on the struggle with the papacy and Spain. But the times had changed. Imbued with a new spirit of independence born of Protestantism, the nation was preparing to claim for itself a larger share in the control of the government. Royal assumptions were met by popular claims, an aggressive king was matched by an aggressive Parliament. There was nothing in James I. to make the new pretensions more acceptable to the nation. His unattractive exterior and undignified bearing were in sharp contrast to the royal carriage of his predecessor, and his shrewd sense and ready wit could not make amends for the coarseness of his uncouth speech. The national sense of decency was shocked by the grossness and unveiled immorality of the court, and national pride was outraged at the elevation of low-born and worthless favorites above the greatest of the nobility.

James I.
1603-1625.

With views so irreconcilable, a conflict between the king and the nation was sure to come. The question was made more complicated, however, and the issue forced by the antagonism between king and people in religious matters.

A large minority, at least, of the English people, were Puritans, impatient of authority, regardless of tradition, and desirous of reform. This was the time of England's real Reformation. The movement of the sixteenth century was more royal than popular, more political than religious. Puritanism, the religious movement of the seventeenth century, struck far deeper into the national life, not merely modifying men's ecclesiastical opinions, but stirring and transforming their spiritual natures. The Puritans had hoped much from James, but the logical outcome of his high ideas of royal prerogative was hostility to independence of thought in religious questions. A conference on ecclesiastical matters, called by the king at Hampton Court, revealed the fact that the weight of his influence would be on the side of the High Church party. To others all freedom of action was denied. "I will make them conform," he said of the Puritans, "or I will harry them out of the land." Although no friend to the Puritans, James had little mind to favor the Catholics, and the penal laws of Elizabeth's reign were strictly enforced. Harassed and irritated, some of the Catholics entered into a conspiracy, the so-called Gunpowder Plot, to destroy king and Parliament. Their plans, however, came to naught. The disappointment of the Puritans found a more legitimate expression in the House of Commons, where they formed a strong element, and the king met with much annoying opposition. Thus, within a twelvemonth of his accession to the throne, the lack of harmony between the king and the nation had been laid bare.

James the Sixth of Scotland and First of England.

Gunpowder Plot. 1604-1605. Managed by Guy Fawkes.

The first year was typical of the whole reign. The king's policy outraged every popular instinct, frustrated every popular wish. Government by statesmen was replaced by the rule of favorites, chief among whom was the Duke of Buckingham, whose only claim was his beauty and graceful manners. Wastefulness and imbecility characterized every department of the administration. James' unvarying purpose was to free himself from all control, but his financial difficulties placed him at the mercy of the Commons, and each appeal for help was met by a demand for redress of grievances. Remonstrances were met by the dissolution of Parliament, and from 1614 to 1621 the king ruled without its aid. To fill his empty treasury he had recourse to many expedients; ancient feudal dues were revived, titles were sold, and customs were levied by proclamation, a practice against which the Commons had twice vigorously protested. The revival of monopolies was a serious evil and served to arouse the nation without adding to the revenue of the government.

James' home and foreign policy were closely connected. To make himself independent of Parliament it was necessary to maintain peace abroad. Moreover, he felt his ability did not lie in war. Proud of his statecraft, he hoped to maintain quiet on the Continent by an alliance with Spain, and proposed the marriage of his son with the Spanish Infanta. There was something to be said in favor of the king's policy, but events rendered it impracticable. In 1618 the long impending struggle between Catholics and Protestants broke out in Germany. James' own son-in-law, the Count Palatine, was involved, and it was impossible for England to stand aloof. The king still strove to play the part of peacemaker, but the nation detested the Spanish alliance, and was eager for war. In this crisis it was necessary to summon Parliament, and at once the

Thirty Years' War. 1618–1648.

storm broke loose. The ancient right of impeachment was revived against the royal ministers. Francis Bacon, the chancellor, was attacked partly for taking bribes, but partly for his support of the prerogative; protests were made against the Catholic alliance, and a declaration of war against Spain was demanded. The temper of the Commons was rising, and a proclamation forbidding all consideration of foreign affairs was met by a resolution that the privilege of discussing these matters was theirs by right as English subjects. The king with his own hand tore the resolution from the journals of the House. "I will govern according to the common weal, but not according to the common will," he said, and ordered the dissolution of Parliament. No words, however, could annul what had been done. In twenty years James had turned respect for the monarchy into contempt, loyalty into hatred. He had insulted Parliament and asserted his authority as no Tudor had ever done, but in spite of his efforts, rather because of them, the constitutional gains of his reign outweighed all that had been achieved since the fall of the House of Lancaster.

Charles I. 1625-1649.

Men hoped much from the accession of Charles I. The dignity of his bearing and the decorum of his life had created a favorable impression, and his known hostility to the Spanish alliance aroused the expectation of a more popular rule. His government, however, was no improvement on the preceding. The king's opposition to Spain was the result of pique, and did not imply an essential change of policy. On the other hand, he believed as strongly as James in the royal prerogative, and had even less comprehension of the popular temper. The enthusiasm with which his accession was greeted soon cooled. His marriage with a French princess and a fancied leaning toward Rome aroused fears of a Catholic reaction, while the continued influence of Buckingham left little hope of more capable action abroad, or more constitutional rule at home. Parliament at once took a suspicious attitude, refusing to grant supplies until grievances were redressed. Buckingham was looked upon as the cause of all difficulties, and at length the Commons, despite the command of the king, proceeded to his impeachment. To save his friend, Charles at once dissolved Parliament, and for the next two years he tried what he could do without one. Everywhere the arbitrary tendencies of the government were apparent. All sorts of illegal means were employed to fill the treasury. The courts of justice were made instruments of the royal tyranny. The collection of a forced loan was ordered and those who resisted were imprisoned at the king's pleasure. A foolish foreign policy involved England in war with both France and Spain, drained the resources of the country and brought the government little credit.

In 1628 Charles was driven by his necessities to call a new Parliament. The Houses met in no favorable temper, and at once proceeded to discuss the condition of the country. All men were stirred by the recent attacks on personal rights. "We must vindicate our ancient liberties," said Sir Thomas Wentworth in words to which his later career lent strange meaning, " we must reënforce the laws made by our ancestors. We must set such a stamp upon them as no licentious spirit shall dare hereafter to invade them." Discussion ended in the drawing up the Petition of Right, second only to Magna Charta in constitutional importance. The right of all men to a fair and speedy trial was asserted, martial law was prohibited in time of peace, and the control of Parliament in all matters of taxation was reaffirmed. Charles was forced to agree to the demands of the Commons, but in his heart he was bent on

Petition of Right.

"Old South Leaflets," General Series, No. 23.

pursuing his old course. He was obliged, however, to act henceforth without the counsels of his favorite, for a few days after the signing of the Petition of Right, Buckingham died by the knife of the assassin. His fall brought no change of policy; it but widened the breach between the king and the nation. Buckingham had borne the brunt of the popular dissatisfaction ; Charles was now forced to take the odium of his own misdeeds.

Personal Government, 1629–1640.

The dissolution of the Houses in 1629 was followed by a period of personal rule. For eleven years no Parliament was called. "We have showed by our frequent meeting our people our love to the use of Parliament ; yet the late abuse having for the present driven us unwillingly out of that course, we shall account it presumption for any to prescribe any time unto us for Parliament." During these years the king governed the realm through ministers, the irresponsible agents of his policy. The ruling spirit in secular affairs was Wentworth, once the champion of English liberties, now the willing servant of despotism. Political conviction as well as personal ambition had led him to forsake the popular cause. His hostility had been directed rather against the influence of Buckingham than against the power of the crown. For the wisdom of the people he had little respect. He saw all the defects of Parliamentary rule, and none of its good points. His ideal was the system of the Tudors, and his purpose was to "make His Majesty as absolute as any king in Christendom, and as little subject to conditions." In Church matters the king's chief adviser was Archbishop Laud. Unity through uniformity was the keynote to Laud's policy. His favor toward Catholics was as marked as his hostility to Puritans, and he strove to enforce conformity while gradually drawing the Church nearer to Rome. With entire sympathy the two ministers labored together

to carry out the policy which they dubbed "Thorough."
The machinery through which they worked was the Privy
Council and the Courts of the Star Chamber and High
Commission. The press was muzzled, the pulpits were
"tuned," the judges bribed or intimidated. Freedom of
speech no longer existed, liberty and property were endangered.
Imprisonment and mutilation were inflicted on
many because of their religion, many more fled to America
to escape persecution. The chief difficulty that beset the
crown was the need of raising a revenue. The royal
forests formed an important source of supply, and by reviving
obsolete laws their boundaries were greatly extended.
Exorbitant fines were exacted for all kinds of petty
offenses. The sale of monopolies was carried to an unheard
of extent. "They sup in our cup," it was later said
of the monopolists, "they dip in our dish, they sit by our
fire. . . . They have marked and sealed us from head
to foot." To secure a fixed revenue, a plan was devised of
exacting ship-money from all the counties, nominally for
the defense of the country. At first the money was used
according to the avowed intention, but the principle was so
capable of extension that Wentworth said of it: "Let the
king only abstain from war for three years that he may
habituate his subjects to the payment of this tax, and in
the end he will find himself more powerful and respected
than any of his predecessors." The nation saw this as
clearly as Wentworth. John Hampden, a gentleman of
Buckinghamshire, undertook to bring the question of the
legality of ship-money before the courts of law. But the
judges were tools of the king, and the decision was in his
favor. One judge declared that *rex* was *lex*, and Chief
Justice Finch asserted "that they are void acts of Parliament
to bind the king not to command the subjects, their
persons and goods, . . . for no acts of Parliament

Court of High Commission, definitely organized in 1583, had jurisdiction in ecclesiastical matters.

The bounds of Rockingham forests were extended from six to sixty miles.

Quarrel with the Scotch, 1637.

make any difference." It was vain to look for justice to courts guided not by the law, but by the will of the king. Hampden's resistance aroused the people, his defeat showed the peril of the situation. Nevertheless action was still delayed. No leader had come forward, the intermission of Parliament left the national temper in doubt, and many of the bolder spirits, despairing of improvement, left the country to seek a home in the Puritan commonwealth beyond the sea. But the stupidity of the king was hastening the crisis. The signal for revolt came from Scotland. The vigorous Puritanism of the north had not been able to hinder the reëstablishment of Episcopacy, but the feeling of the people was openly hostile and it was evident that patience was almost at an end. Nevertheless, Charles and Laud determined to force upon the Scotch a new Church service modeled upon the English prayer book. National pride as well as religious feeling was offended at this innovation from England. The first attempt to use the new liturgy met with opposition which soon ripened into rebellion against the political authority of the king. Charles dared not draw back, however, for fear of the effect in England. Unprepared and unsupported he tried to face a united, determined Scotland. Defeat at length forced him to abandon the policy of the last eleven years and summon Parliament. The Houses came together in no unreasonable spirit, but it was plain that grievances must be redressed before aid would be granted. "Till the liberties of the House and kingdom were cleared, they knew not whether they had anything to give or no."

A Countrywoman.

The Short Parliament, April, 1640.

Money, not debate, was what Charles wanted and Parliament was dissolved with nothing accomplished. The desperate state of affairs in Scotland soon forced the king to summon a second Parliament—the famous Long Parliament of the Rebellion. The nation's temper had changed; men realized that now was their time; Scotland's cause was the cause of English freedom. Ignoring the king's demand for money, the Commons, at the instance of Pym, a marked man in the earlier struggle and the real leader of Parliament, proceeded to a consideration of the evils of the realm. Wentworth, now Earl of Strafford, was the first object of attack. He was regarded as the mainstay of the royal despotism. So long as he lived Charles could not be intrusted with power. His condemnation was a foregone conclusion; a bill of attainder was hurried through both Houses, and received the signature of the king who a few days before had assured him that he should not suffer in "life, honor, or fortune." Strafford paid the penalty of being out of touch with his generation, of endeavoring to restore a constitution which the nation had outgrown.

The Long Parliament, November, 1640.

The overthrow of Strafford was followed by an attack on the powers of the crown. One measure after another was passed limiting the prerogative, and establishing guarantees of constitutional rule. Parliament was to be summoned at least once in three years, the levying of taxes without its consent was forbidden, all irregular courts were abolished. So far as laws could accomplish it, the life, liberty, and property of the subject were made secure.

Thus far the action of Parliament had been practically unanimous. Now, however, division appeared. Some were satisfied with what had been obtained, others deemed additional guarantees necessary. Discussion of ecclesiastical questions showed that while all wished reform, some desired revolution, and would abolish Episcopacy altogether.

These differences of opinion were strengthened by a revival of personal loyalty to the king, standing helpless and almost alone. This was Charles' opportunity. By allying himself frankly and heartily with the moderate reformers he might have cut the ground from under the feet of the radicals. But Charles was incapable of straightforward action, of giving his confidence completely. He called to his counsels Hyde and Falkland, the leaders of the Conservatives, but at the same time he carried on

[*Adapted from Gardiner's School Atlas.*]

secret negotiations with the Scotch and with the army, in the hope of using them against his opponents. An outbreak in Ireland complicated the situation. An army would be necessary to put down the rebellion. Could the

Irish Rebellion. October, 1641.

king be trusted with forces which he might turn against Parliament? Pym and Hampden answered no. Under their leadership the Grand Remonstrance, a statement of grievances, a program for the future, an appeal to the people, was fought through Parliament. This was the crisis of the contest. Failure to pass the Grand Remonstrance would have meant to many the abandonment of the struggle. "Had it been defeated," said Oliver Cromwell, member for Cambridge, "I would have sold tomorrow all I possess and left England forever." Success completed the division of the nation into two parties. Lack of confidence in the king had forced men to extremes. Their violence now led to the formation of a royal party. It was plain that war could not long be delayed. A few weeks later Charles left London, never to return until brought back a prisoner.

Grand Remonstrance. "Old South Leaflets," General Series, No. 21.

The royal standard was raised at Nottingham, Parliament called out the national militia, the country ranged itself on one side or the other. With the king were most of the nobility, many of the gentry, the High Church party; the border counties, also, were royalist in sympathy. A few of the upper classes supported Parliament, but the strength of the Roundhead cause lay with the townspeople and yeomanry. For a time the war dragged. Neither side desired too complete a victory. Many among Charles' supporters feared he would use success to reëstablish what had been overthrown. And some on the opposite side saw in the removal of all restraints a prospect of Parliamentary despotism which they liked no better than royal tyranny. On the whole, success was with the king. The Parliamentary recruits, the offscouring of the towns, were no match for men whose loyalty would lead them to fight for the crown though it "hung in a bush."

The Great Rebellion.

"Roundhead," from the cropped hair of the Puritans.

With the next year Parliament began to retrieve its

1643.

position despite the loss it suffered in the death of Pym, its great leader. His last act had been to secure the alliance of the Scotch by inducing Parliament to accept the Covenant and establish Presbyterianism. In the hands of Oliver Cromwell, now the guiding spirit in military affairs, the army was completely transformed. Cromwell was the first to point out the defect of the Parliamentary forces and to indicate the remedy. "You must get men of a spirit that is likely to go on as far as gentlemen will go." "Men of religion are wanted to withstand these gentlemen of honor." Cavalier loyalty was to be matched by spiritual zeal. None were received into the "New Model," as the reformed army was called, save those of sober Christian life, but all who could fight and pray were made welcome regardless of class or sect. Parliament was dominated by the Presbyterian party, but among Cromwell's Ironsides was a spirit of toleration elsewhere unknown. Such an army was never before seen. It was made up not of adventurers and mercenaries, but of yeomen and tradespeople. The citizen was never lost in the soldier, each man knew for what he was fighting; the end once attained he was eager to return to his home and calling. Such forces were irresistible. Royalist defeat at Marston Moor was followed by royalist rout on the field of Naseby.

Charles was hopelessly beaten in war, but his cause was not yet lost. In the diverse opinions of his foes lay a way of escape. Parliament seemed more desirous of ridding itself of the army with its detestable ideas of toleration than of completing the overthrow of the king. The Scots were ready to furnish Charles with a sufficient force provided he would acknowledge Presbyterianism and suppress Independency. Cromwell and his men wished to restrain both crown and Parliament in the interest of civil and religious liberty. The battle of Naseby, in fact, marked

The Covenant. "Old South Leaflets," General Series, No. 25.

the close of the civil war, and the beginning of a greater struggle, a struggle between conformity and freedom, progress and conservatism. On the one hand stood the army, on the other Parliament and the Scots. Each of the opposing forces was ready to make terms with the king. Parliament insisted on the establishment of Presbyterianism and the control of military forces for twenty years. The proposals of the army were more moderate. "We desire no alteration in the civil government, as little do we desire to interrupt the settlement of the Presbyterian government, only we wish that every good citizen and every man who walks peaceably in a blameless conversation, and is beneficial to the commonwealth, might have liberty and encouragement." With each and all Charles carried on his intrigues, playing off Scots against English, army against Parliament. At length he was rewarded by seeing two of his enemies, the Scots and the army, come to blows. But the patience of the Ironsides was exhausted. A quiet settlement of the country was impossible so long as Charles was alive. With swift success Cromwell's forces overthrew the Scots, and turned "to call Charles Stuart, that man of blood, to an account." Through the forced expulsion of some of its members, the House became a mere tool in the hands of the army, and met the demand that the king be brought to justice by appointing a court whose character left no doubt as to the result. Charles was condemned to death as a tyrant, traitor, murderer. He met his fate like a hero and a saint.

Pride's Purge. Sept., 1648.

> "He nothing common did nor mean,
> Upon that memorable scene."

PURITAN RULE.

The death of the king was followed by the declaration of the Commonwealth. Monarchy and the House of Lords were abolished, and their place was taken by an Executive

The Commonwealth. 1649-1660.

Council and the House of Commons. Power, however, belonged with the army and its leader, and the history of the next ten years is the history of their attempt to rule England. The difficulties were almost insurmountable. A government was to be organized where there was no agreement as to principle. The ideals of Cromwell were not the ideals of the nation. Few cared for religious liberty, fewer still for republicanism. To allow the people to have their way meant to give up most of those things for which he had contended, and for that Cromwell was not ready. He was not, however, a despot by nature. Over and over again he attempted to secure the coöperation of the nation. The Rump, as the mutilated Long Parliament was called, had become corrupt and unmindful of its duty. Cromwell went down to the House, exasperated by its dallying. "I will put an end to this," he cried. "It is not fit you should sit here any longer," and he bade his soldiers clear the hall. He did not wish to rule alone, but he dared not appeal to the nation; a representative Parliament would have been a royalist Parliament. So he called to his aid an assembly of "godly men to rule until the people were fitted to act." But his godly men were visionaries and at once attempted extravagant reforms. Cromwell had too much common sense not to see their mistakes, so the Barebones Parliament went the way of the Rump. Two more attempts were made by Cromwell to establish constitutional rule. Under the Instrument of Government, the first of written constitutions, a protectorate was set up. Later, by giving the Protector the right to name his successor, and by creating a second House, a return was made to the forms of the ancient constitution. Both attempts failed. There was no unanimity of feeling; the members quarreled as to the authority under which they were come together, the nation distrusted Cromwell

1653.

Barebone's Parliament, so called from Praise-God Barebone, member for London.

and his system. Failure forced Cromwell back upon the army, the real mainstay of his power. But though his government was based upon force, there was not much violence or unnecessary severity. Provided his authority was respected, there was but little interference with individual rights. True, the Royalists were taxed more heavily than others, but this was on the ground that their hostility made necessary a large and costly military establishment. Toleration was the principle and, with some exceptions, the practice of Cromwell's government. "Our practice . . . hath been to let all this nation see that whatever pretensions to religion would continue quiet, peaceable, they should enjoy conscience and liberty to themselves." At first there was no interference with the English Church, but within a short time Episcopalian worship was prohibited as tending to stir up disaffection. The proclamation, however, was not very rigorously enforced, and zealous worshipers continued to meet, only more privately.

A Gentlewoman.

Less difficult and more successfully met were the questions of foreign relations. From the first Cromwell adopted a vigorous policy which reflected the temper of the man and the character of the times. Religious considerations as well as political interests determined England's attitude. A proposed alliance with France was arrested until all persecution of Protestants had ceased, and war was waged with Spain, in part at least, because of her traditional position as the great Catholic power of Europe. On the other hand, religious sympathy could not keep peace between England and Protestant Holland, her great rival on the sea.

England's foreign relations.

Commercial interests, in fact, were driving religious questions into the background. In 1651 the Navigation Act was passed, the first of a long series of measures intended to build up English commerce. Its provisions forbade the importation of goods into England except in English vessels, and thus dealt a blow to the Dutch carrying trade. The result was a war with Holland in which the navy, led by Blake, gained many victories and laid the foundations of England's present maritime supremacy. On land as well as on sea the English were successful; Cromwell's force and ability regained for England the place in Europe which she had won under Elizabeth and lost under James.

The triumph of the Commonwealth abroad filled even its opponents with pride. Nor were grounds for some contentment lacking nearer home. Cromwell's rule was stern, but at least order was maintained. All risings whether of Royalists or Levelers were quickly quelled. Gradually the ravages of war were repaired, although ruined hall and mutilated church long bore testimony to the destructive work of the Ironsides. Taxation was heavy, but industry was not crushed, and the country seemed elastic under its burdens. Had Cromwell lived longer he might have effected many improvements in the condition of the people. Reform of the law courts was a matter that he had at heart. The misrepresentation of the country under the existing electoral system was an evil which he recognized and tried to meet. He attempted to equalize representation according to population, and he gave members to Scotland and Ireland.

The Levelers, a party in the army of democratic and socialist tendencies.

Death of Cromwell. 1658.

But Cromwell's work was done. He and his generation were hopelessly at odds. He was as far in advance of his age as Strafford was behind, and before him lay nothing but vexation and disappointment. Under the burden of care and anxiety his health gave way. A storm swept over

England as he lay dying. "The devil is fetching home the soul of the tyrant," said his foes; but the man whom they hated was praying for friends and foes alike. "Lord, Thou hast made me, though very unworthy, a mean instrument to do them some good, and Thee service; and many of them have set too high a value upon me, though others wish and would be glad of my death. Lord, however Thou do dispose of me, continue to go on to do good to them. . . . Teach those who look too much on Thy instruments, to depend more upon Thyself. Pardon such as desire to trample upon the dust of a poor worm, for they are Thy people too. And pardon the folly of this short prayer; even for Jesus Christ's sake. And give us a good night, if it be thy pleasure. Amen."

A Citizen's Wife.

The days of the Commonwealth were numbered. Richard Cromwell was made Protector, but he could not hope to succeed where his father had failed. Conflict arose between the civil and military authorities. One Parliament was expelled and another set up in its place. The nation was weary of army rule, and longed for a restoration of the old order, for a return of the old line. Negotiations were opened with the son of Charles I., living in exile. Vague promises of good government, of religious security, were eagerly accepted. The army, tricked and abandoned by its leaders, could do nothing. A Convention Parliament was hastily summoned which at once recalled Prince Charles, and on May 29, 1660, he entered London attended by rejoicing crowds.

Fall of the Commonwealth.

The Puritan rebellion had ended in apparent failure. In the contest against the despotism of the second Stuart, Parliament and the nation were victorious, but religious differences aroused strife among the conquerors. The right cause triumphed with Cromwell, but it was based on force and found no response in the nation. The result was the reaction which we call the Restoration. The over-severity of the Puritans led to the shamelessness of society under the third Stuart. Toleration at the point of the sword ended in the penal code against dissent. The outcome of the execution of Charles was the doctrine of non-resistance. Nevertheless, Puritanism was far from dead. The spirit that found expression in the writings of Milton and Bunyan left an impress on the national character that might be for a time obscured but never entirely effaced.

THE RESTORATION.

Charles II. 1660-1685.

The recall of the Stuarts did not mean that the nation wished to undo all that had been done; the Convention Parliament contained many Presbyterians, and it insisted at first on a generous treatment of all who were concerned in the Rebellion, and especially that no one was to be "disquieted for difference of opinion which should not disturb the kingdom." But the tide of loyalty was rising fast. The Parliament called in 1661 was fired with devotion to Church and king. Charles was granted what his father never obtained,—a large revenue for life. It was declared that there was no legislative power in Parliament without the royal sanction, that the king was the rightful commander of all forces, and that it was unlawful for either House to make war against the crown.

Declaration of passive obedience: "I, A. B., do declare and believe that it is not lawful upon any pretense whatever to take up arms against the king."

The religious zeal of Parliament was even more marked. Episcopacy was reëstablished, and a stringent Act of Uniformity was passed. From all clergymen and teachers the acceptance of everything in the Prayer Book was required, and as a result two thousand ministers were deprived of their charges. This was the first of a long series of penal statutes directed against dissent, whether Catholic or Protestant. Officeholders in the towns were obliged to subscribe to the doctrine of passive obedience, and to take the sacrament according to the practice of the Anglican Church. Religious meetings of more than five persons outside the family were prohibited unless in accordance with the established forms. A third violation of this requirement was punished by transportation. Another measure was passed under conditions of peculiar infamy. The plague was raging in London, and the clergy had fled in a panic. The Dissenters, a far more earnest set of men, undertook the duties left unperformed, tending the sick and holding services. Parliament, at a safe distance in Oxford, where it had gone to avoid the plague, passed the Five-Mile Act, forbidding all clergymen who had not accepted the Act of Uniformity and the doctrine of passive obedience to teach school, or to come within five miles of any town or borough.

Corporation Act. 1661.

Conventicle Act. 1664.

Five-Mile Act. 1665.

The severity of this legislation against Dissenters was due in a measure to the influence of Hyde, Earl of Clarendon, once a leader in the Long Parliament, then the adviser of Charles I., now the chief minister of his son. Clarendon's ideals were the ideals of the sixteenth century; an Episcopal Church dependent upon the crown, power exercised without restraint by an enlightened and conscientious king. He repeated the mistake of Strafford in endeavoring to make of a Stuart a ruler after the Elizabethan type. Charles II. had far more tact and ability than his father, but, on the other hand, less principle, less earnestness of temper; selfishness, love of pleasure, were the dominant notes in his character. At the outset of his reign he showed little ambition, but, surrounding himself with men of his kind, led a life of dissipation which made the court a national shame. It was folly to expect of such a king

Hyde, Earl of Clarendon.

wisdom and conscientiousness. Inability to realize this was not, however, Clarendon's only mistake. He did not see that the situation abroad had changed. Alliance with France against Spain had been England's traditional policy for more than two generations. But the power of Spain was waning. France, under the ambitious leadership of Louis XIV., was now the menace to the peace and freedom of Europe. Blind to this change, Clarendon allowed England to become involved in a causeless war with Holland, whereas his true policy should have been to establish a close alliance between the two countries against France.

War with Holland. 1665-1667.

The war itself was bad enough; the manner of conducting it was inexcusable. Money voted by Parliament for carrying on the contest was squandered by the king on his pleasures. Unpaid and half starved, the English sailors mutinied, while the Dutch fleet sailed up the Thames and held London in terror for weeks. A storm of indignation swept over the country. An opposition party was formed in Parliament clamoring for Clarendon's overthrow. Charles made little effort to save the minister whose serious life he felt a constant restraint. Clarendon was impeached, but saved himself by flight to France. The crisis resulted in something more than the overthrow of the minister. In the revival of the long disused right of impeachment the Commons had gained a powerful weapon. Moreover, the principle was established that supplies should not be diverted from the use for which they were voted, and that the national accounts should be subject to inspection.

Charles and France.

Clarendon's fall coincided with a certain change in the attitude of the king. It was not that he had become more desirous of playing the despot, but that he had learned that dependence upon Parliament hindered his freedom to do as he liked. He objected to interference in the expenditure of the court, to criticism of his manner of life. Moreover, although an avowed skeptic, his sympathies were with the Catholics, and he was sincere in his wish to relieve them from the oppression of the penal laws. For these reasons it became his purpose henceforth to free himself from the restraint of Parliament. To gain his ends, outside assistance was necessary, and for this he looked to France. Louis met him more than half way. The result of their negotiations was the secret Treaty of Dover. Louis was to give Charles aid in money and troops. In return the French and English were to enter into an alliance against Holland, and the Roman Catholic Church was to be established in England.

Charles II. and a Courtier. From a Scarce Print by Faithorne.

Treaty of Dover. 1670.

This disgraceful treaty was kept a secret even from many of the royal ministers, but its effect at once became apparent. Parliament was prorogued, war was declared against Holland, although an alliance with that country had just been formed, and a Declaration of Indulgence was issued suspending the execution of the penal laws. This was primarily in the interest of the Catholics, but it was hoped it might win over the Dissenters. Its effect, however, was just the reverse. With unusual clear-sightedness, the latter saw the dangerous possibilities in allowing the crown such arbitrary power, and they were the first to appeal against the measure. In spite of the large sums received from France, need of money soon forced Charles to summon Parliament. The first act of the opposition, or "Country party," was to compel the king to withdraw

Test Act. 1673.

the Declaration. It next proceeded to pass the Test Act, requiring all who held any state office to take the sacrament according to the Anglican form, and to make a declaration against the doctrine of transubstantiation. One privilege after another was taken from all who dissented from the established Church. In turn the Church, the universities, municipal office, civil office, were closed to them.

Earl of Danby, Lord Treasurer and leading minister. 1673-1678.

The course of affairs during the next few years seems confused and uncertain. The chief minister was Danby, whose views, on the whole, were those of Clarendon, save that he wished to renew the alliance with Holland. This meant war with France, and here he had the support of Parliament; but Charles was bribed to keep peace. Moreover, Parliament, much as it wanted war, hardly dared trust the king with an army. On the other hand, Louis doubted, and with reason, the good faith of his pensioner, and tried to hold him in check by intriguing with the leaders of the Country party. Peace on the Continent finally made Louis independent of Charles' aid, and he took revenge for the double dealing with which he had been treated by revealing the whole miserable business. Wounded national pride called for vengeance. The king was inviolable, and vengeance fell upon Danby, his unwilling agent. In vain the minister pleaded the royal command; the plea was set aside, and the principle asserted that a minister might not shield himself from responsibility behind the order of the sovereign. If the king could do no wrong, then some one must be made responsible.

Popish Plot. 1678.

The French disclosures and the fall of Danby came just at the time when the country was thrown into a panic by the discovery of the so-called Popish Plot. It was asserted that the papists had conspired to murder the king and set up the Romish Church again. The story rested on the almost unsupported statements of Titus Oates, a man of degraded character, once an Anglican clergyman, later a Jesuit priest. The whole country was beside itself with fright. Men went about armed, and the Commons passed a resolution "that this House is of opinion that there hath been and still is a damnable and hellish plot, carried on by papist recusants, for assassinating and murdering the king, for subverting the government, and rooting out the Protestant religion." Several peers were committed to the Tower and a number of Catholics were put to death. An act was passed disabling papists from sitting in either House. Excitement culminated in the introduction of a bill excluding from the succession the Duke of York, the heir to the throne, on the ground of his being a Catholic. To save his brother, Charles dissolved Parliament and prorogued the new assembly seven times before he dared face it. Signs of a reaction appeared. The country was sharply divided on the question of exclusion. It was at this time that the names of Whig and Tory first appeared. The opposition, those who led the attack on York, were called Whigs, while the supporters of the crown received the name of Tory. When Parliament met again, the Exclusion Bill was still pressed, but it was plain that its supporters had overshot the mark. Their violence led to a revival of loyal feeling which was not yet spent when Charles suddenly died, acknowledging, as he had not before dared to do, his desire to be reconciled with the Roman Catholic Church.

The guiding principle of Charles' policy was contained in his frequent remark, "Whatever else may happen, I have no wish to go again upon my travels." There was never fear that he would press a matter to the point of endangering his crown, and, on the whole, the years of his reign

Disabling Act. 1678.

Whig: a name applied to the Covenanters of the west of Scotland, from the cry of "whiggam," used with horses by the peasants of that region.

Tory: a name given to brigands in Ireland.

were marked by real constitutional progress. Charles made his ministers responsible to himself, but he did not prevent their being held responsible by Parliament. Moreover the establishment of Parliamentary parties was a long stride toward Parliamentary rule, though the principles upon which men divided were not yet clearly understood.

The Stuart restoration coincided with the development in the English nation of intense feeling on certain subjects. An unreasoning devotion to the king and the Church was matched by an equally unreasoning fear and detestation of Puritans and Roman Catholics. Should ever these sentiments come into conflict, it was a question which would gain the mastery. In the reign of James II. the answer was made plain.

James II.
1685-1689.

As a man James was more respectable than his brother, as a king he was more dangerous. In many ways he resembled his father. He had his lack of tact and pliability coupled with even less ability. James' aims were the aims of Charles II., to make himself independent of Parliament, to establish the Roman Catholic Church; but his policy was different. Dependence on France was odious to him. If possible he would achieve his ends in some less humiliating way. If he could obtain from Parliament what he wanted, plenty of money, he would throw England in the scale against France. Or he would try to gain his point through an alliance with the Protestant non-conformists. Only

Charles II. and his Queen. From Heath's Chronicle, 1662.

as a last resort would he become a pensioner of Louis.
The first Parliament of the reign showed the effect of the recent reaction. It was strongly Tory, and readily granted the king a revenue for life; it manifested, however, no willingness to repeal the Test Act and the Habeas Corpus Act, the immediate object of James' desire. Nevertheless after the failure of an insurrection in favor of Monmouth, an illegitimate son of Charles II., who thought his Protestantism would efface the bar sinister, James felt so sure of the national temper that he proceeded to the execution of his plans. Catholics were put into office in defiance of the Test Act, and an attempt was made to form a standing army. But James had misunderstood popular feeling, and he found himself opposed on every point. Violent objection was made to the increase of the army, petitions were pressed against any tampering with the Test Act, and only one half the supplies demanded by the king were granted.

Habeas Corpus Act, passed in 1679, aimed to secure to prisoners their right to be tried or liberated.

Defeated in his hopes of Parliamentary support, James fell back on certain powers of which he held himself possessed. He did not dare at first to dispense with the laws against the Catholics generally, but he made exceptions in individual cases. In this he was supported by the judges who were wholly under his control. Roman Catholics were placed in high offices in the Church and universities. He proceeded also with his plan of forming a standing army. Urged on by the Catholics around him he gained courage for a more sweeping measure, and issued a General Declaration of Indulgence which set aside all religious tests. At the same time an attempt was made to secure a more compliant Parliament by remodeling the town charters and ordering the Lords-Lieutenant of the counties to send up lists of well-disposed men, Catholics or Dissenters. The only effect, however, was to increase dissatisfaction. Matters were brought to a crisis by the publica-

First Declaration of Indulgence. 1687.

Second Declaration of Indulgence. 1688.

tion of a second Declaration of Indulgence which the clergy were ordered to read from the pulpit. The excitement was intense. On the day set, but four of the London clergy attempted to comply with the royal command, and their congregations withdrew from the church as soon as they began to read. The Archbishop of Canterbury and six bishops had taken the lead in the resistance to the king, presenting a petition in which they begged to be excused from performing what they held to be an illegal act. On the ground that their petition was a seditious libel they were brought to trial. The nation watched the proceedings with feverish interest, and the verdict of acquittal was received with tumultuous rejoicings in which even James' army on Hounslow Heath joined.

Trial of the seven bishops.

Nevertheless, matters had not taken a turn for the better. The nation had bided its time, enduring much for the sacred doctrine of non-resistance. It had hoped to see in time an end of its troubles, for James' only children were daughters and Protestants. But just at this juncture the queen gave birth to a son, and at once the aspect of affairs changed. The child was universally held to be supposititious, foisted upon the nation; but, whatever the truth, he was presented as the heir to the throne, and he was sure to be brought up a Catholic. The day of the acquittal of the bishops, a letter signed by prominent men went to William of Orange, the husband of Princess Mary, asking him to come to the rescue of English liberty.

The Revolution of 1688.

William of Orange was the leading Protestant statesman of Europe. He had thrown himself heart and soul into the struggle against France. He saw the advantage of securing the aid of England. But the difficulties in the way were great; English national feeling, Dutch jealousy, the opposition of his continental allies, were all to be met. The unbridled ambition of Louis and the boundless stupidity of James combined to smooth the way. Europe was beginning to see that every nerve must be strained if a limit was to be set to Louis' aggressions. One by one, James drove all elements of the nation into opposition. He continued his attack on the Church and universities, and alienated the army by bringing over Irish Catholic forces. Tories and Whigs, Churchmen and Dissenters, country and town, all alike were brought to feel that political freedom, the Protestant faith, the national honor, were in danger so long as James wore the crown. William no longer hesitated. Before setting sail he issued a manifesto which summed up James' unconstitutional acts, and stated that as the husband of Princess Mary he proposed to go to England to secure a free and legal Parliament by whose decision he would abide. In spite of warnings, James had closed his eyes to what was passing. Forced at last to see his danger, he made concessions right and left. It was too late; one after another of the leading statesmen and generals abandoned him, even his own daughter Anne went over to William. At length, with the fate of his father before his eyes, he fled to France in disguise, and Parliament proceeded solemnly to declare that "King James II., having endeavored to subvert the constitution of the kingdom by breaking the original contract between king and people, and by the advice of Jesuits and other wicked people having violated the fundamental laws, and having withdrawn himself out of the kingdom, had abdicated the government, and that the throne had thereby become vacant." In the place of James, William and Mary were formally called to rule over England. The devotion to the principle of passive obedience had given way before the determination of the people to preserve political freedom and to defend the national Church.

CHAPTER X.

PARTIES AND PARTY GOVERNMENT.

Illustrative Readings.
Esmond; Thackeray.
The Four Georges; McCarthy.
Macaulay's Essays on Chatham and Pitt.
Burke; Morley.

Important Dates.
1693-1694, The Whig Junto.
1701, Act of Settlement.
1701, Death of James II.
1707, Union of England and Scotland.
1715, Jacobite Rising.
1721-1742, Walpole's Ministry.
1745, Rising of the Young Pretender.
1757-1761, Pitt's Ministry.
1763, Peace of Paris.
1770-1782, North's Ministry.
1783, The Coalition Ministry.
1783-1801, Pitt's Ministry.
1793, War with France.

Genealogical Table.

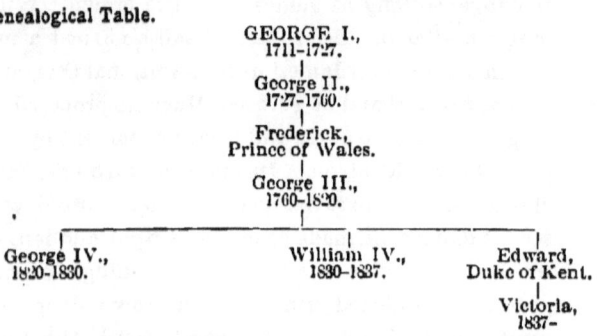

Revolution of 1688.

THE revolution of 1688 marks the overthrow of the Stuart theory of the divine right of kings, and the triumph of the Whig principle that the king reigns by the will of the people. In the place of a sovereign whose word was decisive was established a supreme Parliament, the representative of the nation; government by prerogative gave way to the rule of law. The work was well done; arbitrary taxation and arbitrary legislation could never again be

Its results.

attempted. Little, in fact, was left for the next century to do except to adapt the machinery of government to the new controlling principles. Complete, however, as was the revolution, it was nevertheless essentially conservative. The extravagances of the Rebellion had made men cautious. All unnecessary change was deprecated. Nothing was attacked that could safely be retained. In sharp contrast with the earlier movement was also the peaceful character of the Whig Revolution. Without bloodshed, with but little excitement, a king was deposed and another ruler set in his place and the whole conception of the government changed. Three documents sum up the achievements of 1688. In the simple, restrained language of the Bill of Rights, the fundamental principles of English freedom were reaffirmed, the power and privileges of Parliament were reasserted, the royal prerogative was denied, the rights of the subject over life, liberty, and property were maintained. By the same measure, supplemented by the Act of Settlement, the succession was determined, and henceforth all rulers of England must base their claims to the crown on Parliamentary statutes. Without the aid of the Dissenters the overthrow of James could not have been accomplished; it was impossible to disregard their claims, and in 1689 the Toleration Act was passed, giving to all Protestants liberty of worship. It was not a generous measure; toleration, not equality, was granted; much of the penal legislation of Charles II. was still in force, and nothing was done for the Catholics.

Bill of Rights. "Old South Leaflets," General Series, No. 19.

Act of Settlement. 1701.

Toleration Act.

Within a few weeks the revolution was accomplished; to carry into effect what had been gained was the work of a century. The natural consequence of the supremacy of Parliament was Parliamentary control of the executive, the transformation of the ministers of the king into national ministers responsible to the people, not to the sovereign, and all-powerful if secure of popular support. This was not at first realized. Still less was the means of bringing about the change understood. More than a century of blind, stumbling experiment was necessary to secure the establishment of cabinet government, that is, government by ministers holding the same political views, acting as a unit, in harmony with the prevailing party in the House of Commons, standing or falling, not at the pleasure of the king, but in accordance with the will of the nation as expressed through its representatives.

Nor was the principle of party organization as a controlling political force yet understood, still less its importance as a basis for ministerial rule. Parties existed, but not party government. To overturn the despotism of James, Whigs and Tories had coöperated heartily; but success at once brought out differences of opinion. Although determined to reign constitutionally, William had no mind to become a mere figure-head, and he naturally inclined to the Tory party with its more liberal views of the royal prerogative. On the other hand, gratitude and self-interest bound him to the Whigs who had placed him on the throne. He attempted, therefore, to rule by the support of both parties, including in his ministry Whigs and Tories. The impracticability of this was not at first realized, but the friction that it caused soon became apparent. Quarrels ensued. Accusations of inefficiency and corruption were raised. Parliament did nothing to better the situation, for neither party felt responsible for the government. In the House of Commons there was no assured majority. One day so many Whigs would be off at tennis or a cock-fight that the Tories had everything their own way, but the following day conditions might be reversed. "Nobody," it was said, "can know one day what a House of Commons will do the next." It was the work of the Earl of Sunderland, once the counselor of James, now William's warm supporter, to suggest a remedy for these disorders. Acting under his advice, the king formed his ministry from the Whig party alone, in the belief that by this means political responsibility might be fixed, and a stable support secured. This Whig Junto, as it was called, was of importance in that it was based on the admission that not royal favor, but the coöperation of the Commons was essential to the success of the ministry. Moreover, it was the first recognition of the principle that this coöperation could be best secured through a ministry acting as a unit in representing the dominant opinions of the House.

For twenty years after the Revolution, England's relations with the Continent controlled party politics. William accepted the English crown that he might throw England into the scales against France. Anne, his successor, was completely under the influence of Marlborough, the great military leader, and he was bent on continuing the struggle. The Whigs gave to the contest with Louis XIV. their hearty support. On the other hand, opposition to the war became more and more a part of the Tory policy. On Church questions, also, the two parties divided sharply; toleration was a cardinal Whig principle, while the Tories insisted on maintaining the oppressive laws against dissent. After the death of William the two great parties divided on dynastic questions also. The Whigs were bent on maintaining the Act of Settlement and the claims of the House of Hanover, while the opposing party supported more or less openly the Jacobite cause, and were forming plans for a second Stuart restoration. Their calculations were upset, however, by the unexpected death of Anne, and, before they could act, the energy of the Whig leaders had secured the throne to the Elector of Hanover.

Wars with France. War of the English Succession, 1689–1697. War of the Spanish Succession, 1702–1713.

Whigs and Tories at the beginning of the eighteenth century.

The accession of George I. meant the establishment of

George I.
1714-1727.

George II.
1727-1760.

Parliament in the eighteenth century.

Whig ascendency for forty-five years. A pretender across the water, supported by a strong element among the people, forced the earlier Hanoverians to lean upon the party that placed them on the throne and to accept its principles. Both George I. and his son, foreign in interest and unable to understand English politics, were content to leave everything to the Whig leaders. They were the real rulers of England. But behind the ministry stood a supreme Parliament, and in Parliament power lay with the Commons. Moreover, the course of events since the Revolution had shown that in case of opposition between the two Houses, the Lords would have to give way. Apparently the triumph of the people was complete.

The supremacy of Parliament over the executive did not, however, imply government by the people. The Revolution of 1688 had in fact resulted in the establishment of a kind of aristocratic republic where a few great families ruled the nation in the name of a king who was a mere figure-head, and by the authority of a Parliament which they systematically corrupted. Power had been acquired without a corresponding increase of responsibility. Debates were secret, division lists were never published, public opinion could exert but little influence. Moreover, the electoral system was such that the House in no wise represented the nation. In the counties there had been no change in the franchise since the time of Henry VI. The manner of holding land had been modified and new forms of property had come into existence, but the electors were still the forty-shilling freeholders. The condition of the towns was far worse. Many had fallen under the control of the corporations, and the right of voting was limited to a mere handful of the inhabitants. In others all sorts of anomalous franchises existed. In Weymouth, for example, the title to any share of certain ancient rents constituted the qualification for voting. The report of a commission of inspection showed that several electors voted by right of their claim to an undivided twentieth part of a sixpence. For generations there had been no reapportionment of seats. Population had shifted without a corresponding change of representation. Much injustice was the result. Lancashire, with nearly one and a half million inhabitants, had fourteen representatives; Cornwall's three hundred thousand inhabitants returned forty-four mem-

The Election. Canvassing for Votes. Hogarth.

bers. Great cities like Birmingham and Manchester were unrepresented, while old Sarum, with but one house, and Dunwich, which had disappeared under the waves of the North Sea, still returned their two members. It was a system of "represented ruins and unrepresented cities." Such a condition of things naturally invited corruption. Many of the towns were "pocket" or nomination boroughs controlled by some neighboring noble or landowner. Others were put up publicly for sale, the customary price being about £4,000. Contested elections when they occurred involved the expenditure of immense sums of money. One Yorkshire election cost nearly £150,000. Under this condition of things, systematic bribery seemed the only means of securing party success or of giving stability to the government. Corruption began with the meanest voter and ended in the cabinet. Large sums were expended in the purchase of seats. Places and pensions and titles were the rewards held out to the supporters of the administration. In the first Parliament of George I., two hundred and seventy-one of the members held offices or pensions. One of the most arduous duties of the ministers was the disposal of the secret service funds. At one time an office was established at the Treasury for the purchase of members, and more than twenty thousand pounds are said to have been spent in a single day. The example of the government was followed by all the great lords. Careful estimates showed that at least three fifths of the members of the House were returned by the crown and one hundred and sixty-two private individuals.

Walpole's Ministry. 1721-1742.

By no one was this system of corruption so well understood or so successfully applied as by Sir Robert Walpole, the great Whig minister. He came into power soon after the accession of George I., and with statesmanlike appreciation of the situation took for the keynote of his policy "peace at home and abroad." All agitation was discouraged, the most needed reforms were left unconsidered. "Better let sleeping dogs lie," was Walpole's maxim. For almost twenty years this policy was pursued. A spirit of apathy seemed to have seized upon the country, but, in reality, the nation was making good what it had gained by the overthrow of the Stuarts. The ascendency of the Whigs during these years was undisputed, for the Tories, linked to a lost cause, were hopelessly discredited with the nation. Success and long tenure of power brought out, however, elements of opposition within the dominant party. Personal feeling, dislike of Walpole's methods, dissatisfaction with his persistent peace policy, combined to form the party of "Patriots." Their efforts ended in the overthrow of Walpole and the reversal of his foreign policy. Politically, however, there was but little change. Walpole's methods were the methods of his successors. The same clique of great families controlled the government; politics were dominated by corruption, reforms were frowned down. But a change was at hand. In 1756 the Seven Years' War broke out. England could not safely hold aloof, in fact ever since 1748 her colonies had been waging a desultory war with the French. It soon became apparent, however, that she was in no condition to fight. A storm of indignation greeted the revelation of ministerial incompetence. At this critical moment there came forward a man capable of inspiring the nation with courage for the contest, William Pitt, one of the Young Patriots. "I know that I can save this nation, and that nobody else can," he declared. Disliked by king and politicians, he leaned not upon the House, but upon the nation, and his summons to the control of affairs meant the triumph of the popular will. His statesmanlike views and brilliant oratory, no less than the integrity of his character and the ardor of his patriotism, won the devotion of England. He breathed a new spirit into the administration. The army and navy were reorganized and supplies were raised. Under the inspiration of the "Great Commoner," England was winning victories from India to America when the king suddenly died. During his life George II. had had little influence on the government, but his death marks an epoch in England's constitutional development. For more than forty years the Whigs had

War with Spain. 1739. War with France. 1744.

Ministry of William Pitt.

been in control. Long tenure of power had brought the usual results, corruption and neglect of public interest. Politics meant little more than a greedy scramble for office. The Whigs had done a great work in defending religious and political freedom against the House of Stuart, they had remained true to the principles of 1688, under their rule persecution had ceased, justice had been administered, the supremacy of Parliament had been established; but they had ceased to be a party of progress. Demands for reform met with no response, the needs of the many were lost sight of in the interests of the few.

Just at the moment when the country was growing weary of Whig rule, the Tories, after years of political insignificance, reappeared, organized on a new basis, inspired by different principles. So long as Toryism meant Jacobitism, its revival was out of the question; the nation was too strongly Protestant and Hanoverian to favor a Stuart restoration. But Jacobitism came to an end in 1745, with the failure of a third attempt to bring back the Stuarts. In the writings of Bolingbroke, greatest of Tory thinkers, was furnished the basis of a purified, reorganized party. Under his inspiration the Tories were brought to accept the principles of the Revolution, and to support the Hanoverian rule while holding fast to the idea of authority as opposed to the Whig cry of liberty. In their opposition to the Whigs, they were sure of a leader in the young king. George III. had been trained by his mother in the spirit of Bolingbroke's Patriot King. His ideal was a strong monarch governing by his own will, but in the interest of the whole nation. He came to the throne with a carefully considered plan for overthrowing the Whig clique and ruling through ministers dependent upon his pleasure. Parties, he maintained, were at an end, and he purposed to act, not as a party leader, but as the head of the whole

Rising of the Highlanders in support of the Young Pretender.

George III. 1760–1820.

nation. In this he was sure of the support of the people to whom party government meant simply the domination of a few great families ruling in their own interest. The first ten years of his reign were spent in efforts to establish this policy. Supported by the nation in his war against the Whigs, and aided by divisions in the party, George soon succeeded in driving Pitt from power and in appointing ministers dependent upon himself. He discovered, however, that the nation, while willing to strengthen the crown against the Whigs, acted in the interests of a more popular government, and was far from accepting his views of the royal functions. The Bute ministry was soon overthrown, and for a short time the Whigs were again in power. But the illness of Pitt and the rise of the American question gave George a second opportunity of putting his plans into execution. What he before attempted in alliance with the nation he now accomplished with the support of the Tory party. In 1770 a Tory ministry under Lord North was established, and for the next twelve years George "ruled as well as reigned." The national policy was the king's policy, the ministers were his agents, Parliament was his tool. Bribery was carried to lengths heretofore unknown. Preferment in Church or State was made the reward of political usefulness, and loss of office followed refusal to support the royal policy. George did not disdain to make use of his direct personal influence to gain his ends. In a letter to Lord North he wrote in reference to a recent vote in Parliament, " I wish a list could be prepared of those that went away and those that deserted to the minority. This would be a rule for my conduct in the drawing-room to-morrow." By such means the king commanded a steady majority. Royal authority was based on a Parliament which was bought and sold.

North's Ministry. 1770-1782.

The attempt of the nation to throw off the domination

of the landed aristocracy had ended in the triumph of the king and a policy of repression. All popular movements were put down; Parliamentary reform at home, self-government in the colonies, were met by determined opposition. George was willing to govern in the interest of the people, but he was not willing that they should govern themselves. On the whole, the royal policy met with little resistance. The American war was at first popular with the mass of the people. Commercial interest and national pride were enlisted on the side of the king. To many of the opposition party, however, the question appeared in a different light. Exclusion from power was transforming the Whigs into a party of reform. Pitt and his following had long called attention to the defects of the Parliamentary and administrative system, but in vain; the Whigs felt no need of change so long as they were in control. Now, however, they realized the evils of court influence when used against themselves, they saw the need of reforms which might turn to their advantage. In the resistance of the colonists their own interests were at stake; triumph of the royal policy in America meant its firm establishment in England. Accordingly, under the vigorous leadership of Burke and Pitt, now Earl of Chatham, they made the cause of the revolted colonies their own, at the same time giving a steady support to every demand for reform. For a time they could make but little headway against the general approval of the war and the apathy of the masses. But failure in America and the heavy burden of taxation changed the current of feeling. Moreover, the struggle of the colonists for liberty had not been without effect in arousing Englishmen to the evils of their own system of government. The reform movement assumed formidable dimensions. Great meetings were held throughout the country with the intention of bringing public opinion to bear on Parliament. Petitions demanding reform in the administration, and signed by thousands, were presented in the House. One measure after another was brought forward. Burke introduced his celebrated measure for economic reform, and a bill to deprive revenue officers of their votes was followed by another demanding the exclusion of contractors from the House. The Duke of Richmond brought in a motion for Parliamentary reform, asking for annual Parliaments, manhood suffrage, and equal electoral districts. Finally, a startling resolution was carried to the effect "that the influence of the crown was increased, is increasing, and ought to be diminished." It was plain that the royal policy had failed. Before the combined pressure of defeat in America and demand for reform at home, the king was forced to give way. Lord North resigned and the Whigs returned to power. But the treaties which closed the war were mismanaged, control of the government cooled the desire for reform. The hostility of the king and the dissatisfaction of the nation soon brought about the downfall of the new ministry. In its place was set up a coalition ministry, an "unholy combination" of Lord North and Fox, the leader of the progressive wing of the Whigs. Popular indignation was aroused at an alliance formed apparently for the sole purpose of securing power. The king led the attack upon the coalition, and, regardless of the fact that it had the support of the House of Commons, turned it out and called upon William Pitt, a son of the Great Commoner, to form a ministry. Pitt, although only twenty-four, had already made his mark in the House. He had none of the fire of his father, but his tact and sagacity were unerring. A tremendous struggle ensued. It was the king, Pitt, and the nation against the coalition and Parliament. On one vote after another Pitt was defeated, but he maintained his place, declaring with truth

Richmond's plan for electoral reform.

The Coalition Ministry. 1783.

that the House did not represent the nation. The contest ended in Pitt's triumph and the establishment of the royal policy until the conclusion of the reign.

Pitt's Ministry. 1871-1801. 1804-1806.

Pitt, however, was too strong to be a tool as North had been, and so long as he remained in power his was the guiding mind in English affairs. He might act under royal authority, accepting the Tory doctrine that to the king belonged the choice of ministers, but nevertheless he preserved a large measure of independence. He had entered public life a Whig, his policy was liberal, and he should have received the support of the Whigs; lacking that, he leaned more and more on the Tory party. Insensibly his views were modified by his relations with the king and by his party associations. Nevertheless he still favored reform and introduced a bill which, however, was not thoroughgoing and which recognized the right of property in a seat in the House of Commons. The measure was defeated, for the demand for reform was subsiding; there was even yet very little intelligent public interest in the subject. Pitt's especial ability lay in finance. He met the national evil of smuggling by lowering the customs. The falling off in revenue he made good through an excise. Careful management turned the deficit into a surplus which was applied to paying off the national debt. Pitt also attempted, although without success, to give to Ireland the commercial freedom which would have done so much to disarm rebellion.

French Revolution. 1789.

All things pointed to a period of cautious reform when suddenly the country was startled by the outbreak of the French Revolution. At first public opinion was divided. To the timid and conservative the rising of the French people meant the complete overthrow of the established order, the beginning of anarchy; but by many progressive Englishmen it was hailed with enthusiasm. The excesses

of the Reign of Terror, however, turned the current of
feeling. Men recoiled from deeds so un-English, and the
champions of popular liberty were silenced. The attacks
of the French were directed against the crown and the
privileged classes. In England, as a result, the Tories, the
king's party, became the champions of vested interests.
The clergy, the aristocracy, the wealthy middle classes
rallied around the king in defense of privilege and property.
The cause of reform received a fatal blow. Burke,
once the advocate of political progress, became now the
mouthpiece of reaction, and in his "Reflections on the
French Revolution" issued the manifesto of a crusade
against democracy. The opposition dwindled to a mere
handful. Fox's following numbered only sixty, a hopeless
minority. It became, however, what it had never been
before, a party of popular reform; but it had little influence
in politics, it could scarcely obtain a hearing. The
propagandist attitude of the French revolutionists aroused
a panic of alarm in England. The abolition of monarchy
and the execution of Louis XVI. at length determined the
government to join hands with royalist Europe in an
attack on the new republic. At the outset this was a war
against opinion, and men might honestly doubt its justice.
When the republic was transformed into an empire with
conquest as its watchword, it became a struggle of self-defense
and the nation threw itself heart and soul into the
contest. It was in the beginning a Tory war, and its continuance
meant the continuance of Tory ascendency.
More and more the party became an aristocratic party,
actuated by motives of class aggrandizement, incapable of
looking at public affairs except from a class point of view.
Every popular movement was repressed. Motions for Parliamentary
reform were thrown out by large majorities,
freedom of speech and of the press was abridged, public

1793.

Grey's motion for Parliamentary reform thrown out by a vote of 232 to 41 in 1793, of 256 to 91 in 1797.

Irish Rebellion. 1798.

Act of Union. 1800.

meetings were prohibited. The chronic discontent of the Irish gave opportunity for French interference. A rising in 1798 was cruelly repressed by the English government, and led to the Act of Union, carried in 1800, in face of the opposition of the "whole unbribed intellect of Ireland." Everywhere a policy of high-handed repression was pursued. For twenty years all progress was checked, and the prospect of reform, so bright in 1780, seemed, thirty years later, hopelessly deferred.* More than a century had elapsed since the overthrow of the Stuart despotism but England had apparently made no advance toward popular government. Parliament was the agent of the classes, the king could still impose his will upon the nation. Nevertheless, much had been gained. In the organization of parties and the development of the cabinet, governmental forms had been established, well fitted to give effect to the will of the people and to make possible successful democratic rule.

---

* From 1688 to 1815, the country was involved in seven great wars. Only sixty-two years, or less than half the whole period, were exempt.

War of the English Succession, 1689-97............................cost £	32,648,764
War of the Spanish Succession, 1702-13..............................cost	50,084,956
War of the Austrian Succession, 1739-48 ....cost	43,655,192
Seven Years' War, 1756-63...cost	82,623,738
War of American Independence, 1776-83...........................cost	97,599,496
The Napoleonic Wars, 1793-1815..cost	831,446,449
Total cost..	£1,138,653,595

CHAPTER XI.

GROWTH OF DEMOCRACY.

Illustrative Readings.
Adam Bede; George Eliot.
Alton Locke; Kingsley.
Coningsby; Disraeli.
Locksley Hall; Tennyson.
Locksley Hall Seventy Years After.
John Halifax, Gentleman; Miss Muloch.

The Sovereigns.
George IV., 1820-1830.
William IV., 1830-1837.
Victoria, 1837-

The Prime Ministers.
Lord Liverpool, Tory, 1812-1827.
Mr. Canning, progressive Tory, 1827.
Duke of Wellington, Tory, 1828-1830.
Lord Grey, Whig, 1830-1831.
Lord Melbourne, Whig, 1835-1841.
Sir Robert Peel, progressive Tory, 1841-1846.
Lord Russell, Liberal, 1846-1852.
Lord Derby, Conservative, 1852.
Lord Aberdeen, Whig and Peelite coalition, 1852-1855.
Lord Palmerston, Liberal, 1855-1858.
Lord Derby, Conservative, 1858-1859.
Lord Palmerston, Liberal, 1859-1865.
Lord Russell, Liberal, 1865-1866.
Lord Derby, Conservative, 1866-1868.
Mr. Gladstone, Liberal, 1868-1874.
Mr. Disraeli, Conservative, 1874-1880.
Mr. Gladstone, Liberal, 1880-1886.
Lord Salisbury, Conservative, 1886-1893.
Mr. Gladstone, Liberal, 1893-1894.
Lord Rosebery, Liberal, 1894-

NINETEENTH century England has undergone a political revolution no less significant than that achieved under the Stuarts. This transformation might rather be termed an evolution than a revolution, since it has been wrought out, not by civil war and the overthrow of kings, but by the more peaceful and permanent method of Parliamentary legislation reënforced by public opinion. The great reforms of the present century would have been impossible but for the quickened intelligence and increased influence of the common people. Industrial betterment and popular education have inspired the masses with new purposes

First Parliamentary grant in aid of schools, 1833. School attendance required of all children, 1870.

and larger aspirations. Never, perhaps, since the fourteenth century has the English nation been stirred to hopes so eager and far-reaching.

The democratic movement in England has gathered animus from the popular revolutions that have three times in the past hundred years convulsed the Continent. In 1789, in 1830, and again in 1848, have king, clergy, and aristocracy been called to account by the people, and bidden show cause why they should monopolize wealth and place and power. In France, in Spain, in Italy, Belgium, and Germany, the old order so challenged could make but a lame defense. Overcome by superior strength, the privileged classes made unlimited concessions to the *demos* whom they could no longer control—concessions which were, however, quickly recalled when, the strength of the people being spent, the forces of reaction were again dominant. In every continental state, political progress has been spasmodic—epochs of rapid advance being followed by intervals of retrogression. England, on the other hand, remote from Jacobin passion and exempt from the devastating wars that troubled the Continent, was left free to develop along natural lines. The conservative temper of the people deterred them from rash innovations, while the real services rendered by the aristocracy to their dependents mitigated the bitterness of class antagonism. Without revolution, almost without bloodshed, without violent breach with the old order, England has achieved a government which is a juster expression of the national will than that of France. The best of the medieval constitution has been conserved and adapted to the needs of the present day.

An Alarmist.

Growth of Democracy.

The first effect produced by the French Revolution on English thought was a strong aversion to the political philosophy that could give birth to such horrors. A wave of reaction passed over England, discrediting progressive statesmen and sweeping all reform projects into oblivion. But England could not long remain ignorant of the deeper significance of that tremendous revolt of a people against its tyrants. France was indeed conquered in 1815, and the Bourbons restored, but the great achievements of the Revolution were not undone. Just laws and a liberal constitution were secured to the people by the very monarchs who had undertaken the war in behalf of Louis XVI. During this same twenty years, the cause of English liberty had lost much and gained nothing. Absorbed in the long struggle with Napoleon, the Tory ministers had given little thought to the national well-being. Enthusiasm for the war, pride in its triumphant conclusion and in the new prestige acquired by England, the champion of oppressed nationalities, together with a certain fictitious prosperity accruing to trade and manufactures, had blinded men's eyes to the heavy cost of the conflict. Peace once declared, the nation began to balance accounts. The war debt amounted to £831,000,000. The financial stringency was such that the Bank of England suspended specie payment, and for twenty-two years the country had to be content with a depreciating currency. The consequent rise in

Influence of the French Revolution. 1789-95.

Influence of the Napoleonic wars. 1793-1815.

Extinction of Napoleon.

1797-1819.

prices was exaggerated by the failure of trade with the Continent and by a series of bad harvests which brought corn up to famine rates. The Corn Laws, which protected English agriculture against foreign competition, were vigorously maintained by the landlord class who secured the lion's share of the profits. The prosperity of the landlord and the farmer was not shared, however, by the agricultural laborer who, during these years of extraordinary

Price of wheat rose to 171s. a quarter, or $5 a bushel, in 1812 and 1813. None might be imported under 80s. a quarter.

Napoleon in Chains following Britannia's Triumphal Car.

prices, was steadily sinking into misery and want. Wages fell below the subsistence level and had to be supplemented from the poor rates. At the moment when England attained the acme of her military renown, her laboring people were being reduced to pauperism.

National glory won at such a cost was not cause for congratulation. Men were found bold enough to assert that while pursuing a crusade against Jacobin violence, England allowed more hateful cruelties to pass unchallenged within her own boundaries. Might not one cherish the watchwords proclaimed by the Revolution—liberty, equality, fraternity—while condemning its mad excesses? A revulsion of feeling characterized the second and third decades of the nineteenth century. The writers of the day were the first to recognize that the revolutionary ideals were far in advance of English conceptions of justice and right. Wordsworth, the poet of the people, had greeted with rapture the birth of democracy in France, but the violence of the Jacobins filled him with such despair as to chill his faith in the ability of the people for self-government. Shelley's democratic idealism, could, however, ignore the ugly facts of the Revolution. Byron, an aristocrat by birth and temper, but at war with his order, struck

See Browning's "The Lost Leader."

A Short Way with Corn Merchants.

telling blows for freedom in his wild revolt against convention and dogma, while Burns, the Ayrshire plowman, voiced the people's protest against class inequalities:

> " For a' that and a' that,
> Our toil's obscure, and a' that,
> The rank is but the guinea's stamp,
> The man's the gowd for a' that."

Democracy had yet more strenuous advocates in the Radicals. The radical movement originated with Cobbett's "Weekly Political Register," a twopenny sheet that had a wide circulation and enormous influence among the working classes. The "Register" voiced the prevailing discontent, and proposed reforms aiming to give the people more effective control of the government. Redistribution of the representation, universal suffrage, and annual Parliaments were presented as the necessary steps toward the

The Radical party. Name assumed in 1819.

vindication of the popular will. In order that the unrepresented people might make their purpose felt, mass meetings were held, secret associations were formed, and propagandist literature scattered far and wide. The government, unreasonably suspicious of any popular movement, determined to crush the malcontents. A political demonstration at Spa Fields in 1816 was broken up by the police.* Three years later, a convention held in Manchester for the purpose of electing a "legislatorial representative" for that unenfranchised town, was raided by a military force and seventy persons were injured. The Manchester Massacre, or the Battle of Peterloo, as it was derisively called, roused intense indignation. It was becoming every year more evident that the government was quite independent of the people since Parliament represented only the aristocracy and the upper middle classes.

The Hampden clubs.

Tax Collectors.

The convention was held in St. Peter's Field.

The continental revolutions of 1830, which substituted constitutional for absolute monarchy in France and Belgium and several of the German states, produced a marked effect in England. They seemed to prove that fundamental

---

* A placard was paraded at this meeting entitled "The present state of Great Britain."
"Four millions in distress!!!
Four millions embarrassed!!!
One million and a half fear distress!!!
Half a million live in splendid luxury!!!
Our brothers in Ireland are in a worse state.
The climax of misery is complete—it can go no farther.
Death would now be a relief to millions."

reforms could be accomplished without anarchy, and Englishmen began to question whether, after all, their medieval constitution might not safely be modified to suit modern needs. In the elections that followed immediately upon the death of George IV., the Liberals won a signal victory. The Tories lost fifty seats and Wellington was obliged to resign. Lord Grey, who was called to take his place, had been for forty years the stanch champion of Parliamentary reform. A Reform Bill was framed by the ministry and introduced in the House of Commons by Lord John Russell (March 1, 1831). It provided for the disfranchisement of the rotten boroughs, the redistribution of seats among the counties and hitherto unrepresented towns, and the extension of the borough franchise to all ten-pound householders. The bill was received with derisive cheers from the opposition benches and, though cordially endorsed by the king and maintained by all the influence the ministry could bring to bear, it was defeated on the third reading by a majority of eight. The government determined to have recourse to the people. The dissolution of Parliament was declared by the king in person on April 22d, and through May and June the country rang with the excitement of the campaign. The result was even better than the government had hoped. When the bill came again to its third reading (September 21), it passed the House by a majority of one hundred and nine. It had still, however, to run the gauntlet of the Peers. The Upper House did not deign to admit the bill to consideration, but threw it out on the first reading by a majority of forty-one.

William IV. 1830-1837.

Struggle for Parliamentary reform.

Cobbett on the Stump.

This haughty rejection of a measure which had the enthusiastic support of the great majority of the nation by a privileged and non-representative body, roused intense indignation throughout the country. Political unions were formed with a view to bringing public opinion to bear upon the reactionary legislators. A reform program was announced, which went so far as to propose the abolition of all hereditary privileges and distinctions of rank. The Lords could not but be influenced by the popular agitation, violent and ill-advised though it sometimes was. When the new Reform Bill came up for its second reading in the House of Lords, the ministry succeeded in obtaining a majority of nine. A motion to postpone final action, was, nevertheless, carried. Driven to extremities, Lord Grey appealed to the king to swamp the opposing majority by the creation of Peers. This was refused and the ministry resigned. An attempt to form a Conservative cabinet under the Duke of Wellington failed. The popular protest was overwhelming. The Liberal papers came out in mourning and petitions were sent up to Parliament signed by thousands of the unrepresented. The unions announced their determination to march to London in numbers sufficient to compel regard for the nation's will. Wellington dared not resort to force. The military could not be trusted to fight against the people. Finally the king recalled Lord Grey and sent a circular letter to the Peers requesting them to withdraw their opposition.

April 14, 1832.

"Orator" Hunt.
A leading radical.

May 15, 1832.

So compelled, the House of Lords approved the bill. *June 4, 1832.* The Reform Act was a signal triumph of the popular will over vested right and hereditary privilege. Fifty-six rotten boroughs were disfranchised and thirty were deprived of one member each. The one hundred and forty-three memberships so vacated were divided between the more populous counties and thirty-nine unrepresented towns. Thus, after an interval of nearly two hundred years, the electoral reform proposed by Cromwell was resumed. Representation was not yet, however, exactly proportioned to population. Universal suffrage and annual Parliaments were not even broached; but the people had got a foothold in the House of Commons and might bide their time. The Reform Act of 1832 transferred the balance of power from the landed aristocracy to the manufacturers and merchants —the dominant classes of newly enfranchised towns. The populace, though it had borne the brunt of the agitation, was not yet entrusted with the ballot. But fifty Radicals were returned to the new Parliament. With the change in the character of representation and the consequent change of policy, new party names were adopted. The Whigs, dominated henceforth by the progressive contingent, called themselves Liberals; while the Tories, conceiving their function to be the preservation of a time-honored constitution, preferred to be known as Conservatives. *The Reform Act of 1832.*

The reforms undertaken by the first Parliament elected on the new basis were directed by middle class interests and fell far short of popular expectation. An act was passed (1833) emancipating the slaves on the West Indian plantations, but with heavy compensation to their owners. The Poor Law was revised (1834) with a view to checking the growth of pauperism. The new act was based on the wholesome principles of the Elizabethan Law, but it was bitterly resented by the working classes accustomed, for a century past, to regard parish aid as a poor man's right. More popular measures, *c. g.*, the Factory Act (1833) and the reform in municipal government (1835), were not initiated in the House of Commons, but were forced upon its notice by public agitation.

Beneficent and necessary as was much of this legislation, it did not remove the sense of grievance from the minds of the common people. They had supported the Reform Act in the hope that it was but the preliminary to more radical legislation. The bulk of the Liberal party was, however, well content with the results attained. Lord John Russell declared in the first Parliament convened after the accession of Victoria that reform could not safely be pushed further. The disappointment and indignation of the Radicals was intense. Convinced that the people would never get their rights till they could send spokesmen to the House of Commons, they entered with renewed zeal upon a crusade for popular representation. A conference between certain prominent Radicals and the working-class leaders was called in 1838, and a program for the new campaign agreed upon. The "six points" of the People's Charter were: (1) annual Parliaments, (2) manhood suffrage, (3) vote by ballot, (4) the division of the country into equal electoral districts, (5) abolition of the property qualification for members of the Lower House, (6) salaries for the people's representatives. The Chartists, as the agitators called themselves, advocated Parliamentary reform only as means to an end. The exact nature of that end was as yet undefined. Socialistic, even anarchistic, schemes were in the air and awakened consternation among the propertied and order-loving classes. Malcontents, on the other hand, of whatever shade of belief, were naturally attracted to the ranks of the reformers. "Universal suffrage," said a Radical orator, "the meaning of universal suffrage is that every

Victoria. 1837.

Chartism.

working man in the land has a right to a good coat, a good hat, a good roof, a good dinner, no more work than will keep him in health, and as much wages as will keep him in plenty."

No effective means of propagating the new gospel was neglected. Newspapers and local organizations were maintained in every principal town. Mass meetings were called at frequent intervals, and in 1839 the Chartists held a national convention. A huge petition was sent to the House of Commons bearing 1,200,000 signatures. The contemptuous rejection of the petition was followed by riotous outbreaks in divers parts of the kingdom. A second petition was presented in 1842 and met with a like fate. This time the petitioners, some 3,000,000 men, demanded not only the "six points," but the repeal of all class legislation, the abolition of monopolies and the redistribution of property. Demonstrations and riots grew so serious that even the Tory ministry recognized that something must be done. The repeal of the Corn Laws had long been advocated by enlightened Liberals, who held that the interests of the great manufacturing communities ought not to be subordinated to that of the landlord class. The Irish famine brought matters to a crisis. Early in 1846 Sir Robert Peel, much to the scandal of the Tories who thought him a traitor, and of the Liberals who accused him of stealing their thunder, proposed a Corn Bill which provided for a rapid reduction of duties on imported grains. Despite the protests of disappointed politicians, it passed both Houses, and England was thereby committed to the policy of free trade. Wheat fell to seventy-five shillings a quarter, and the ruinous fluctuation in prices ceased. There is no doubt that the removal of the tax on grains greatly relieved the sufferings of the poor, but it was scouted by the Chartists as a mere sop to Cerberus. They were bent on popular government.

Repeal of the Corn Laws. Ebenezer Elliott wrote "The Corn Law Chimes," in the interest of repeal.

The year 1848 witnessed a second epidemic of revolutions throughout the Continent. Not only France, Germany, and Italy, but Austria, the stronghold of despotism, was convulsed by the upheaval. Paris, the city of insurrections, was mastered by the combined strength of Republicans and socialists and a working-class republic was established. This signal success of their brothers across the water could not but stir the English Chartists to new exertions. The democratic movement came to a head. A national convention was called at London, April sixth, and arrangements were made for a mighty demonstration of the popular will. A monster petition, boasting 5,000,000 signatures, was to be carried to Westminster on the tenth, by a body of 500,000 men. The government was, however, amply forewarned. The Duke of Wellington was put in charge of the defense, and competent arrangements were made to suppress disorder. The Chartists were at odds among themselves as to whether they should or should not use force. The more timid and level-headed among them withdrew from a project which could only result in failure or defeat. Some 25,000 finally gathered on Kennington Common, but they were frightened by the force arrayed against them and meekly consented to send their petition to the House of Commons in a cab. When submitted to examination, the 5,000,000 signatures dwindled to 2,000,000, many of these evidently bogus. So the most formidable working-class movement England has yet seen ended in *fiasco*. When brought to the test, Chartism proved to be a mere wind-bag blown to portentous dimensions by demagogues and would-be politicians. Yet the agitation had its valuable results. The people were trained to think, to search for the causes of their misery, to look for legislative reform. The "classes" were compelled to inquire into the condition of the "masses," to recognize their own responsibility for

Chartist demonstration, 1848, led by Feargus O'Connor.

Permanent results.

the national well-being, and to set about measures of redress. The essential clauses of the Charter have since been attained—not by insurrections and mob violence, but by the characteristically English method of free discussion and Parliamentary enactment.

The Chartists failed, but the advocacy of Parliamentary reform was taken up by the Liberal party. Extension of the suffrage was repeatedly recommended in the queen's speech, and bills proposing to lower the franchise were introduced in the House of Commons in 1851, 1859, and 1860. Not, however, till the death of Palmerston left the more progressive element of the Liberal party in the ascendant, was the work of reform undertaken in earnest. Immediately upon his accession to the premiership, Lord Russell, the life-long champion of suffrage extension, framed a measure on which he staked the success of his administration. The measure was introduced in the House of Commons by Mr. Gladstone, a young Peelite, lately turned Liberal. He defended the bill with remarkable eloquence and was ably supported by the free trade Radical, John Bright. But the measure was a timid makeshift and failed to secure the support of the Liberals themselves. It was defeated in committee and Lord Russell's government immediately resigned.

Struggle for extension of the suffrage led by Gladstone.

The discontented were dubbed "Adullamites."

The new ministry under Lord Derby was made up of stiff Conservatives, but they found themselves forced by public feeling to broach the question of the suffrage. A Reform League was formed by the Radicals and working-class leaders, who plainly signified a determination not to be defrauded of their rights by factious politicians. The country was agitated by popular demonstrations, such as had extorted the first Reform Act. An attempt to hold a mass meeting in Hyde Park resulted in something very like a riot. Having no choice but to bring in a reform bill or to resign office, the ministry finally yielded. The measure originally introduced by Disraeli was meant to provide against throwing the balance of power into the hands of the masses; but the bill was amended again and again, the government yielding point by point, until it emerged a more radical measure than the Liberals themselves would have proposed. Borough suffrage was extended to all householders paying taxes and to all lodgers paying £10 annual rent. In the counties all persons owning property of £5 annual value and occupiers paying £12 a year were entitled to vote. This was the legalization of democracy. Lord Derby characterized the measure as a "leap in the dark," and many other Conservatives feared for the result; but the party as a whole supported the measure, having, as Disraeli said, "been educated by events."

<small>Reform Act, 1867.</small>

The history of English politics, during the past twenty-five years, is hardly intelligible without some comprehension of the Irish question. Since Cromwell's conquest of Ireland established English rule, the relations between the two races have been strained and unhappy. The English mind was naturally filled with distrust of Ireland, the maintainer of the Stuarts and Roman Catholicism, while the Irish people had abundant reason to fear and hate their conquerors. Irish estates were confiscated and made over to English landlords. Irish industries were systematically discouraged, the manufacture of woolens being prohibited and trade being limited to such produce as did not come into competition with English goods. Penal laws were enacted banishing Catholic priests, obliging all subjects to attend Protestant worship, and requiring that children of Catholic parents should be educated by Protestant teachers. Though Roman Catholics formed three fourths of the population, they were ineligible to office. The Act of Union redressed none of these wrongs, while it deprived Ireland of

<small>The Irish Question.</small>

Growth of Democracy. 253

the last vestige of self-government, her national Parliament. Under the terms of the Union, the two Parliaments were united at Westminster, thirty-two Irish peers, four spiritual and twenty-eight temporal, being added to the House of Lords, while one hundred representatives of the Irish counties and boroughs were to sit in the House of Commons. The Union was meant to secure to Ireland a non-sectarian government and legislation uniform with that for England and Scotland; but the Irish people have never ceased to protest against it, and the nineteenth century has been occupied by persistent effort to attain political independence. Agitation first took the form of a demand for the removal of political disabilities. The Catholic Association was organized to this end, and petition after petition was sent up to Parliament. The successive Tory governments held out against popular pressure until 1829, when Peel declared for emancipation and carried a bill providing that a Roman Catholic who would take oath to support the State and not to injure the Church should be eligible to office. This was an important concession, but it did not satisfy the Irish leaders. Admitted to Parliament, they continued to agitate, and that with renewed vigor, for the repeal of the Act of Union. "Young Ireland," the political organization formed by O'Connell, gained immense influence with the people. Monster mass meetings were held after the fashion of the contemporary Chartist demonstrations, French aid was solicited, and a formidable insurrection seemed imminent. The government had resort to coercion, forbade the political conventions, arrested and transported the ring-leaders. Ireland was in a fair way to be subdued by physical force when the famine of 1846 gave a new turn to the struggle. Thousands of the helpless people died of starvation, thousands more, evicted by the landlords, to whom they could pay no rent, drifted

Catholic Emancipation Act. 1829.

Agitation for repeal of the Union led by O'Connell, 1829-1843.

into pauperism, those who had money to buy passage took ship for America. The population decreased by a million and a half in these years of unparalleled misery. Ireland was silenced, but her cause was urged with redoubled energy by her loyal sons in America. The Fenians, as this Irish-American party called themselves, did not stop at repeal of the Union. They advocated nothing less than complete separation. The project was too wild to meet with a large measure of support, and the movement, in spite of its brilliant leadership, proved abortive. Fenianism had, however, effected an important change in English opinion. It had become apparent even to partisan observers that conditions giving rise to such persistent hatred must be seriously wrong. Coercion had been maintained for thirty-five years without avail. Why not try the effect of reform?

Population of Ireland in 1841, 8,175,124; in 1851, 6,552,385.

The Liberal party led by Gladstone accepted the task of ascertaining the actual situation and endeavoring to meet Irish discontent with adequate measures of relief. In pursuance of this policy, the Liberal leaders have been led to propose three successive measures of reform, viz., the disestablishment of the Irish Church, the modification of land laws in the interest of the tenant, and the restoration of the Irish Parliament. The initial measure was introduced by Mr. Gladstone in the first Parliament elected on the reformed basis in 1868. The Liberals were in the ascendant and the bill passed the Commons by a majority of one hundred. Indeed, it was difficult to find ground for defense of the Episcopal establishment in Ireland. Its annual income from tithes and ecclesiastical lands was £600,000, yet it ministered to not more than one tenth of the population. An Irish member declared that he paid tithes in eight parishes, in not one of which was there a church or a resident clergyman. The exclusive privileges of the Anglican Church were a direct affront to the Roman

Disestablishment of the Protestant Church in Ireland. 1869.

Catholic population obliged to contribute to its support. The bill was, nevertheless, hotly debated in the House of Lords and amended so as to secure larger compensation to the disestablished clergy. The House of Commons insisted on the original form and the Lords were forced to accept a compromise not at all to their liking. The disestablishment of the Protestant Church in Ireland was quickly followed by the Land Bill, which provided that the so-called "Ulster right," the form of land tenure customary in the northern counties, should be legal throughout Ireland. This measure proposed to secure the three "f's," fair rent, fixity of tenure, and free sale of the tenants' interest in improvements, but since landlords were able to contract themselves out of the requirements of the act, it proved ineffective. In the Irish University Bill, Mr. Gladstone went a step too far and lost his Parliamentary majority. The object of the measure was to remove religious tests and provide a non-sectarian education for all who desired to avail themselves of it. It was opposed by the priests who objected to secular education and by a large body of the Liberals who dreaded Roman Catholic ascendency. Gladstone dissolved Parliament and appealed to the country. The elections of 1874 gave the Conservatives a majority of fifty, and Gladstone had no choice but to resign.

The Irish Land Act. 1870.

Irish University Bill. 1873.

Defeat of Gladstone's Ministry. 1874.

This sudden and overwhelming defeat of a reform ministry so soon after the extension of the suffrage seems at first inexplicable. Gladstone's government had fulfilled all its pledges. In addition to the legislation having special reference to Ireland, Parliament had provided for national compulsory education and a secret ballot, had opened the civil service to public competition, had abolished the purchase of commissions in the army, and introduced a bill for the reform of the law courts. The reaction in favor of conservatism had originated not in the failure of the Liberal party to achieve the proposed reforms, but in the constitutional inability of the English nation to digest so rich and varied a menu. Reform had gone too fast and too far. The national temper, essentially conservative, shrank from such rapid change. Disraeli's denunciation of Gladstone's policy expressed the sentiment of the country. "You have had four years of it; you have despoiled churches, you have threatened every corporation and endowment in the country, you have examined into everybody's affairs, you have criticized every profession and vexed every trade, no one is certain of his property, no one knows what duties he may have to perform to-morrow." Furthermore the Liberal government, in its zeal for domestic improvement, had somewhat neglected foreign affairs. In India and in Africa, English interests were threatened, and the government, preferring negotiation to war, had pursued a policy repugnant to the national pride.

Disraeli, Lord Beaconsfield.

Disraeli succeeded to the premiership in 1874, pledged to maintain the domestic *status quo* and to vindicate the national honor in foreign fields. The Russo-Turkish War gave the new government an opportunity to show its aggressive foreign policy. Russia's rapid successes and temperate use of her victory rendered it unnecessary for England to proceed to war; but national excitement ran high and the blustering policy of the government was warmly approved.*

Jingoism.

In relation to internal affairs, Beaconsfield's government was less successful. The Conservative party, expressed a benevolent concern for the well-being of the laborer, and certain members, at least, showed a strong disposition to legislate in the direction of technical schools, public provision for recreation, rural artisans' dwellings, an eight-

---
* Popular sentiment was voiced and a term for the ministerial policy suggested in a street song of the day.
"We don't want to fight, but by jingo, if we do,
We've got the ships, we've got the men,
And we've got the money too."

hour day, etc.; but the government was resolved to move
slowly, and little was accomplished beyond an Agricultural
Holdings Act, securing compensation for improvements
to English tenants, and the Laborers' Dwellings Act which
empowered town corporations to purchase land and erect
buildings for the accommodation of workmen's families.

Toward Irish discontent the government showed an uncompromising severity. The recent reforms, liberal and
thoroughgoing though they were, had apparently not
reached the root of the difficulty. Agitation increased
with every concession. Hardly had the Land Bill become
law when the Irish party, under the lead of Isaac Butt,
brought forward a demand for Home Rule. The new leader
declared that Ireland could no longer consent to receive
her laws at the hands of a Parliament, the great majority of
whose members were Englishmen and Scotchmen. She
must have an independent legislature, but wished to retain
such relations to the British Parliament as an American
commonwealth bears to the government of the United
States. To the impartial outsider there appears to be
nothing unreasonable in this proposal. It would indeed
seem expedient that not only Ireland, but Wales and Scotland, should have local parliaments, and that the four
originally independent kingdoms should form a federal
union after the American plan. The several interests are
as diverse as those of our states, and would be better served
by sectional legislation. Moreover, the mass of business
involved in the care of domestic, colonial, and foreign interests augments from year to year. It already exceeds the
capacity of a single legislative assembly. To relieve Parliament of local legislation would greatly facilitate the conduct of imperial affairs. Nevertheless, the demand for
Home Rule met with small favor among Englishmen.
Race prejudice lent weight to the argument that an Irish

Isaac Butt and the demand for Home Rule.

Parliament could not be trusted to deal fairly with the Protestants or the landed interests involved. Controlling but a small minority (fifty or sixty members) in the House of Commons, the Nationalist faction remained in sulky isolation until Parnell taught them how to compel attention. Charles Stuart Parnell, a man of cool head and steady nerve and an expert parliamentarian, succeeded to the leadership of his party in 1877. His policy was, in one word, obstruction. The House of Commons was to be hindered in the prosecution of any and every measure until Irish interests were considered. By moving amendments and forcing divisions, by making interminable speeches and dragging in irrelevant issues, the ordinary course of business was effectually checked. In despair of getting anything done, the government resorted to extreme measures. Parnell and other unruly members were censured by the House, and rules were adopted enabling the Speaker to coerce an obstinate minority. Nevertheless, the obstructionists succeeded so far as to bring upon the government the charge of timid inefficiency.

<small>Parnell and Irish obstruction.</small>

<small>*e. g.*, the closure, a method of cutting off debate by calling for the previous question.</small>

Parliament was dissolved and new elections were held in the spring of 1880. Beaconsfield appealed to the country for support on the ground that the Conservative party could alone be trusted to maintain England's ascendency in the councils of Europe or to defend the empire against threatening disintegration. The Liberal platform, on the other hand, announced an "anti-jingo" foreign policy, progressive domestic legislation, redress for Irish grievances, but firm and consistent resistance to Home Rule. The election results showed that the tide had turned. The Liberals secured a clear majority of fifty-five, and Gladstone was free to inaugurate a program of reform. Campaign pledges were redeemed in the Irish Land Act (1881) which provided that rents should be fixed by land courts, and in

<small>Result of the elections of 1880. Liberals, 355; Conservatives, 238; Nationalists, 62</small>

the Reform Act (1884) which further extended the suffrage to the agricultural laborers. The county franchise was now made identical with that of the boroughs and all adult males paying £10 room or house rent were entrusted with the ballot. The manhood suffrage demanded by the Chartists was thus practically secured. Another of the "six points," equal electoral districts, was attained in the next year. Counties and boroughs are now divided into election divisions containing from 50,000 to 60,000 voters each. Each returns but one member to the House of Commons.

Reform Act. 1884.

Four fifths of the 5,000,000 voters in the United Kingdom are qualified as householders.

Gladstone had amply fulfilled his promise of internal reform, but he failed a second time to meet the approval of the people in the conduct of foreign affairs. A vote of censure on the Egyptian policy of the government failed by only fourteen votes, and in June of 1885 the ministry was defeated on an amendment to the tax bill. Lord Salisbury was called to the prime ministry, but the Conservatives were not strong enough to hold their own unaided. Lord Randolph Churchill, the leader of the "fourth party," as the progressive Tories were called, was summoned to the cabinet. The Conservative party was thus committed to various projects for social and industrial improvement little akin to its former policy. Churchill, furthermore, negotiated an alliance with the Nationalists, always ready to cast in their lot with either party that showed any inclination to concede Home Rule. Thus, by currying favor with Tory reformers and Irish Home Rulers, the government was enabled to control a majority in the House of Commons, but little important business was put through. Both parties were making ready for a critical campaign.

Lord Randolph Churchill.

In the coming elections the agricultural laborers were to cast their first ballots and no man could surmise how their vote would affect the political future. The ministry relied on the influence of the clergy and the landed gentry to keep the rustics under party control, but the opposition candidates drew glowing pictures of the benefits to be expected from a Liberal administration. Laborers' allotments, free schools, reform in local government, disestablishment of the Scotch Church, these and other legislative tid-bits, Gladstone's more radical followers did not hesitate to offer. The unnatural alliance between Conservatives and Home Rulers was maintained through the campaign. Parnell instructed his party to vote Conservative wherever there was no Nationalist candidate. The result of the elections abundantly justified his tactics. The Liberals secured 333 seats, the Conservatives 251, but Ireland, outside of Ulster county, had gone solid for Home Rule. Parnell could count on eighty-six members and could by uniting forces with the ministry outvote the opposition. He had, therefore, the balance of power in his hands, and was in a position to extort concessions. Gladstone was directly converted to Home Rule. The result of the elections was no sooner known than he issued a manifesto favoring the Nationalist claims. The opportunity to introduce a Home Rule Bill was soon vouchsafed him. In an amendment to the address, the government was defeated by a vote of 329 to 258. Nationalists and Radicals voted with the opposition, while a few dissentient Liberals joined the Conservative ranks.

Elections of 1885.

Gladstone's Home Rule Bill provided for the establishment in Ireland of a separate executive government solely responsible to a legislature sitting in Dublin and empowered to deal with all non-imperial business. Irish representation in the British Parliament was to be discontinued. It was closely followed by the Land Purchase Bill designed to enable Irish tenants to buy up their holdings by means of a loan from the imperial government. This

The Home Rule Bill, April 8, 1886.

complete surrender to the demands of the Nationalist faction roused intense indignation throughout England. Not even such popularity as Gladstone's could survive the storm of abuse heaped upon the author of this "scheme of disintegration." The "grand old man" was denounced as a political turncoat, a traitor to his party and to his country. His change of front was no more reprehensible than Peel's desertion of the Corn Laws in 1846, but Home Rule was a more contentious issue since it challenged race feeling. The breach occasioned in the Liberal party was deep and irreparable. The seceders, under the lead of Lord Hartington and Mr. Goshen (Whigs), Joseph Chamberlain and John Bright (Radicals), called themselves Liberal Unionists, but joined forces with the Conservatives who now declared that the Irish question could only be settled by coercion. With forces so depleted Gladstone could not carry his measure and the Home Rule Bill was voted down 341 to 311. The only chance of success was an appeal to the country. In the elections of July, 1886, the Conservatives had an easy victory in the English constituencies, but Ireland, Scotland, and Wales stood loyally by Gladstone and Home Rule. The Conservatives returned 316 members, the Liberal Unionists 74, the Gladstone Liberals 196, the Parnellites 84. The defeat was so decisive that Gladstone resigned, and Salisbury was summoned to form a ministry before Parliament convened.

June 7, 1886.

Elections of 1886. The popular vote in favor of Home Rule was: In Ireland, 4½ to 1; in Scotland, 3 to 1; in Wales, 5 to 1.

In the autumn of '86 the Conservatives entered upon a long lease of power. The six years of their administration was marked by no legislation of first importance except the Local Government Act. By this measure, the anti-Home Rule ministry undertook to meet the demand for self-government by establishing county councils elected by the freeholders and responsible for all purely local business. The defeat of Home Rule occasioned a series of riotous outbreaks in Ireland which the government put down with a strong hand. England, on the contrary, was well content with the decision, and the Conservative party seemed securely intrenched within an insurmountable bulwark of national prejudice.

Signs of reaction, however, began soon to be discerned in working-class quarters. A new party had arisen. Social and industrial questions were pressing for solution and a Conservative government could hardly be expected to give them adequate treatment. Propositions for an eight-hour day, for land-tenure reform, for repeal of the Septennial Act, for payment of members of Parliament, were rejected, to the great indignation of the people. Under the pressure brought to bear by popular feeling, the ministerial ranks thinned until Salisbury could no longer be sure of his majority and dissolved Parliament. The election returns of June, 1892, reversed the verdict given in 1886. Gladstonians and Nationalists combined could boast a majority of forty-two, and the Conservative government was readily defeated by an amendment to the address. The Home Rule Bill, spite of dissensions in the Nationalist ranks, passed the House of Commons by a vote of 347 to 304, but it met with unexpected defeat in the Upper House. Since Lord Grey forced the first Reform Bill through the House

Lord Salisbury Rejects the People's Bills.

Election returns of 1892. Gladstonians, 271; Nationalists, 81; Labor party, 4; Conservatives, 268; Liberal Unionists, 46.

The second Home Rule Bill thrown out by the Lords.

of Lords, that honorable body had not ventured to reject a measure sent up from the House of Commons and endorsed by popular support. It was generally supposed that its veto power, like that of the crown, had passed into "innocuous desuetude." To the scandal of all believers in popular

The House of Lords Disposes of the Home Rule Bill.

government, this measure, which had been approved by 2,477,856 out of 4,752,698 voters in the recent elections, was rejected by a body of men who could lay no claim to voice the will of the nation. Unionists argued in their defense that this extraordinary prerogative might be exercised in a case where an extra-constitutional measure was in question. The Lords, it was said, would never presume to interfere in the course of ordinary legislation. But the Upper House, dominated by Lord Salisbury, has since plucked up courage to defeat other Liberal projects.* The Radicals had for years been protesting that the House of Lords was an anachronism—a clog on the wheels of progress, but so long as this degenerate descendant of the Witenagemot was content to remain a mere handful of idle old gentlemen who amused themselves with ratifying the bills passed in the Lower House, its abolition would hardly have been seriously considered. Recent obstruction

Labor.   Salisbury.   Archbishop of Canterbury.

of Liberal measures has, however, laid them open to attack. Mr. Labouchere, the inveterate foe of hereditary privilege, recently introduced into the House of Commons a resolution stating that "the power now enjoyed by persons who were not elected to Parliament by the usual process of the franchise, yet who are able to prevent the passage of bills, shall cease." The proposition had not been foreseen and half the members were absent. To the surprise and amusement of the House it was carried by a vote of 147 to 145. Both Mr. Gladstone and Lord Rosebery (appointed

Proposed abolition of the House of Lords, March 13, 1894.

March, 1894.

---

* *E. g.,* the Parish Councils Bill, which aims to take local interests out of the hands of the squire and the parson and entrust them to the people, was weakened by the amendments of the Upper House.

premier on the resignation of Gladstone) have given expression to the conviction that the House of Lords must be reformed if it is to remain a part of the English constitution, but the government could hardly adopt so hasty and

Types of our Hereditary Legislators.

ill-considered a measure. It was allowed to drop, but the end is not yet. Not only are the Radicals bent on the destruction of every remnant of political privilege, but the growing Labor party menaces all aristocratic claim.

The political reforms achieved during the past hundred years amount to a complete transformation of the English constitution. The oligarchic monarchy of the Georges has become the democratic monarchy of to-day. The people, through their representatives in the House of Commons, control the ministry and the ministerial policy in every detail of domestic and imperial legislation.

NOTE.—The illustrations in this chapter are contemporary caricatures.

CHAPTER XII.

INDUSTRIAL PROGRESS DURING THE EIGHTEENTH AND NINETEENTH CENTURIES.

Illustrative Readings.	Principal Inventions.
Shirley; Brontë.	Fly shuttle, Kay, 1738.
Sybil; Disraeli.	Spinning-jenny, Hargreaves, 1767.
All Sorts and Conditions of Men; Besant.	Throstle, Arkwright, 1709.
	Spinning-mule, Crompton, 1779.
The Children of Gibeon; Besant.	Steam engine, Watt, 1775.
Marcella; Mrs. Humphry Ward.	Power loom, Cartwright, 1785.
In Darkest England; General Booth.	Cotton gin, Whitney, 1793.
	Steamboat, Fulton, 1811.
Life and Labour of the People; Charles Booth.	Railroad, Stephenson, 1825.

THE industrial history of the seventeeth century offers little that is noteworthy. The disorders of the civil war caused a rise in prices which was made good only in part by the rise in wages. On the whole, however, there was little economic disturbance. Gradually population had adjusted itself to the changes consequent upon the agrarian revolution of the Tudor period. The growth of domestic industries and the improvement in methods of agriculture brought increased demand for labor, and by the beginning of the eighteenth century the rural classes were in a fairly prosperous condition.

AGRICULTURE.

A second movement toward enclosure comparable in extent and significance to that which transformed the face of Tudor England, characterized the eighteenth century. This second onslaught on peasant holdings was due, not to the demand for pasture land, but to improved methods of tillage. Scientific agriculture, eloquently advocated by such men as Markham and Arthur Young, had become the fashion among English landlords. Assiduous attention was given to stock-raising. Clover and rich grasses were introduced and better breeds of cattle were kept. To the arable land, marl and other manures were applied, while methods of cultivation were carefully studied. The open field system, with its numerous proprietors and cumbersome regulations, was abandoned. The land was redivided in such fashion that each man who could justify his title received his share in a single lot. This could be cultivated to much better advantage than the scattered holdings of the old-time tenure. These and other improvements so increased the productive power of the soil that wheat crops averaged twenty and thirty bushels to the acre, four times the thirteenth century rate. The weight of sheep and cattle was raised in the same proportion.

<small>Improved methods of agriculture.</small>

From the standpoint of the scientific agriculturist, the wasteful and petty methods of the medieval system were intolerable. Writing in 1771 of the small farms in Buckinghamshire, Young says: "Nearly the whole country is open field land; and all lies in broad, high, crooked ridges." With the farmers using four or five horses to a plow, "the tillage is miserable," the wheat crop yielding not more than fifteen bushels per acre. "In no part of the country have I met with husbandry that requires greater amendment than this; such crops are, their soil considered, contemptible." "As to the landlords, what in the name of wonder can be the reason of their not enclosing! All this vale would make as fine meadows as any in the world!" In Norfolk, on the other hand, where the common fields had long since disappeared, conditions were, according to Young, all that could be desired. "No small farmers could effect such great things as have been done in Norfolk. Enclosing, marling, and keeping a flock of sheep large enough for folding, belong absolutely and exclusively to great farmers. . . . Great farms have been the soul of the Norfolk culture; split them into tenures of an hundred pounds a year, you will find nothing but beggars and weeds in the whole country. The rich man keeps his land rich and clean."

Progress of Enclosure. The progress of enclosure was accelerated by a new demand for land. Merchants, grown suddenly rich in the East India trade, and clothiers who had amassed fortunes in manufacture, were eager to buy country estates and to secure a place among the landed gentry. Under the spur of rising prices the zeal for enclosing overcame all obstacles. Between 1710 and 1760, 334,974 acres were enclosed, while the land so redistributed from 1760 to 1830 amounted to nearly 7,000,000 acres. In the second period, 4,000 Enclosure Acts were passed affecting 4,000 out of the 10,000 parishes in England. The transformation was most complete in the southern and eastern counties. In Cumberland and the West Riding of Yorkshire, in Scotland, Wales, and Ireland, the small holdings still per-

The Water Supply.

sist. The Enclosure Acts were framed by a Parliament made up of landowners who gave but slight consideration to the rights of tenants and freeholders. Unable to defend themselves against their powerful neighbors, small proprietors yielded, not without protest, to unjust encroachment, or finding that they could not compete in the same market with the new cultivators, they sold their little holdings and dropped to the rank of the landless laborer. Even Arthur Young laments the disappearance of the freeholders. The stalwart yeomen who had been the main support of Cromwell and the Puritan revolution were hardly to be found in England at the close of the eighteenth century. They had been driven from the land to make room for improved agriculture under the tenant-farmer.

MANUFACTURES.

The decay of the yeomanry was hastened by the changed conditions of the textile industries. With the failure of the gilds, the cloth manufacture had fallen largely into the hands of the peasant farmers. Spinning and weaving were carried on as a by-industry in thousands of cottage homes. The first fifty years of the eighteenth century was an epoch of marked prosperity for the woolen industry. Protective legislation shut out foreign goods, and the rural manufacturers found a ready market for their homespun broadcloths and serges. The income so obtained was a welcome addition to the produce of their scanty fields. Defoe describes the cloth industry near Halifax in glowing terms. "Not only the valleys, but the sides of the hills, which were very steep every way, were spread with houses and that very thick; for the land being divided into small enclosures, that is to say from two acres to six or seven acres each, seldom more, every three or four pieces of land had a house belonging to it. . . . We found the country in short one continued village—hardly a house standing out of speaking distance from another. . . . At almost every house there was a tenter and on almost every tenter a

Epoch of domestic manufacture. See Burns' "Cotter's Saturday Night."

Daniel Defoe, "Tour through Great Britain."

piece of cloth. . . I thought it was the most agreeable sight I ever saw. . . Look which way we would, high to the tops or low to the bottoms, it was all the same; innumerable houses and tenters and a white piece on every tenter. At every considerable house was a manufactory or work-house (dyeing houses, scouring shops, etc.). . . Among the manufacturers' houses are likewise scattered an

Traveling in the Eighteenth Century.

infinite number of cottages or small dwellings in which dwell the workmen which are employed, the women and children of whom are always busy carding, spinning, etc., so that no hands being unemployed, all can gain their bread even from the youngest to the ancient; *hardly anything above four years old, but its hands are sufficient to itself.* . . . This whole country is infinitely full of people and those people all full of business; not a beggar, not an idle person to be seen, except here and there an almshouse, where people ancient, decrepit, and past labor might perhaps be found."

The eastern counties were no less prosperous. "When we come into Norfolk, we see a face of diligence spread over the whole country; the vast manufactures carried on by the Norwich weavers employ all the country round in spinning yarn for them, besides many packs of yarn which they receive from other countries, even from as far as York-

Chief centers of the woolen industry were Norfolk, Wiltshire, and the West Riding of Yorkshire.

shire and Westmoreland." The manufacturers assured Defoe that "there was not in all the eastern and middle part of Norfolk any hand unemployed if they would work; and that the very children after four or five years of age could every one earn their own bread." Many of these people were self-employed — like the medieval master-craftsmen, owning their own looms and spinning-wheels, buying their own material and carrying the finished stuff to market; but some who were not able to set up for themselves were working for the manufacturers. These furnished the yarn and even the looms, paying the employees for their labor, much as do the clothing contractors of to-day. Defoe describes the market held in the High Street of Leeds, where from £10,000 to £20,000 worth of cloth was bought and sold twice a week. "Early in the morning, there are tressels placed in two rows in the street, sometimes two rows on a side, but always one row at least. Then there are boards laid cross those tressels, so that the boards lie like long counters on either side from one end of the street to the other. The clothiers come early in the morning with their cloth, and, as few clothiers bring more than one piece, the markets being so frequent, they go into the inns and public houses with it and there set it down. . . . At seven o'clock in the morning, the market bell rings. It would surprise a stranger to see in how few minutes, without hurry or noise, and not the least disorder, the whole market is filled; all the boards upon the tressels are covered with cloth, close to one another as the pieces can lie longways by one another, and behind every piece of cloth, the

A local market.

Lamplighting.

clothiers standing to sell it. . . . As soon as the bell has done ringing the merchants and factors and buyers of all sorts come down and coming along the spaces between the rows of boards, they walk up the rows and down as their occasions direct. . . . When they see any cloths to their colors or that suit their occasions, they reach over to the clothier and *whisper*, and in the fewest words imaginable the price is stated; one asks, the other bids; and 'tis agree or not agree in a moment."

Inventions.

Until 1750, the implements employed in textile industry were nearly as simple as those of India. The distaff and spindle had been displaced by the spinning-wheel in the fifteenth century, but the loom contained as yet no essential improvement on that used under the Pharaohs. In 1738, one John Kay invented an attachment for the loom, the fly shuttle, which enabled one man to run the machine that had heretofore required two. At the same time, the productive power was doubled. The fly shuttle came rapidly into general use, and, since the efficiency of the weaver was quadrupled, the looms soon outstripped the spinning-wheels. It was difficult to provide sufficient yarn to afford employment for all. In 1767 Hargreaves stumbled upon an invention that restored proportion. Upsetting a spinning-wheel and observing it still moving, he caught the idea of an automatic arrangement of several spindles set in motion by one wheel. The spinning-jenny, as his machine was called, carried at first eight threads, then sixteen, twenty, one hundred and twenty, etc. At about the same time, Richard Arkwright secured a patent for a spinning-machine (the throstle) constructed on a different principle and spinning a harder, firmer thread than the jenny. The best features of the two machines were combined in the mule-jenny patented by Samuel Crompton in 1779. The new spinner has been improved till it now

The fly shuttle. 1738.

The spinning-jenny. 1767.

The mule-jenny. 1779.

Industrial Progress. 273

carries 2,000 spindles and requires so little attention that several machines can be managed by one man. These inventions gave a marvelous impulse to textile industry, since the spinners were once more able to supply the weavers with yarn. The new machinery was used to great advantage in making up not only silk, wool, and flax, but the far more difficult fiber cotton. The manufacture of cotton had been neglected as impracticable and the importation of cotton cloth was prohibited lest it should come into injurious competition with the native woolen goods. But Hargreaves' jenny spun a fine, strong thread that could be woven into the best cambric. Business enterprise caught at this new opportunity. Mills were built and machinery perfected, vast quantities of raw material were imported, and cotton cloth became one of the principal products of English industry. The zealous manufacturers soon cast aside hand power as quite too slow for their purpose. Horse power and water power were utilized in turn. Finally Watt's steam engine furnished a motor, at once the most convenient and the most efficient. Cartwright's power loom was invented in 1787 and was immediately adopted in the cotton factories. In the manufacture of silk and wool the hand looms held their own, however, for fifty years longer.

The invention of the cotton gin (1793) greatly reduced the cost of preparing the raw material.

The power loom. 1787.

The inventors who wrought this marvelous transformation in the textile industries were, with few exceptions, men of humble birth. Hargreaves was an ignorant weaver; Crompton, a spinner and a farmer's son; Arkwright was a poor wig-maker; Cartwright alone of the great inventors was a gentleman born. "It is not extravagant to say that the experiments of these humble mechanics have in their results added more to the power of England than all the colonies ever acquired by her arms."

The modern factory was the direct result of these inventions. The several processes, carding, spinning, weaving, etc., could not long be carried on in scattered cottages, but must be brought together under one roof in order that the machinery might be run by the central motive power, whether steam or water. Concentration of processes involved massing of operatives—and here the changing conditions of manufacture coöperated with changing conditions of agriculture to bring about a remarkable movement of population. The displaced yeomen and the agricultural laborers, deprived of work by the improved methods of tillage, flocked to the factories in search of employment. People began to migrate from the country to the towns, from the agricultural regions of the south to Yorkshire and Lancashire where water power was abundant and stores of coal furnished an inexhaustible fuel. The movement has not yet ceased and its ultimate results are still problematic, but it has already transformed the agricultural England of the Middle Ages into the manufacturing and mercantile England of the present day.

Movement of population.

Furthermore, with the introduction of costly machinery, capital acquired an entirely new significance in industry. Labor had heretofore been the all-important element in production, but from the time that money was required to build and furnish a mill, capital has played the principal part. The man who could bring to bear upon the new industrial opportunity not only a considerable fortune but business ability and organizing genius, was easily master of the situation. He might direct the forces at his disposal as absolutely and as dexterously as a general maneuvers his regiments and artillery. The laborer, on the other hand, was degraded to the position of a dependent. Working on material and with machinery that belonged to another, with no share in the product beyond his wages, he lost all personal concern for his work. The

Antagonism between capital and labor.

e. g., Sir Richard Arkwright, Sir Robert Peel, Robert Owen.

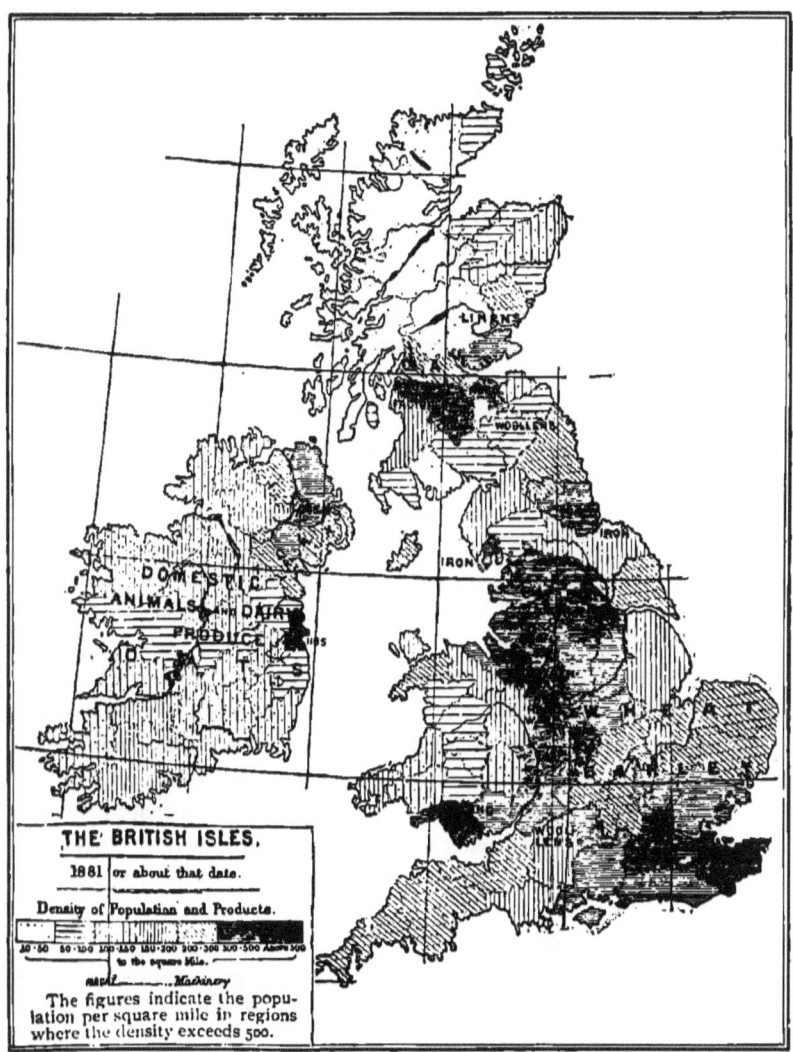

[Reproduced from Chisholm's "Handbook of Commercial Geography," by permission of Longmans, Green & Co.]

interests of employer and employed, no longer identical, came frequently into direct conflict. Misunderstanding and distrust grew into a well-defined hostility. With the factory organization of industry, arose the modern antagonism between capital and labor.

Deterioration of the laborers.

The deterioration of the laboring classes in the first five decades of the factory system goes far to justify this hostility. Machinery has rendered muscle and skill unnecessary. In the factory operative, who has but to overlook a self-impelled mechanism, the essential quality is patient, unremitting attention. Endurance is more important than strength or ingenuity. The craftsman suddenly found his labor a drug in the market, for unskilled laborers, women, the very children, could do the work required as well as he. Women and children were even preferred because they were more dexterous and docile. The effect was to reverse the relations of the home. Wives and children became the bread-winners, while grown men vainly sought employment or degenerated into contented idleness. It is true that new industries were being developed by the requirements of the factory. Machinery was to be constructed and mills put up. England's inexhaustible supplies of coal and iron were discovered and must be brought to the surface. Railroads and steamship lines were opened up to carry the products of English looms to distant markets. The factory era, indeed, witnessed a marvelous expansion in all departments of industry; but the new opportunities fell to the succeeding generation. The spinners and weavers thrown out of work by the recent inventions could not immediately secure employment as miners and machinists. The enlarged demand for labor might ultimately absorb the whole labor supply, but it could not avert temporary distress. Quite as serious as the displacement of skilled laborers were the evil effects of the inferior conditions of

Textile statistics, 1890. Factories, 7,190; spindles, 53,641,062; looms, 822,489; employees, 1,084,631; women, 410,608; children, 86,499.

Industrial Progress. 277

employment on the operatives. Machinery knows no fatigue. In order to get as much as possible out of his investment, the master was tempted to work his employees as long and hard as was humanly possible. Hours varied with the policy of the individual employer, but a fifteen-hour day was not thought excessive, and cases are recorded where operatives were regularly kept at work for eighteen

An Iron Furnace.

hours out of the twenty-four. Motives of economy dictated that the mills should be cheaply built. Poor light, bad ventilation, defective drainage, were the rule. Conditions outside the factory were even more deplorable. People crowded into the factory towns far in excess of house accommodations. Huddled together in attics and cellars and hastily built tenements, they were forced to live under conditions that bred disease. The physique of the factory operative rapidly degenerated, while the death rate, markedly higher in manufacturing towns than elsewhere, told a sad tale of misery.

In Manchester one tenth of the population lived in cellars.

The suffering of the laboring classes was hardly noted by economists and statesmen of that day. All energies were engaged in the accumulation of wealth, all attention was fixed upon the marvelous inventions by which production was multiplied a hundredfold. Enormous fortunes were amassed in manufactures and trade, and the national

Wealth of Great Britain in million pounds:
1774, 1,100
1800, 1,740
1812, 2,100
1822, 2,600
1833, 3,750
1840, 4,100
1865, 6,113
1875, 8,584
1885, 10,037

wealth augmented by leaps and bounds. The increase of population, then regarded as a sure index of prosperity, was not less marked. England's population has been quadrupled and her wealth multiplied by ten in the past one hundred years.

REVOLT OF LABOR.

The laborers were, however, not consoled by the ultimate advantages of the use of machinery. They saw plainly enough that the immediate results were disastrous, and blindly thought to set the matter right by destroying their dangerous rival. Kay's fly shuttle was so resented that the inventor was forced to flee the kingdom. Hargreaves'

Machine breaking.

house was broken open and his spinning-jenny smashed in pieces. Arkwright's mill was wrecked by an infuriated mob, and Peel's factory at Altham suffered a similar fate. Serious riots broke out among the silk-weavers of Spital-

Luddite Riots.

field and Blackburn. In 1811, a formidable insurrection was set on foot by the hosiers of Nottingham. Forming themselves into secret associations, the mutinous laborers attacked the houses of the manufacturers and destroyed the dreaded knitting frames. Such outbreaks of popular frenzy were summarily suppressed as offenses against public tranquillity.

The strike was a more rational method of resistance.

Trades unions and strikes.

This, however, involved concerted action on the part of the laborers, and was hardly less incriminating than open violence. The manufacturers readily secured assistance from Parliament. The Coalition Act of 1800 reasserted the old-time prohibition against "covin and conspiracy." Any persons combining to advance the rate of wages, reduce the hours of labor, or in any manner coerce the masters of a trade, were condemned to jail and hard labor. Repressive legislation was, however, found to be of no avail. Secret associations existed wherever laborers were congregated in the factory towns, and their methods were more desperate because illegal. The policy of repression was maintained for twenty-five years. In 1824 Parliament appointed a commission to inquire into the effect of the Coalition Act. It was reported that "those laws had not only not been efficient to prevent combinations either of masters or workmen, but, on the contrary, had, in the opinion of many of both parties, a tendency to produce mutual irritation and distrust, and to give a violent character to the combinations, and to render them highly dangerous to the peace of the community." The statute was therefore repealed. A sudden and marked increase in the number of strikes induced this employers' Parliament to impose certain restraints on trades societies in the following year, but absolute prohibition was never again attempted. In the Trades Union Acts of 1871 and 1876, such associations were given a legal status. For the past fifty years the unions have been a notable influence. They have accomplished not merely a considerable advance of wages, but they have united to bring about a legal limitation on the hours of labor, and to denounce such conditions in mine and workshop as militate against the wellbeing of the laborer.

Repeal of the Coalition Act. 1824.

Average rise of wages from 1835 to 1885, 70 per cent.

The Postman.

The trades unions have not been alone in their endeavor to secure for the operatives higher wages, shorter hours, and better conditions of labor. Throughout the nineteenth century the cause of the working class has been championed by philanthropists and statesmen who have thought it wiser to protect the laborer against degrading

Factory legislation.

conditions than to build hospitals and almshouses for the victims of an iniquitous system. First to protest against the injurious effects of factory labor was Sir Robert Peel, who called attention to the sufferings of the so-called apprentices—the children sent from the parish poorhouses to be bound out to the manufacturers. The Act of 1802 applied only to apprenticed children working in cotton and woolen mills. It required that they should have suitable lodging, clothing, and instruction; their working day was limited to twelve hours, between six in the morning and nine at night; and the factory where they were employed was to be "lime-washed twice a year and duly ventilated." The law was evaded by unscrupulous manufacturers, who had no difficulty in hiring free children from their needy parents and guardians. Owen and Peel pressed for further legislation that should protect these no less unfortunate victims of the new order. A series of abortive measures prepared the way for the searching investigation conducted by the Factory Commission of 1833. The report revealed a state of things that roused the country to horrified protest. Children of tender years were employed for long hours and under unwholesome conditions. Robbed of sleep and healthful recreation, these toiling little ones fell an easy prey to diseases and deformities incident to the nature of their work. Deprived of opportunity for education, subjected to demoralizing influences, they rapidly degenerated into weakness, brutality, vice. England stood aghast at the evident degradation of her working classes. A vigorous effort was made in the interests of industrial freedom to prevent remedial legislation; but the economists were overborne by the weight of evidence against the "let-alone" policy, and the eager advocates of national aggrandizement were silenced. The Act of 1833 forbade the employment in factories of children under nine years. Children between nine and thirteen years of age might be employed but eight hours a day, while no person under twenty-one years and no woman might be employed at night. Subsequent legislation has provided schooling for factory children on the "half-time" system, regulated the use of children as chimney sweeps, and forbidden the employment of children or women underground. In 1847, after a battle royal between the champions of protection and the advocates of *laissez faire*, the Ten Hours Act was passed, reducing to ten the number of hours in the working day for women and children. This practically meant a ten-hour day for all factory employees, since the men could not profitably be kept at work after their nimble assistants were withdrawn. Recent legislation has extended the blessings of protection to every factory and workshop where women and children are employed. Safe and wholesome conditions of work are secured by minute requirements as to ventilation and drainage and the guarding of machinery. Legislation is now pending designed to render the employer liable to damage in case of accident for which he can reasonably be held responsible.

<small>Children required to be in school on alternate days or half days.</small>

<small>Ten Hours Act, 1847.</small>

<small>Employer's Liability Bill voted down by the House of Lords, 1893.</small>

The well-being of the factory operative is now far in advance of that of the agricultural laborer. In the condition of the rural population there is still much to deplore. Unsanitary cottages, low wages, excessive hours of toil, the employment of women and children at brutalizing tasks—these and many other evils have alarmed the philanthropist and attracted attention to the need of reform. Little has as yet been accomplished here. The Agricultural Union movement so bravely inaugurated by Joseph Arch, and protective legislation forced through against the bitter opposition of the landed interest, have alike proved ineffective. The degradation of the agricultural laborer is to-day a blot on the fair fame of England.

<small>Agricultural Children's Act, 1873, repealed in 1876.</small>

PAUPERISM.

Any review of the social and industrial conditions of modern England would be incomplete without some notice of the growth of pauperism and the efforts made to check this menace to the nation's health. The industrial upheaval of the last century accomplished, like the corres-

Old-time Fire Engine.

ponding revolution in the sixteenth century, results both good and bad. In each case an immense gain in material wealth was achieved at the expense of the well-being of the laborers. Machinery, no less than the sheep pastures, deprived thousands of the means of self-support and drove them to seek aid at the hands of parish officers or private almsgivers. From 1750 to 1820, the years in which the factory system was becoming established, the growth of pauperism was appalling. The poor rate augmented till it reached the alarming proportions of one fourth the national revenue, and became to the taxpayer an intolerable burden. The phenomenal increase in the number of paupers was due in part to unwise methods of relief, in part to the demoralizing effect of the Napoleonic wars, in part to the mischievous corn laws that not infrequently raised the price of bread to famine rates; but the main cause was the in-

Poor rate per head of population:
1750, 2s. 2d.
1760, 3s.
1770, 3s. 6d.
1780, 4s. 5d.
1790, 5s. 11d.
1800, 8s. 5d.
1810, 10s. 3d.
1818, 13s. 4d.
1820, 12s. 2d.
1830, 9s. 9d.
* * * *
1890, 5s. 9d.

dustrial change that rendered opportunity for employment uncertain and left the laborer dependent on precarious wages. No legislation has yet touched the fundamental difficulty. Parliament has undertaken little more than the regulation of relief. The burden of the poor rate is now but one third of what it was in 1834, and the number of paupers has been greatly reduced, but there is still the problem of the "submerged tenth."

The most hopeful feature of the times is the awakening of the social conscience. People's Palaces, Toynbee Halls, improved tenements, university extension, these and as many more generous efforts to better the conditions of life and labor for the working classes bear witness to the new spirit of brotherhood that controls the thought of to-day. This new ideal astir in England, has found noble expression through the voices of Carlyle, Ruskin, and William Morris.

Salisbury.   Archbishop of Canterbury.
"PROPUTTY, PROPUTTY, PROPUTTY."

"Doesn't thou 'ear my 'erse's legs, as they canters awaay?
Proputty, proputty, proputty—that's what I 'ears 'em saay. . .
Proputty, proputty's iv'rything 'ere, an', Sammy, I'm blest
If it isn't the saame oop yonder, fur them as 'as it it's the best. . .
Coom oop, proputty, proputty—that's what I 'ears 'em saay,
Proputty, proputty, proputty, canter an' canter awaay."
—*Tennyson's "Northern Farmer: New Style."*

CHAPTER XIII.

THE EXPANSION OF ENGLAND.

Illustrative Readings.

History of Ireland; McCarthy.
The Virginians; Thackeray.
The Lady of Fort St. John; Mrs. Catherwood.

Macaulay's Essays on Clive and Hastings.
Tales from the Hills; Kipling.

THE BRITISH ISLES.

THE United Kingdom of Great Britain and Ireland had no existence before the seventeenth century. Scotland was an independent and jealous state. Ireland was but half conquered and wholly uncivilized, the English within "the Pale" existing as an alien colony in the midst of a hostile race. The amalgamation of the three kingdoms was accomplished under the Stuarts and the Commonwealth. The accession of James I. established a dynastic connection between England and Scotland, while the civil war afforded Cromwell opportunity to reduce the Irish to subjection. The formal union with Scotland was not, however, effected until 1707, while the incorporation of Ireland was delayed till 1800. The reconciliation of conflicting interests has been a delicate matter. In the case of Scotland, race feeling and religious differences were outweighed by the signal industrial advantage of free trade with England and England's colonies; but the breach between England and Ireland has not been so readily healed. Both kingdoms are represented in the English Parliament, and are thus secured a proportionate influence in national legislation.

Union with Scotland, 1707; with Ireland, 1800.

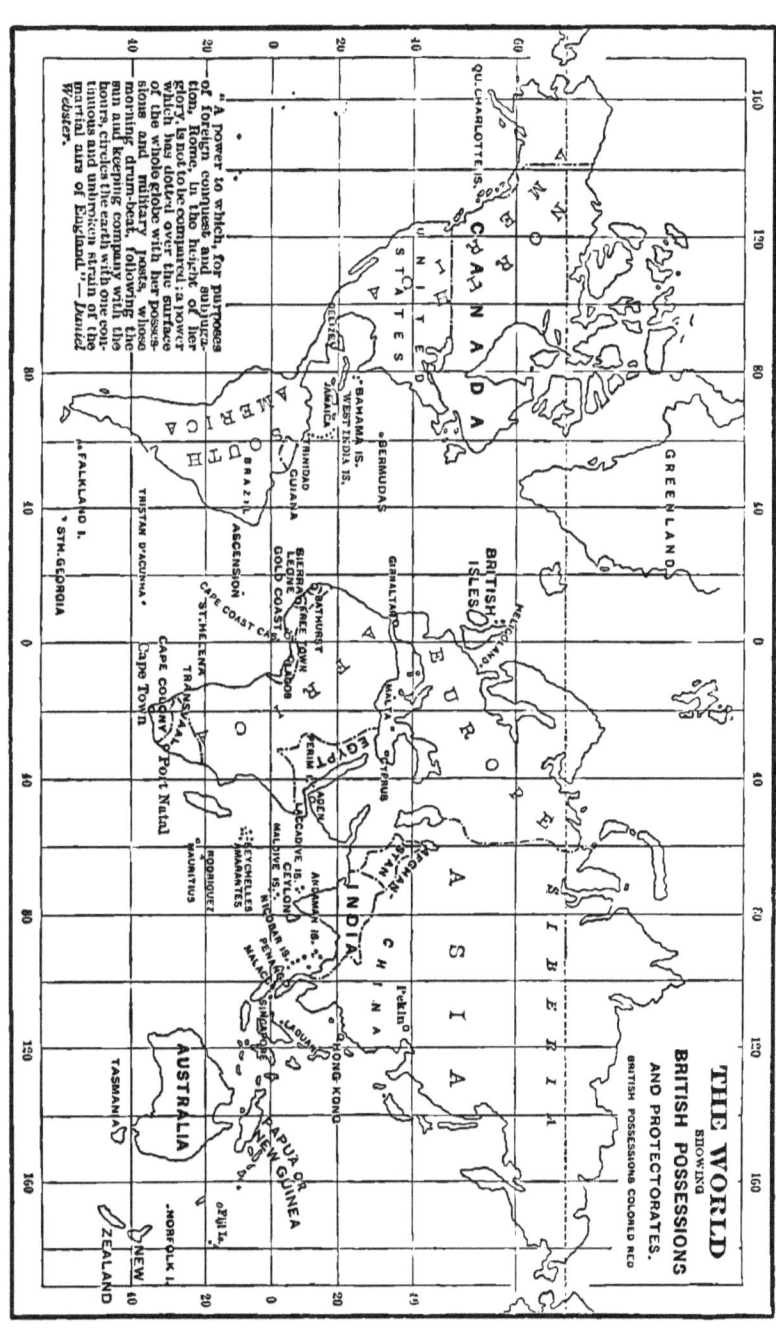

COLONIAL EXPANSION.

The discovery of America and of the new route to India by way of the Cape of Good Hope revealed two new worlds, an eastern and a western, to the maritime enterprise of Europe, and the explorations of the sixteenth century opened up vast realms of untold wealth inviting conquest and colonization. The seafaring nations of western Europe were not slow to respond to the call. Spain, being first in the field, took possession of the richest regions, Mexico, Peru, and the West Indies. Portugal, more enterprising but less fortunate, pushed her interests in the East Indies, in West Africa, and in Brazil. Holland followed in the wake of Spain and Portugal. Getting a foothold in the East Indies, she established trade relations with the spice islands of the Indian Archipelago. At the Cape of Good Hope, moreover, and along the Hudson River, she planted flourishing colonies. France entered later upon the quest, but secured extensive domains on the Western Continent. Early in the seventeenth century her adventurous mariners explored the St. Lawrence River and the Great Lakes, crossed to the Mississippi and so on to the Gulf of Mexico, thereby establishing exclusive right to the two great river valleys. The French settlements were, however, mere military posts maintained to secure trade with the Indians and to protect the Jesuit mission stations. Despotism, civil and religious, such as characterized the France of Louis XIV., was not favorable to the growth of colonies.

It is a significant fact that England was the last of the great European powers to enter upon colonial enterprise. The Cabots had been assisted by Henry VII. to undertake a voyage of discovery. They explored the North American coast from Cape Breton to Albemarle Sound, and to this portion of the New World the English thus secured preëmptive right. Unsuccessful attempts to plant colonies

Discovery and colonization of the American continent.

John and Sebastian Cabot. 1498.

Frobisher. 1576.
Raleigh. 1584.

were made in the reign of Elizabeth by the doughty sea-captain, Frobisher, and the courtly gentleman, Sir Walter Raleigh, but no permanent settlements were effected till the seventeenth century. Ultimate success was due not so much to the trading companies established by James I. as

The English colonies.

to the determination of the colonists who came, some in pursuit of gain, but more to seek in the New World the political and religious freedom that was denied them at home. The Puritan settlements struck deep root in the virgin soil of America and thrived under the beneficent neglect of a government too much occupied with home politics to concern itself with colonial interests. Not till the close of the century did England awake to the fact that this chain of seaboard colonies might become a source of strength and profit to the mother country, and must be defended against their dangerous French rivals.

England's part in the European wars of the eighteenth century was determined by her purpose of winning and maintaining a predominant interest in America. From the continental point of view, the occasion for the war was usually dynastic, but England's object was uniformly the extension of commercial and colonial interests. It was

Commercial wars.

one long duel between France and England, "a second hundred years' war." The contending armies fought not only on European battle-fields, but in Acadian forests, on the heights above Quebec, before the rude fortresses that controlled the unknown valleys of the Ohio and the Mississippi. England won nothing in Europe beyond an added prestige, but wide territories were annexed to her American domain. By the Peace of Utrecht (1713) she gained Nova Scotia and Newfoundland. In the Peace of Paris (1763), France was forced to surrender the bulk of her American possessions, Canada and all the rich region east of the Mississippi, together with her islands in the West Indies.

In the American campaigns, efficient aid had been rendered by the English settlers, who, being not priests and soldiers but *bona fide* colonists, took up arms against the French, not merely out of loyalty to the mother country, but in defense of their homes. Grown prosperous and strong in the wholesome conditions afforded in the unspoiled wilderness, they had established representative governments far more liberal than the English model, opened a profitable trade with the West Indies, set up manufactures of their own, and were in a fair way to become independent. Turgot, a wise French statesman of the day, compared colonies to fruit which hangs on the tree only until it is ripe. England's colonies in America were nearly ripe, but the English government failed to perceive it. The colonial policy of George III. and his cabinet was suggested by the perverted notion prevalent in that day of the use to be made of such dependencies. A colony was regarded not as an extension of national territory—an opportunity for national expansion—but as a piece of property, an estate to be exploited in the interest of the country owning it. Spain, Portugal, and Holland treated their foreign possessions as mere sources of supply for gold and silver, tropical fruits, and spices. England's colonies produced none of these, but they might be made a market for home products and a source of raw material for the rising manufactures of England. "The only use of American colonies or West Indian islands," said Lord Sheffield, "is the monopoly of their consumption and the carriage of their produce." In conformity with this frankly expressed doctrine of national greed, the English government imposed restrictions on colonial trade which were calculated to insure its profits to the home country. All exports must be sent to England, and all trade must be carried on in English vessels. Colonial industries were discouraged, the

England's colonial policy.

manufacture of woolen goods and the smelting of iron being actually forbidden. The Americans, having protested against this partisan legislation in vain, were devising means of securing some constitutional representation of their interest in Parliament, when the home government assumed the questionable right of taxing the colonies. This was resisted, and, resistance being met by compulsion, the colonists declared themselves independent of the mother country. In the war that ensued, England was handicapped by the three thousand miles of stormy sea that lay between her and her unruly subjects, while the colonists had the advantage of fighting on familiar ground. France, moreover, was glad to wipe out old scores by lending aid to the Americans. In the end, England lost the thirteen original colonies, together with all the territory lying east of the Mississippi, the better part of her American dominion.

The American War. 1776-1783.

In the Eastern hemisphere, as well as in the Western, the superabundant energy of the English race found opportunity for achievement. During the seventeenth century, trade interests had been developed in India by the East India Company, and three fortified posts, Madras, Bombay, and Calcutta, had been established. French merchants had also opened commercial relations with the Orient, and had secured Indian trading posts—notably Pondicherry, a town on the east coast but a few miles from Madras. Conflict between the rival races was inevitable. Both companies took advantage of dissensions between the native princes to extend their power, while the home governments supported each its own subjects. The East Indian wars were but one phase of the contest for supremacy that was being fought out during this century in Europe and America. The same year that achieved the transfer of the best part of America from France to Eng-

Conquest of India. 1748-1763.

land witnessed the expulsion of the French from India. By this victory the English Company was left to the unhampered pursuit of its own interests. There was slight capacity for resistance in the native peoples. India was but a "geographical expression." The dense population was made up of many races, alien and hostile. The Mussulman Empire had fallen into decay, and government was reduced to anarchy. Rival princes and satraps levied tribute and waged war to the infinite woe of the people. It was not a difficult matter for men who could command the superior military and diplomatic tactics of Europe to gain ascendency amid such weakness and confusion. Clive and Hastings made the most of their opportunity. Sometimes by treachery, sometimes by force, sometimes by legitimate negotiation, the native princes were induced to surrender their sovereignty, and one province after another was compelled to pay tribute. In 1773, the Company's charter was renewed on terms which gave the English government the right to supervise Indian affairs. The civil administration was made responsible to the crown, and the unblushing greed which had characterized earlier relations with the natives gave way to a sense of responsibility for the well-being of the country. Still the English rule was both alien and corrupt, and was bitterly resented by upper-class Hindoos. A widespread mutiny among the native troops convinced the home government that radical reform was imperative. In 1858, the East India Company's charter was withdrawn, and the country so long under its control became a dependency of the crown. The oriental empire thus acquired is ten times the area of the United Kingdom and more than half as large as the United States. Its population amounts to one seventh that of the whole globe. One hundred different languages are spoken within its confines.

Misgovernment of India.

Queen Victoria declared Empress of India. 1877.

This apparently splendid acquisition has thus far been of but dubious advantage to England. The government of India is a heavy responsibility, far more perplexing than that of Ireland. Vexed questions of race and religion baffle the ministry at every turn, and frustrate the efforts of the best-intentioned officers. The administration is as un-English as might well be—a bureaucratic service maintaining itself by military force. India can never be Anglicized, for the climate is an impossible one for the English race. According to the last census, there were but 100,000 British-born living in India. It is true that the commercial interests are very great and tend constantly to grow more profitable, but England pays dear for her practical monopoly of the Indian trade. Russia is her jealous neighbor, and conflict of interests on the Bosphorus and in the Orient have more than once involved England in war.

<small>Exports to England, £32,234,389. Imports from England, £31,177,968.</small>

<small>e. g., Crimean War. 1854-56.</small>

During the nineteenth century a new colonial empire has been built up in the far East, by successive discoveries and colonization. Australasia was visited by both Portuguese and Dutch explorers early in the sixteenth century, but it remained for the famous English navigator, Captain Cook, to identify the new continent. Colonization followed close upon discovery. The new acquisition was at first used as a dumping-ground for convicted criminals, but the country was opened to free colonization in 1821. The rich grazing lands attracted immigrants and the several colonies developed steadily in wealth and population. The discovery of gold fields in 1851 confirmed this industrial prosperity.

<small>Discovery of Australia. 1709-1777.</small>

As Britain's colonial dependencies developed in wealth and population, the question of self-government was sure to be broached. Agitation in favor of "home rule" took shape first in Canada. The attempt to suppress the movement having failed, Parliament, profiting by the unhappy experience of 1776, granted a responsible government. Since

<small>1837-40.</small>

1867 Canada has had a constitution "similar in principle to that of the United Kingdom." The governor-general, acting for the queen, has only authority to appoint the ministry that can command a majority of the legislative body. Responsible government has subsequently been extended to the Australian provinces and to Cape Colony, and sanguine statesmen look forward to the day when all British colonies shall be joined in a great federation, each bearing such relations to the imperial Parliament as one of the United States bears to our general government.

BRITISH COLONIAL POSSESSIONS, 1891.

*The colonies form three classes: (1) The crown colonies, which are entirely controlled by the home government; (2) those possessing representative institutions, in which the crown has no more veto on legislation, but the home government retains the control of public officers; and (3) those possessing responsible government, in which the home government has no control over any public officer, though the crown still retains a veto on legislation. There are also protectorates with a more or less organized government administered by the crown.

Name of Colony, etc.	Form of government.	Date of acquisition.	Area in square miles.	Population.
EUROPE:				
Gibraltar	Crown.	1704	1¾	25,880
Heligoland	"	1807	0¼	2,001
Malta and (Gozo)	Representative.	1800	117	165,062
Total, Europe			119⅞	193,532
ASIA:				
Aden	Crown.	1838	75	31,771
Brunei	Protectorate.	1888	3,000	175,000
Ceylon	Representative.	1796	25,364	3,008,466
Cyprus	"	1878	3,584	209,286
Hong-Kong	Crown.	1843	30	221,441
India, British	"	1625–1885	1,064,720	221,172,952
India, Feudatory States	"	"	714,758	55,101,742
Keeling Islands	"	"	8	400
Kuria Muria Islands	"	"	21	34
Labuan	Independent.	1846	30	5,853
North Borneo	Crown.	1840	31,106	175,000
Perim	Protectorate.	1855	4	150
Sarawak	"	1888	35,000	300,000
Straits Settlement	Crown.	1785–1819	1,472	512,312
Straits, Feudatory States	"		24,660	357,000
Total, Asia			1,903,832	281,304,437
AFRICA:				
Ascension Islands	Crown.	1815	35	360
Basutoland	Protectorate.	1868	10,250	218,902
Bechuanaland	Crown.	1885	162,000	60,576
Berbera and vicinity	"	1881	(?)	?
British East Africa	Independent.	1888	75,000	1,527,224
Cape Colony	Responsible.	1806–1877	219,700	14,536
Gambia	Crown.	1831	69	1,905,000
Gold Coast	"	1861	29,400	100,000
Lagos	"	1861	1,071	
Matabeleland, etc. to Zambesi	Protectorate.	1888	250,000	
Mauritius	Crown.	1810	708	371,655
Natal	Representative.	1838	18,765	543,913

* Statesman's Year-book, 1891.

British Colonial Possessions, 1891—Continued.

Name of Colony, etc.	Form of government.	Date of acquisition.	Area in square miles.	Population.
Niger districts	Crown.	1885	(?)	(?)
St. Helena	"	1651	47	4,116
St. Paul and Amsterdam	"		28	(?)
Sierra Leone	"	1787	468	180,000
Socotra	"	1875	1,000	4,000
Tristan Da Cunha	"	1818	45	50
Zululand	Protectorate.	1886	8,000	
Total, Africa			776,566	4,929,862
America:				
Bahamas	Representative.	1670	5,450	47,565
Barbadoes	"	1605	166	182,306
Bermudas	"	1609	20	15,123
Canada	Responsible.	1625–1760	3,170,382	4,832,679
Falkland Islands	Crown.	1832	6,500	1,789
Guiana	Representative.	1803	109,000	288,328
Honduras	Crown.	1783–1786	7,562	31,471
Jamaica and Turks Island	"	1629–1655	4,424	585,582
Leeward Islands	Representative.	1625–1763	479	127,723
Newfoundland	Responsible.	1583	40,200	197,934
South Georgia	Crown.		1,570	
Trinidad and Tobago	"	1797	1,670	228,415
Windward Islands	Representative.	1605–1803	623	137,322
Total, America			3,648,256	6,666,387
Australasia:				
Cook Archipelago	Protectorate.	1888	300	8,000
Fiji and Rotumah Islands	Crown.	1874, 1881	7,754	125,402
Kermadec Islands	"	1886	21	(?)
New South Wales and Norfolk Islands	Responsible.	1787	325,000	350,000
New Guinea	Crown.	1884	86,457	626,658
New Zealand	Responsible.	1841	104,458	223,779
Queensland	"	1859	668,497	320,431
South Australia	"	1836	903,690	146,667
Tasmania	"	1803	26,215	1,140,405
Victoria	Representative.	1787	87,884	49,782
Western Australia	"	1829	1,060,000	
Auckland, Lord Howe, Caroline, Starbuck, Malden, and Fanning Islands	Crown.		256	(?)
Total, Australasia			3,270,582	2,857,724
Grand total, British colonies and dependencies			9,599,305⅝	296,011,892

INDEX.

Abbey lands, the, distributed by Henry VIII., 173; not restored, 177.
"Adullamites," the, 251.
Adulterine castles, 72.
Agincourt, 150.
Agricola, 25.
Agricultural Holdings Act, 257.
Agriculture, under the Romans, 26; in the twelfth century, 72; under the Tudors, 188; in the eighteenth century, 266-269.
Aidan, 37.
Alfred, saves Wessex, 30; reorganizes the kingdom, 40.
American War, the, 233-235, 238.
Anderida, 29.
Angevins, the, characteristics of, 71.
Angles, the, invade Britain, 27, 29.
Anglesey, 25. See Mona.
Anglo-Saxons, the, characteristics of, 32-35.
Anjou, 62; lost by John, 89; finally lost, 153.
Anne, 222, 227.
Anne Boleyn, 171.
Anselm, comes to England, 63; quarrels with Henry I., 66, 90.
Apprentices, Statute of, 187.
Aquitaine, duchy of, dowry of Eleanor, 73; finally lost, 153.
Arkwright, Richard, 272, 273, 278.
Armada, the, 10; destruction of, 185, 187.
Arthur, nephew of John, 89.
Arthur, son of Henry VII., 168.
Articles, the ten, 173; the six, 174; the forty-two, 176; the thirty-nine, 182.
Artisans, the, 136-138; in the nineteenth century, 276.
Aryans, true, 22.
Athelney, Alfred takes refuge in, 39.
Augustine, converts Kent, 35.
Australia, 14, 17; discovery of, 290.
Avignon, 132.
Babington Plot, 185.
Bacon, Francis, 195; impeached, 200.
Bacon, Roger, 97, 125.
Badon, Mount. See Mount Badon.
Baeda, 37, 40.
Ball, John, 142; put to death, 144.
Balliol, John, declared king of Scotland, 106.

Bank of England, suspends specie payment, 241.
Bannockburn, 108.
Barebone's Parliament, origin of the name, 210.
Barnet, 157.
Barons' War, the, 98, 102, 103.
Barri, Gerald de, 83.
Beaconsfield, Earl of, becomes prime minister, 256; defeated, 258.
Beaufort, Henry, Bishop of Winchester, 152.
Becket. See Thomas, Archbishop of Canterbury.
Bede, "Ecclesiastical History" of, 37, 40.
Bedford, John, Duke of, 152; dies, 153.
Benedictines, the, 72.
Benevolences, 158; declared illegal, 159.
Bernicia, 29.
Black Death, the, 119, 139.
Black Prince, the, 116, 117; dies, 119, 120.
Blake, Admiral, gains victories over Holland, 211.
Bolingbroke, viscount, 232.
Bosworth, 159.
Bothwell, Earl of, career of, 182.
Bouvines, 92.
Bretigny, Peace of, 117.
Bright, John, supports reform, 251; opposes Home Rule, 261.
Britain, origin of name, 22; invaded by the Romans, 24; under Roman rule, 25-27; conquered by the Saxons, 30.
Britons, the, early condition, 22, 24-27; conquered by the Saxons, 28-30.
Bruce, Robert, 108.
Buckingham, George Villiers, Duke of, 199; impeached, 201; dies, 202.
Bunyan, 213.
Burgh, Hubert de, justiciar under Henry III., 94, 95.
Burke, Edmund, supports Americans, 234; attacks French Revolution, 237.
Burns, 243.
Bute, Earl of, 233.
Butt, Isaac, leads Irish party, 257.
Byron, Lord, 243.
Cabinet, the, defined, 226; corruption in, 230; established, 238.

295

Cade, Jack, 154.
Cædmon, 37.
Cæsar, describes the Celts, 22, 23; invades Britain, 24.
Calais, 153; lost, 179.
"Canterbury Tales," the, 124-127.
Cartwright, invents the power loom, 273.
Catharine of Arragon, marries Prince Arthur, 168; divorce of, 170-172.
Catholic Association, the, 253.
Catholic emancipation, 253.
Catholics, the Roman, legislation against, 182-184; enforced by James I., 198; favored by Laud, 202; disabilities increased, 214, 217, 218; favored by Charles II. and James II., 216, 220; nothing done at Revolution of 1688, 225; disabilities removed, 253.
Caxton, William, 165.
Celts, the, 14, 22, 23, 30.
Chamberlain, Joseph, opposes Home Rule, 261.
Charles I., 200-209.
Charles II., 213-220.
Charles VI., of France, 150, 151.
Chartists, the, 248-251, 259.
Chatham, Earl of, 234. See Pitt, William (the Elder).
Chaucer, Geoffrey, 124, 127, 131.
Chronicle, the Anglo-Saxon, 40; quotations from, 49, 51, 58.
Churchill, Lord Randolph, leader of "fourth party," 259.
Cistercians, the, 65, 72.
Clarence, Duke of, 154.
Clarendon, Earl of, 214-216. See Hyde, Edward.
Clarendon, Assize of, 74; Constitutions of, 75.
Closure, defined, 258.
Cnut, 44, 45.
Coalition Act, 278, 279. See Covin and conspiracy.
Coalition ministry of Fox and North, 235.
Cobbett, 243.
Colet, 194.
Colonial expansion, 285-291.
Columba, 37.
Commerce, 190, 191, 211, 286.
Common lands, 188.
Commons, House of, origin of, 106, 118, 119; electors of, 162; in the eighteenth century, 228; reformed, 247, 252, 259.
Commonwealth, the, 209-213.
Compurgation, system of, 34.
Confirmation of the Charter, 108, 111.
Conservatives. See Parliamentary parties.
Conventicle Act, 214.
Convention Parliament, 213.
Corn Laws, 242; repealed, 249.

Copyhold, 162.
Corporation Act, 214.
Country party. See Parliamentary parties.
Covenant, accepted by Parliament, 207.
Covin and conspiracy, statute against, 140.
Cranmer, Archbishop of Canterbury, 178.
Crecy, 116.
Crompton, invents the mule-jenny, 272, 273.
Cromwell, Oliver, 206-213, 247, 252.
Cromwell, Richard, 212, 213.
Cromwell, Thomas, 172-175.
Curia Regis, 55, 74, 76.
Danby, Earl of, 217; impeached, 218.
Danelaw, the, formation of, 39; conquered by Wessex, 40.
Danes, the, invade England, 38-40; conquered, 41; return, 43-45.
Darnley, Henry, Lord, marries Mary, 181, 182.
Declaration of Indulgence, issued by Charles II., 217; by James II., 221.
Deira, kingdom of, 29.
Deorham, 30.
Derby, Earl of, forms ministry, 251, 252.
Disabling Act, the, 218.
Dispensers, the, 113, 114.
Disraeli, 252, 256. See Beaconsfield, Earl of.
Domesday Survey, 55, 56, 67, 69.
Dominic, St., 96.
Dominicans, the, land in England, 96.
Douay, college at, 184.
Dover, Treaty of, 216.
Druids, the, described by Cæsar, 23, 25, 26.
Dunstan, 41.
Ealdormen, the, Saxon leaders, 32, 34; power of, 42, 43; disarmed by Cnut, 44.
Earldoms under Cnut, 44.
Earls, the, 32, 44, 45.
East Anglia, 31, 42.
East India Company, incorporated, 191; conquers India, 288; misgoverns, 289.
Ecclesiastical courts, jurisdiction of, 65; quarrel over, 75, 76, 78.
Edgar, 40, 41.
Edgar, the Atheling, 50-52, 59.
Edmund Ironsides, 44.
Edward, the Confessor, 45, 46.
Edward I. and the barons, 101; at Evesham, 102, 103; reign of, 103-108.
Edward II., 112-114.
Edward III., 114-120.
Edward IV., crowned king, 155; rule of, 156-158.

Index. 297

Edward V., 158–159.
Edward, Prince of Wales. See Black Prince.
Edward, Prince of Wales, son of Henry VI., born, 154; claims set aside, 155; slain, 157.
Edward VI., 175–177.
Edwin, king of Northumberland, 31; accepts Christianity, 36.
Egbert, king of Wessex, unites England, 31, 38.
Eleanor, of Aquitaine, marries Henry II., 73; dies, 89.
Elizabeth, 179–186, 190, 191.
England, character of the country, 14–16.
Enclosures, 188, 208.
Erasmus, 194.
Essex, 29; conquered, 31.
Ethandun, 39.
Ethelbert, 35.
Ethelred, 43, 44.
Evesham, 102.
Evictions, 188.
Exchequer, Court of, 74.
Exclusion Bill, 218, 219.
Factory Legislation, 279–281.
Falkland, viscount, 206.
Fawkes, Guy, 198.
Fenians, the, 254.
Feudalism, in England, 42, 43; described, 54, 55.
Five-Mile Act, 214.
Flambard, Ranulf, 57, 65.
Flanders, controlled by France, 121; trade with, 136, 187.
Flemings, the, come to England, 136, 190.
Folk-moot, described, 34.
Fox, Charles James, 235, 237.
France, feudalism in, 42; invaded by Northmen, 47; war with, 78, 89, 106, 107, 115–118, 150–153; becomes a centralized state, 167; war renewed, 179; rival of Spain, 179; war renewed, 201; alliance with, 215, 216; 237, 241, 286.
Francis d' Assisi, St., 96.
Franciscans, the, 96, 131.
French Revolution, the, 237, 241.
Friars, the, 95–97, 133.
Fyrd, the, 39.
Gaels, the, 22.
Gaul, 24.
Gaunt, John of, 120, 121; attacks the Church, 133, 134.
Gaveston, Piers, 113.
George I., 227, 228.
George II., 228, dies, 231.
George III., policy of, 232; reign of, 232–235.
George IV., 245.
Gesiths, the, 32.
Gilds, the, 85, 86; craft-gilds, 137–139; under the Tudors, 189.
Gladstone, William Ewart, 251; leads Liberals, 254; defeated, 255;

prime minister, 258; brings in Home Rule Bill, 260; defeated, 261; becomes prime minister, 262; on the House of Lords, 265.
Gloucester, Robert of, 82.
Gloucester, Duke of, son of Edward III., 121.
Gloucester, Duke of, brother of Henry V., 151, 152.
Gloucester, Duke of, brother of Edward IV., 158, 159. See Richard III.
Godwin, Earl of Wessex, 44, 45.
Good Parliament, 120.
Grand Remonstrance, 206.
Great Council, 55, 77; composition, 93; name changes, 100.
Great Charter, 82, 93–94.
Gregory VII., 65, 66.
Grey, Earl of, 237; becomes prime minister, 245, 246.
Grey, Elizabeth, marries Edward IV., 156.
Grey, Lady Jane, 177.
Grosseteste, Bishop of Lincoln, 96, 99.
Gualo, papal legate, 94.
Guises, the, 184.
Gunpowder Plot, the, 198.
Habeas Corpus Act, 220.
Hampden, John, resists ship-money, 203; in Long Parliament, 206.
Hampton Court conference, 198.
Hanover, House of, given the throne, 227.
Hargreaves, invents the spinning-jenny, 272, 273.
Harold, son of Godwin, 45; crowned king, 50; dies, 51.
Hartington, Lord, 261.
Hastings, Battle of, 51.
Hastings, Warren, 289.
Henry I., 59; dies, 60.
Henry II., 62; comes to throne, 71; reforms of, 72–77; dies, 78; work, 79.
Henry III., crowned, 94; misrule of, 98–103.
Henry IV., 147–149.
Henry V., 149; invades France, 150; dies, 151.
Henry VI., 151; crowned, 152; becomes insane, 153, 154; overthrown, 155; dies, 157.
Henry VII., 159; reign of, 167–169.
Henry VIII., 169; wishes divorce, 170–172; attacks Church, 172–174; popularity, 175.
Henry of Navarre, 185.
Hereford, Duke of, 122. See Henry IV.
Heretics, Statute for the burning of, 148.
Hereward, the Wake, 53.
High Commission, Court of, 203.
Holland, rivalry with, 211; war with, 215, 216.

Home Rule, 290; demand for, 257; supported by Gladstone, 260.
Home Rule Bill, first, 260; defeated, 261; second, passes the House of Commons, 262; thrown out by the Lords, 263.
Huguenots, the, 183, 185.
Hundred court, 33.
Huntington, Henry of, 83.
Hyde, 206. See Clarendon, Earl of.
Iberians, the, 22.
India, conquest of, 288; misgovernment of, 289.
Innocent III., 90, 91.
Instrument of Government, 210.
Interdict, England under, 90.
Iona, 9; monastery in, 37.
Ireland, physical characteristics of, 9, 14, 19, 20; Henry II. in, 77; rebellion in, 206; represented in Parliament, 212; union with England, 238; relations with England since Cromwell, 252, 253; population of, 254; Church in, 254-255. See Home Rule.
Irish Land Act, 255, 258.
Irish question, the, 252-262.
Irish University Bill, 255.
Ironsides, Cromwell's, 207, 208, 211.
Isabel, wife of Edward II., 114.
Jacobins, the, 240, 242, 243.
Jacobites, the, 227, 232.
James I., obtains crown, 197; character of reign, 198-200.
James II., Duke of York, attempt to exclude from throne, 218; character of, 220; issues Declaration of Indulgence, 221; dethroned, 222, 223.
Jesuits, the, 184.
Jesus, Society of, 183.
Jewish money-lenders, 111.
Jingoism, 256.
Joan of Arc, 152.
John, intrigues of, 79, 80, 81; character of, 88; loses Normandy, 89; quarrels with pope, 90; with barons, 91, 92; grants Charter, 93; dies, 94.
Junto, the Whig, 227.
Juries, system of, 74, 82.
Justice, early system of, 33.
Jutes, the, 27-29.
Kay, John, invents fly shuttle, 272, 278.
Kent, settled by Jutes, 28; converted to Christianity, 35.
King's Bench, Court of, 104.
Knights of the shire, in Parliament, 106, 119.
Laborers, 187-188, 191-193, 276-281.
Laborers' Dwellings Act, 257.
Laborers, Statute of, 139, 140.
Labouchere, proposes to abolish House of Lords, 264.
Lancaster, House of, 157, 158.
Lancaster, Thomas of, 113.

Land Purchase Bill, 260.
Lanfranc, Archbishop of Canterbury, 66.
Langland, William, 124, 127-129.
Langton, Stephen, made archbishop, 90; leads the barons, 92, 94, 95.
Latimer, Bishop, 163; put to death, 178.
Latimer, Lord, 120, 121.
Laud, Archbishop, 202, 204.
Leicester, Earl of. See Montfort, Simon de.
Levelers, the, 211.
Lewes, 102.
Liberals. See Parliamentary parties.
Litany, English, 176.
Liveries. See Maintenance and livery.
Lollards, the, 135, 141; legislation against, 148; put down, 150.
London, under the Romans, 26; taken by the Saxons, 29; acquires self-government, 84; center of trade, 187.
Longchamp, William, justiciar, 80, 81.
Long Parliament, 205; dissolved, 209.
Lords, House of, origin, 118; abolished, 209; restored, 210; resists reform, 245-247; resists Home Rule, 262; proposal to abolish, 264, 265.
Lords Appellant, 121, 122.
Lords Ordainers, 113.
Louis IX. of France, 102.
Louis XIV. of France, 215-217, 222.
Luther, Martin, 170.
Lyons, 120, 121.
Magna Charta, 88. See Great Charter.
Maine, conquered by William I., 50; lost by John, 89.
Maintenance and livery, 161, 162; statutes against enforced, 168.
Malmesbury, William of, 49, 83.
Manchester Massacre, the, 244.
Maletot, 108.
Manufactures, 138, 189, 269.
Map, Walter de, 83.
March, Earl of, 149.
Margaret of Anjou, 153, 155-157.
Marlborough, Duke of, 227.
Marston Moor, 208.
Mary II., wife of William III., 222, 223.
Mary Stuart, 181, 182; put to death, 185.
Mary Tudor, 170, 177-179.
Matilda, daughter of Henry I., claims the crown, 60-62.
Mercia, 29; supremacy of, 31; accepts Christianity, 36.
Merciless Parliament, 121, 122.
Model Parliament, 106.

Index.   299

Monasteries, dissolution of, 173.
Monmouth, Duke of, 220.
Monmouth, Geoffrey of, 83.
Monopolies, protested against, 191; revived, 199, 203.
Montfort, Simon de, 101; leads the barons, 102; killed, 103.
More, Sir Thomas, put to death, 173; and the Renaissance, 194, 195.
Mortimer, Roger, 114.
Mount Badon, 29.
Napoleon, 241.
Naseby, 208.
Navigation Act, 211.
Navy, the, 39; under the Tudors, 190; under Cromwell, 211.
Netherlands, the, revolt against Spain, 183, 184.
New Model army, 207.
Norman Conquest, 50-56; results of, 62-70.
Normandy, 48; reunited with England, 59; revolts against Henry II., 78; lost, 89.
Normans, the, 48, 49; in England, 62, 82.
North, Lord, 233; resigns, 235.
Northampton, 155.
Northmen, the, 38; on the Continent, 43, 47.
Northumberland, 29; conquered, 31, 40; accepts Christianity, 36, 37.
Nottingham, 206.
Oates, Titus, 218.
O'Connell, Daniel, 253.
O'Connor, Feargus, 250.
Odo, Bishop of Bayeux, 58.
Offa, 31.
Oldcastle, Sir John, 150.
Old Sarum, 229.
Open field, described, 188.
Orange, William of, 222.
Ordeal, the, 34.
Oswiu, 36, 37.
Oxford, Parliament of, 101.
Oxford, University of, beginning of, 64, 70; importance of, 84; effect of friars on, 96.
Palmerston, viscount, 251.
Papal jurisdiction in England, abolished, 173; restored, 177; abolished, 180.
Paris, Peace of, 286.
Parliament, 100; of Simon de Montfort, 102; Model, 106; of 1322, 114; acquired power, 118, 224, 225. See Great council, Witenagemot.
Parliamentary corruption, 228-230, 233.
Parliamentary reform, 237-238, 245-246, 252, 259.
Parnell, Charles Stuart, 258.
Parties, Parliamentary, country party, 217; Whig, 219, 226, 227, 230, 232, 233, 236; Tory, 219, 226, 227, 232, 237; Patriot, 231; Liberal, 247, 251, 254, 256, 258, 260, 261; Conservative, 247, 256, 258, 259, 261, 262; Liberal Unionists, 261; Nationalists, 258-262; Radical, 247, 248, 251, 264.
Paston, Clement, 163.
Paulinus, 36, 37.
Pauperism, 191-193, 282-283.
Peasants' Revolt, the, 134, 141-144.
Peel, Sir Robert, 249, 253, 280.
Pembroke, Earl of, 94.
Penda, king of Mercia, 31, 36.
People's Charter, the, 248.
Petition of Right, 201.
"Piers the Plowman," 127-130.
Pilgrimage of Grace, 173.
Pitt, William (the Elder), 231, 234.
Pitt, William (the Younger), 235, 236.
Poitiers, 116, 117.
Poor Law, Elizabethan, 193; of 1834, 247, 283.
Popish Plot, 218.
Praemunire, Statute of. 131.
Prayer Book, the, 176, 180, 211.
Presbyterian party in Parliament, 207, 208.
Pride's Purge, 209.
Protection, 242, 249.
Protectorate, the, 210-213.
Provisions of Oxford, the, 101.
Provisors, Statute of, 131.
Puritanism, 198, 213.
Puritans, the, rise of, 183, 198; persecuted by Laud, 202.
Purveyance, 112.
Pym, 205, 206; dies, 207.
Recognitions, 71.
Reform acts. See Parliamentary reform.
Reformation, the, in England, 166-168, 198.
Reign of Terror, 237.
Renaissance, the, 194, 195.
Retainers, 161.
Revolution of 1688, 222, 223; results of, 224-226.
Richard I., 80-82.
Richard II., 121-123.
Richard III., 159. See Gloucester, Duke of.
Richmond, Duke of, 235.
Ridley, Bishop of London, 178.
Ridolfi Plot, 185.
Rights, Bill of, 225.
Rising in the North, 182.
Rizzio, 181.
Robert, Duke of Normandy, 57-59.
Rollo, the Ganger, 48.
Romans, the, invade Britain, 24-28.
Rosebery, Lord, 265.
Rump Parliament, 209.
Russell, Lord John, 245, 248, 251.
St. Albans, 155.
Salisbury oath, 55, 56.
Salisbury, Marquis of, 259, 263.
Saxon shore, the defense of, 28.
Saxons, the, conquer Britain, 27-32; characteristics of, 32-35.

Scotland, physical characteristics, 17; language, 22; succession to throne of, 105; war with, 106, 108; under Mary Stuart, 181, 182; resists Charles I., 204-205; supports Long Parliament, 207; intrigues with Charles I., 208; united with England, 284.
Scutage, 78, 93.
Senlac, 51.
Serf, 68, 69; in the fourteenth century, 138-140, 145.
Settlement, Act of, 225, 227.
Seven Years' War, 231.
Shelley, 243.
Ship-money, 203.
Somerset, Edward Beaufort, Duke of, 154, 155.
Somerset, Duke of, protector under Edward VI., 175, 176.
Spain, 167, 169; connection with England, 177; at war with England, 184-185, 201, 211.
Star Chamber, Court of, 168, 203.
Stephen, claims the crown, 60-62.
Strafford, Earl of. See Wentworth, Sir Thomas.
Stourbridge, fair at, 86, 87.
Suetonius Paullinus, 24, 25.
Supremacy, Act of, 173, 177, 180.
Tallage, 82.
Ten Hours Act, 281.
Test Act, 182, 217, 220.
Teutons, the, invade Britain, 27-30. See Anglo-Saxons.
Thegns, 32, 42.
Thirty Years' War, 199.
Thomas, Archbishop of Canterbury, 75-77.
"Thorough," policy of, 203.
Tinchebrai, 59.
Toleration, 207, 208, 210.
Toleration Act, 225.
Tory. See Parliamentary parties.
Tostig, brother of Harold, 50.
Towns, growth of, 69, 70, 84.
Towton, 155.
Trades Union Acts, 279.
Troyes, Treaty of, 151, 152.
Tyler, Wat, 143, 144.
Tyndale, William, 170.
"Ulster right," 255.
Uniformity, Act of, 180, 214.
Union with Scotland, 284; with Ireland, 284.
Universities, the, 64, 84, 96, 97.
Utopia, 195.
Utrecht, Peace of, 286.
Villeins. See Serf.

Vortigern, 28.
Wales, physical characteristics of, 14, 16, 17; population of, 20; speech of, 22; unconquered, 30; conquered, 40; subdued by Edward I., 104, 105.
Wallace, Sir William, 108.
Wallingford, Treaty of, 62; executed, 72.
Wakefield, 155.
Walls, the Roman, 25.
Walpole, Sir Robert, 230, 231.
Walter, Hubert, minister of Richard I. and John, 81, 90.
Wars of the Roses, 155-157; effects, 159, 160.
Warwick, Richard Neville, Earl of, 156, 157.
Warwick, Earl of, minister of Edward VI., 176, 177.
Watling Street, 39.
Watt, James, invents steam engine, 273.
Wedmore, Treaty of, 39.
Wellington, Duke of, 245, 246, 250.
Wentworth, Sir Thomas, attacks Buckingham, 201; supports Charles I., 202, 203, 205.
Wessex, supremacy of, 31; overrun by the Danes, 39; conquers the North, 40.
West Indies, 285.
West Saxons, 29. See Wessex.
Whig. See Parliamentary parties.
Whitby, 37.
Wight, Isle of, 9, 121.
William I. (the Conqueror), 49; conquers England, 50-56.
William II. (Rufus), 57, 58.
William III. (Prince of Orange), 222; offered the crown, 223; character of reign, 226, 227.
Winchester, Statute of, 104.
Winwaed, 36.
Witenagemot, described, 42; continued in great council, 55.
Wolsey, Thomas, cardinal, 169, 170; overthrown, 171, 172.
Wordsworth, 242.
Wyclif, John, 124; and Church reform, 132-135; doctrines accepted, 148.
York, 25, 26.
York, James, Duke of, 218. See James II.
York, Richard, Duke of, 154, 155.
Young, Arthur, 267, 269.
"Young Ireland," 253.

www.ingramcontent.com/pod-product-compliance
Lightning Source LLC
Chambersburg PA
CBHW022050230426
43672CB00008B/1130